Advance Praise for *The Pioneer's Way*

"Dr. Jennifer Epperson's *The Pioneer's Way* is a fascinating look at pioneering leaders—a topic that is not often covered in leadership books. Dr. Epperson is a wonderful storyteller, and she uses them to highlight the characteristics of this rare breed and to make a convincing case for their importance. The result is a thoroughly delightful book that is simultaneously informative and enjoyable."

—PROF. GLENN SUNSHINE, Central Connecticut State University

"This fascinating book marches us onto the stage of a New Frontier—presenting the old term 'Pioneer' and highlighting its new relevance for today. All Pioneers are clearly leaders, however, most leaders are not Pioneers. Yet if by God's design you are one, your eyes will be opened to the freedom to live as a Pioneer and your mind will be challenged to be both a life changer and culture changer He created you to be."

—JUNE HUNT, Founder, HOPE FOR THE HEART and The Hope Center, Author, *Counseling Through Your Bible Handbook*

"Jennifer's book highlights the branched winding paths that true pioneers traveled to achieve their goals. In telling the stories of these pioneers, she gives us insight into her own journey as a pioneer through a profession riddled with roadblocks and inequities—yet she is successful. Using the incredible feat of landing a man on the moon as an opening scenario, she intrigues the reader to 'go where no one has gone before' and illuminates the path with the tools to get there."

—DAVID W. SHELLMAN, Ed.D., Dissertation Professor and former Executive Leadership Studies Chairman, Gardner-Webb University

"*The first.* Who me? Yes, indeed, perhaps you. That's the message of Jennifer Epperson's book about some of the extraordinary men and women who fit the description: pioneer. Whether a familiar name or, perhaps even more intriguingly, an *unknown* trailblazer, this book reveals the secret of those who were willing to forge a new path and achieve significant accomplishment in a wide span of endeavors. It's fascinating reading and an ideal guide for any pioneer who is grappling with how to move from an inherent passion to the fulfillment of life purpose."

—PEGGY CAMPBELL, President, Ambassador Advertising Agency

"Get ready to take a captivating journey into the world of pioneering leadership. This is not your 'run of the mill' leadership book. Rather, this book is for those who have a passion to affect change in some way for the common good and are willing to take the risks to achieve their vision. A pioneer leader herself, Dr. Epperson shares her exceptional talent at storytelling, weaving together cleverly written tales of leaders from all walks of life who have realized success through great resilience and persistence. It is through thought-provoking questions and the parallels drawn between these inspiring leadership stories that Dr. Epperson connects the dots for us and distills the 'Points for Your Compass.' These insightful nuggets are essential tools for the leader's toolbox. And, as the author so aptly points out, 'You need the right tool for the right job.' This unique book is definitely that tool."

—**KATHY HARTLEY,** President, Friends of Hearthside, Inc., Former President, Leadership Rhode Island

"The term *pioneer* typically evokes images of prairie landscapes, covered wagons, trailblazers carving out mountain trails, and trappers catching various critters for food and fur. But the pioneer spirit and drive goes far beyond those things. Pioneers have advanced medicine, space exploration, sports, mental health, mapping, engineering, business, and virtually every other field of study and practice that most of us take for granted. What motivates such people? What process do they go through in order to accomplish all that they do? What personal and professional standards do they typically adhere to? In short, how do they bring about such surprising and welcomed change? Jennifer Epperson answers these questions and more in her timely and insightful book, *The Pioneer's Way.* Do you want to be a change-maker? Do you want to be on the cutting edge in whatever is your passion? Follow *The Pioneer's Way.* You'll find that Epperson is just the guide you need."

—**WILLIAM D. WATKINS,** Award-winning author, speaker, and founder and president of Literary Solutions

"I've read many books on leadership, but none quite like this. Jennifer Hayden Epperson's book methodically and creatively maps out a path for pioneering leaders. It's full of relevant examples, fascinating anecdotes, time-proven principles, practical tips, and deep-dive self-assessment tools. Yet, it doesn't read like a dry college textbook. It stirs your imagination as you step into the lives of pioneers past and present. I think you'll enjoy it and find it very helpful."

—**DREW M. CRANDALL,** President, Keep In Touch, Former President, Friends of the Prudence Crandall Museum

"*The Pioneer's Way* is a thought-provoking book offering encouragement to any entrepreneur as they blaze their own trail. Dr. Epperson captures the essence of the pioneering spirit in today's complicated culture and offers a calm assurance to the reader that, though our individual contexts may differ, we can indeed find common ground with notable world changers. This work offers timely truths especially in light of the monumental challenges modern leaders face. A must read!"

—**HEIDI BOGUE,** Entrepreneur, Wife, Mother of Six, Owner,
Coach, and Director of Operations, CrossFit HighGear,
Owner, Creekside Labradors

"In *The Pioneer's Way*, Dr. Epperson has produced a seminal work of leadership literature that counterbalances today's mentality of managing risk. With beautifully descriptive prose, she helps us understand the gamechangers the world is indebted to. Through recounting pioneering stories (including her own) in fields such as science, civil rights, and exploration, she inspires us to see we all can be a pioneer in something we feel called to—if we will only answer the call. Thank you, Jennifer, for being the example of a pioneer to the rest of us and for writing this essential work to call forth the next generation of pioneers!"

—**ROBERT MCFARLAND,** President, Transformational Impact LLC,
Bestselling Author, *Dear Boss: What Your Employees Wish You Knew*

"If you want to know what a pioneer looks like, this book takes you on an exciting, full-color adventure! Jennifer has exhibited a tone and style that immediately launch the reader into a 'kaleidoscope of pioneers.' She weaves real and relatable examples of men and women into this masterfully crafted book. Jennifer has demonstrated how everyday people have gone into uncharted territory, carving out a niche for themselves, not just out of mere curiosity, but as a result of their own dogged passion for discovery and transformation.

I am convinced, like Jennifer, that 'once you know the truth, you cannot unknow it.' So, I am recommending this book to anyone who must take on what may seem like gigantic barriers and tread rough patches in order to pioneer change. Once you hop on this adventure, there is no going back."

—**BISHOP DR. SUNDAY NDUKWO ONUOHA,**
President and Founder, Vision Africa

THE
PIONEER'S
WAY

LEADING A TRAILBLAZING LIFE
THAT BUILDS MEANING FOR YOUR
FAMILY, YOUR COMMUNITY, AND YOU

JENNIFER HAYDEN EPPERSON

BOMBARDIER
BOOKS

A BOMBARDIER BOOKS BOOK
An Imprint of Post Hill Press
ISBN: 978-1-64293-457-1
ISBN (eBook): 978-1-64293-458-8

The Pioneer's Way:
Leading a Trailblazing Life that Builds Meaning for Your Family,
Your Community, and You
© 2020 by Jennifer Hayden Epperson
All Rights Reserved

Cover art by Cody Corcoran

BOMBARDIER BOOKS

Post Hill Press
PRESS

Post Hill Press
New York • Nashville
posthillpress.com

Published in the United States of America

This book is in memory of my mother, Elizabeth "Betty" Hayden (née Moffett), who took me on my first adventures and is now on one of her own. Her unflagging example of courage, conviction, and a conquering spirit remains in the hearts of many.

CONTENTS

Hope lies in dreams, in imagination, and in the courage of those who dare to make dreams into reality.

—Jonas Salk

FOREWORD

Have you ever read a book that deeply moved you because you were discovering something profound and revealing about yourself? That was the result when I reached the end of Jennifer Epperson's book, *The Pioneer's Way: Leading a Trailblazing Life That Builds Meaning for Your Family, Your Community, and You.* It brought more clarity to me as to why I do the things I do.

Full disclosure: I am one of the pioneers in this book. And that wasn't always what marked my life.

For the first thirty years of my career, I had employment in corporate America. My life was comfortable and full of family, friends, hobbies like hot-air ballooning, and just about anything else I wanted. But in 2011, I stepped away from this life and moved my family to Mozambique, Africa. I saw a great need for which I had the skills to help make effective change. I founded and became the CEO of Sunshine Nut Company. I am proving out a business model designed to transform the lives of the poor, widowed, and orphaned of sub-Saharan Africa using food factories as the engines for transformation. During this time of tremendous change, we have overcome great odds and significant obstacles to build the Sunshine Nut Company. The task has been tough sometimes, but I now live with a mission toward my destiny. And I do not consider this work; I consider this life—a genuinely abundant life.

What drew Jennifer to me was her discovery that our cashew brand was in the finest stores across the USA, which prompted her to investigate the story behind the brand. When she reached out to me, it was clear that she had done her research on me and my past and wanted to learn more about the traits of a pioneer exhibited in my life. Now I have been called many things over the years, such as a thrill-seeker, a risk-taker, and a turn-around specialist, but I had never been classified as a pioneer. But Jennifer helped me realize that this is what I am. And not just me. In *The Pioneer's Way*, she wants all of us to see the pioneers among us, and she wants to inspire us to join their ranks either as pioneers ourselves or as their followers and supporters. She wants the world to be a better place, and she sees the work of pioneers as critical to this vision.

The Pioneer's Way is filled with the stories of pioneers both past and present. Jennifer shares their backstories and what drove them to achieve their accomplishments. Jennifer comes from a long line of pioneers herself and is fascinated by the traits that lead people to overcome all odds in a quest to make the world better. She has created a mesmerizing read that masterfully breaks down what it means to be a pioneer, the steps of the pioneering process, and the traits pioneers typically possess.

Jennifer details the lives and motivations of pioneers who have made significant impacts in the world. She delves into the motivations that set people on the path that would define them as a pioneer. This book is not just about the pioneers' accomplishments, though. It is also about the process along the way—the slogging, the suffering, the tenacity, the principles—that keep the pioneer moving forward despite overwhelming odds. After all, there is territory to take. There is good to be done. There are people suffering who need relief and support and a better way to live.

Jennifer captures what leads a pioneer to do what they do. She tells you why the pioneer selects a path in life to the detriment of other interests, which involves sacrifice for this great possibility of good. She describes the processes along the way and the making of decisions that set the pioneer's course—a course on which there is no turning back. Jennifer points out that persuasiveness is a key trait for pioneers, where they cast a vision and sacrifice much to see it realized. People follow pioneers because they see the wholehearted devotion to the cause, and they get hooked into the desire to see it happen. But pioneering is not just leadership; it involves an extra element of persistence, of having skin in the game, among other essential traits.

Jennifer's style of presentation is compelling. She doesn't give a pioneer's story all at once. Instead she breaks up the various stories, returning to them to give us more as she unpacks the pioneering process and the traits pioneers exhibit. This approach cements into readers' minds the key points she wants to make while also enabling readers to thoroughly enjoy the stories. She teases you to keep reading as she unfolds so many fascinating journeys into the frontier of pioneering. The excitement that leaps from the pages has the power to propel the meekest, quietest soul, the one who prefers to stay in the background, to build the motivation to step out and go on a quest in their circle of influence to increase the greater good. It is the everyday lives of people that form the basis of visions that will break the paradigm of the status quo. Will you be encouraged to break with routine to go where nobody has gone before or has tried but never succeeded?

As I read this book, I could relate to the processes that Jennifer explained and illustrated. Her book was encouraging, refreshing, and validating. Being a pioneer can be a lonely journey. But the excitement of innovation against the boredom of the status quo keeps the pioneer on his or her path. The paths of pioneers lead to where the world becomes a better place.

The book clarifies so much that every pioneer or would-be pioneer needs to understand. We can all learn from each other. What was especially helpful to learn is how pioneers have handled their teams. A common misconception is that pioneers are out there on their own on the bleeding edge of achievement. Jennifer documents that pioneers not only have teams but also the traits of humbleness and service. Pioneers roll up their sleeves and lead their teams by example. They never ask of others what they are unwilling to give themselves. They don't stand back and watch. They dig in, sharing the trenches with those who have agreed to dig with them.

Reading *The Pioneer's Way* was healthy for my soul as I am right in the middle of the fight to overcome the obstacles preventing people from flourishing in life. I started the book worn down by the grind of the pursuit. I finished the book full of new energy and vigor. Jennifer states that living in the "not yet" or "with hope," as some might say it, is not for the feeble-hearted. Having said that, those with the strong traits described in these pages need a word to bolster their courage as well as an acknowledgment of the hardships they experience.

The front of our Sunshine Nut cashew bags highlights our company's motto: "Hope Never Tasted So Good." My hope in my pioneering vision is for millions of people to come out of poverty. My hope is for people to flourish in life. Many of the pioneers in this book had similar convictions. What is a conviction in your life? What burning desire do you have that could be the answer to helping people? This book can help you realize that you, too, have a pioneer spirit in you.

My three children have joined me in my pioneering journey, and I will ask them to read Jennifer's book to inspire and inform them of the pioneer's way. We can learn much from the past in order to do great good for the future. The reward is beyond the monetary. My wife gave up everything to be at my side, and she now runs the philanthropic arm of our company. As a family who owns 100 percent of Sunshine Nut Company, we have pledged 90 percent of our profits to be donated back to the goal of helping those less fortunate break the bonds of poverty. We are all involved in the day-to-day transformation of these people to give them hope and opportunity. We have a long way to go to realize the fullness of our vision, but true to the aspect Jennifer outlines in her book, the pioneer never accepts failure. We learn from our mistakes and continue moving forward toward the goal. Jennifer documents the less glorious aspects of being a pioneer, such as the pain, the suffering, and the many things we go without. She gets it right when she writes that the selection of a path causes the pioneer to move on out and never look back. Regret is not an option because the prospect of achieving the vision far outweighs the comfort of the status quo left behind.

Do you consider yourself an explorer, a game-changer, a warrior, a champion, a conqueror, a visionary? Then read this book. As you read through it, you will either see these traits in yourself or you will see them in others. You will be encouraged to persevere or you will be in a position to encourage those who are on the quest for adventure in their uncharted territories to make discoveries that will benefit all of us.

No matter where you are in life and what type of individual you are, this book has something for you. When you are done reading it, I will meet you on the road to destiny as you discover the ability to pioneer your way to a better world. I wish you a journey filled with fascination. May you be filled with the wisdom to persevere through to your goal—to the vision that keeps you awake at night, to the situation that needs addressed in order to bring a better life to those who need it.

Don Larson
Founder and CEO, Sunshine Nut Company
Mozambique, Africa

Wanted: New Pioneers for New Frontiers

"LIZZIE, STAY AWAY FROM THAT BUBBLER!"

My mother recalled her own father bellowing at her to step back from the water fountain when she was a child. His voice caused her to recoil, which was exactly the effect he wanted to impress upon her. A child born at the tail end of the silent generation (1925–1945), Mom never forgot her father's dread of public drinking outlets. There was a time in the not-too-distant past when a thirsty soul avoided public drinking fountains like the plague. This was because there actually *was* an active plague, believed to be transmitted through water. The terror it caused has largely been forgotten as the memory of it has sunk into the lengthening shadows of history. However, those who lived through it, like my own parents, have not, and cannot, forget its impact.

My grandfather wasn't alone in his apprehension. Millions of other parents had the same grave concern as the ghostly poliomyelitis disease swept across the world. Known more simply as polio, it was at the height of its outbreak when Mom was a child in the early 1950s. By then, its paralyzing fingers had touched many children her age. With their central nervous systems compromised, some polio patients were placed in a tank respirator, known as the iron lung, to enable them to continue breathing if too many chest muscles had been paralyzed. The disease permanently crippled others, as muscles warped and growing limbs contorted. Posters with children standing with the assistance of crutches and braces proliferated, many of these requesting financial help to invest in beating the disease.

The mysterious nature of polio added to the panic. Swimming pools were avoided, and other public activities were curtailed or abandoned altogether. Children were encouraged to avoid overexertion or becoming chilled, and to stay clean. People still enjoyed a highly anticipated movie at the theater, but they viewed it at their own risk and were warned not to sit too closely to a person they didn't know. Life changed as the public did their best to avoid the silent predator, yet they still remained unsure that any of their efforts might ward off the unwelcome interloper.

The polio pandemic mobilized a global army of medical personnel to treat polio victims, as well as medical researchers to help find a cure. It was estimated that up to fifteen thousand people per year fell victim to polio in the United States alone.[1] With every sweep of the clock's hands and turn of the calendar's page, more and more people were infected. Who could put a stop to it? A terrified public hoped and waited.

Among the researchers joining the battle was Jonas Salk. Believing that a safe, effective remedy could come from an inactive virus, Dr. Salk initially administered his vaccine to himself, his family, and his lab scientist. None of these initial volunteers fell prey to the virus. In fact, they all developed anti-bodies to ward off the disease. Next in line to receive the vaccine were the "polio pioneers"—children who would be part of a historic test in the war on the disease. "In 1954, national testing began on one million children, ages six to nine.... On April 12, 1955, the results were announced: the vaccine was safe and effective. In the two years before the vaccine was widely available, the average number of polio cases in the U.S. was more than 45,000. By 1962, that number had dropped to 910."[2]

With the success of the vaccine, Jonas Salk was hailed a miracle worker. His altruistic nature kept him from patenting his discovery. Rather, he immediately facilitated its global distribution without personal financial benefit. On April 22, 1955, just ten days after the announcement that the vaccine had been a success, Salk stood in the Rose Garden at the White House with President Eisenhower. The president paused after reading a commendation in his honor. Then he added these heartfelt remarks:

> Dr. Salk, before I hand you this citation, I should like to say to you that when I think of the countless thousands of American parents and grandparents who are hereafter to be spared the agonizing fears of the annual epidemic on poliomyelitis, when I think of all the agony that those people will be spared seeing their loved ones suffering in bed, I must say to you I have no words in which adequately to express the thanks of myself and all the people I know—all 164 million Americans, to say nothing of all the people in the world that will profit from your discovery. I am very, very happy to hand this to you.[3]

Even just one year after Jonas Salk's pioneering efforts, his vaccine continued to free people from the crippling effects of polio and the public paralysis that accompanied the fear of the disease—all to the great relief of the world.

A popular science fiction television show released in the mid-1960s opens with the declaration that "space [is] the final frontier." Set in the twenty-third century, space may indeed be the final frontier that humanity faces in the distant future. In the meantime, people are still needed to step up and be today's trailblazing pioneers. When Dr. Jonas Salk died at age eighty in 1995, he was still pioneering. He was on the search for the cure to another insidious plague caused by the human immunodeficiency virus (HIV). Many had hoped that the one who had given the world the polio vaccine might also conquer this dreaded predator, but it wasn't to be. The world is still waiting.

The world is also waiting for an entire spectrum of breakthroughs, not just in medicine, but in new mechanical and technological wonders, education, politics, law enforcement, psychology, civil rights, and just about any other area that yearns for needed change to advance the common good. But these discoveries desperately need discoverers to blaze the trail and unravel the mysteries that keep the benefits for humanity just out of reach. Almost all worthwhile benefits to human life began with one or more individuals who identified a need and worked hard, sometimes with great personal sacrifice, to meet it. These individuals stepped up and have done the hard intellectual, experimental, and sometimes dangerous work to turn their ideas into reality. This job is far from over. We desperately need more people who will embrace the challenge, taking on these tasks in their areas of influence.

The rest of this book is about some of the other pioneers who came before us and what their pioneering work shows us about what it takes to step into their shoes and successfully pioneer new vistas in our day and time. But before we launch into that, we need to be clear about what and who a pioneer is.

A Pioneer Is...

When we hear the word *pioneer*, specific pictures come to mind, and they could vary greatly among us. In the realm of science, we might think of a researcher whose indefatigable persistence yielded an advancement in medicine previously never achieved, such as the cure for leprosy, a disease feared by people for centuries. Or we might think of a human being who boldly entered a place for the very first time, such as astronaut Neil Armstrong, the first person on the moon, or James Cameron, who piloted the submersible Deepsea Challenger into the lowest point of the earth on March 26, 2012. A history class might bring to mind the masses of people in the United States who left an East-coast life with dreams of greater freedom and prosperity in a new prairied context. Still others might call up the present trend of some who are making the leap to live "off the grid." While others among us may imagine Dr. Ben Carson, who against the backdrop of a challenging childhood emerged a surgeon and figured out how to successfully perform the first separation of twins conjoined at the back of their heads.

As a group, pioneers were men and women who ventured into uncharted lands to discover what was there and to carve out new lives. As individuals, however, pioneers are still among us. They come from diverse cultures and languages and span the entire range of human skin tone. Their lifestyles and choices vary, as do their perspectives and practices. Yet, when we think about them as a whole, there seems to be something rare about them, some uncommon ingredient that sets them apart. And when we stand back and view their achievements, we are struck with wonder: "How did she build that?" "How did he think to solve that problem in that way?" "Why did they risk their lives to go to that place?" Part of our amazement is in knowing that to be named a pioneer is to be bestowed an honor. After all, pioneers are individuals or groups who seized the opportunity to be first at something—and succeeded! We seem to intuitively understand that to be a pioneer is to be, in some way, different from the rest of us. And this difference is a good and welcomed thing—a difference that ends up benefiting us all.

Our Fascination with Pioneers

In 1975, the United States was on the verge of celebrating two hundred years of "life, liberty and the pursuit of happiness." It seems everyone was busy planning celebrations, unfurling flags, and cooking up campaigns to get Americans into the "Spirit of '76." John F. Horgan Elementary School in West Warwick, Rhode Island was no different in its desire to join the national party. Basketball backboards in the gym were repainted in red, white, and blue, bookmarks listing the U.S. Presidents along with the school name were distributed, and the powers-that-be decided that the school needed a mascot. The final mascot choice turned out to be a pioneer. Long-time art instructor Peggy Ramsier was pressed into service to transform the concept into a visual reality.

Mrs. Ramsier, as we students knew her, got to work designing the character that would soon adorn school bulletin boards, T-shirts, and sweatshirts. I even wore one of the sweatshirts in navy blue for my fifth-grade class picture. She wisely depicted the new icon as a child, marching happily with determination to somewhere...westward, perhaps? We were in West Warwick, after all. But, really, who knew exactly where that coonskin-hatted, grinning child was going or what discoveries would be uncovered on the way? It was enough that the pioneering youngster was on a quest and was happy about it. It was an apt and inspirational symbol for all of us students who were just beginning our own life's journey. Technically, in name only I suppose, that is when I, along with the rest of my classmates, became "pioneers," though we had not pioneered anything on our own yet. We were in process: learning the historical whos, whats, whys, and whens that would eventually lead to doing, and perhaps some of that doing might lead to pioneering.

There were, however, a myriad of pioneering efforts that stimulated the culture during this particular period in the 1960s and 1970s. My mother shared with me that she had stood me in front of the television for the live broadcast of astronaut Neil Armstrong's first step on the moon. For the life of me, I don't remember it, but I appreciate her desire for me to witness that giant leap for mankind as it happened, even as I was taking the first small steps of my own. I have relived blurry images of the astronauts descending to the surface of the moon through video archives. I also recall the hours I spent mesmerized by *Star Trek* reruns several years later. I never seemed to tire of watching those three television seasons again and again. My skin would tingle every time I heard William Shatner's voice declare that he and the Enterprise crew were "boldly going where no man had gone before." At the time, it didn't even occur to me that the male reference might exclude me as a girl-child. But I saw Lieutenant Uhura on board the Enterprise, showing me that a woman could go on space adventures. And in my imagination, I would join the crew darting around the galaxies. I learned, along with many other young viewers, that I could also boldly go and seek out something new in my civilization, or in another, if I wanted. As I think about it, this was probably a significant factor in my decision to major in French. Sadly, I didn't have a snazzy universal translator like Lt. Uhura had. If I wanted to speak to people who were different from me, I'd have to learn to do it myself.

Walter Cronkite, the CBS news anchor of the first moonwalk, said of the event, "Man has landed there, and man has taken his first steps there. I wonder just what there is to add to that?"[4] Given the enormity of what Cronkite had just witnessed, such a question is understandable. In reality, however, even the day after the moonwalk, human beings continued to innovate, and our lives have been better for it. In the decades after the moon landing, humanity has realized a myriad of advances in medicine, industry, technology, social sciences, and more. Yet no one would argue that there remains further need for innovation. As long as there are problems to be solved, products to be improved, pristine places to explore, and people who need relief, the world is still in need of daring souls to pioneer.

Who Is a Pioneer?

People have been curious since the dawn of the human race. It is in our nature to ask questions such as why? who? what? and how? But the pioneers among us don't just ask the pertinent questions. They pose them about problems yet unsolved, and not just any problems, as we'll see. Then they pursue possible solutions with a dogged determination that will not be denied.

So how should we describe such visionary explorers? And what sets them apart from others? The word *pioneer* seems to fit them the best.

Pioneer originally developed from the word *paon*, an early Latin-Franco term for "foot."[5] It wasn't just a reference to a part of the human body, though. It also pointed to military personnel who used their feet as a means to execute their primary operational task.[6] In other words, we're talking about the infantry—those who advanced military interests while on foot. Another early French word for "foot" is *pion* (or *peon*), recognizable in modern use as somebody in lower social standing performing menial or unskilled labor. In English, the word *paon*, like *peon*, developed into *pawn*, another related word with a similar meaning. However, instead of taking on a demeaning connotation as the word typically does today, I see the root of this word demonstrating an "all in" participation. A peon's work is a holistic effort; it presses the spirit, mind, and body into service for missional achievement. In other words, these people have their own skin in the game.

As words often do over time, this one morphed in spelling and meaning. Eventually, the word *pion* in French became *pionnier,* which brings to mind something like "one who hoofs it." It entered English in the early 1500s in the form we know today—*pioneer*. The word has been assigned several meanings, including "one of the first to settle in a territory" and "a person or group that originates or helps open up a new line of thought or activity or a new method or technical development."[7] Pioneer has even taken on verb status and is often linked with a mission in its usage, such as "Marie Curie pioneered the theory of radioactivity."

Pioneering or Leading?

Many pioneers are thought of as leaders in their field. They have served as the tip of the spear into new geographical areas or fields of inquiry. In this way, they are considered individuals on the "leading edge," paving the way for the rest of us to follow and potentially benefit from their efforts.

But are leaders and pioneers interchangeable in their purpose?

Do they possess qualities that are similar or are they divergent in significant ways?

Do leaders and pioneers accomplish their objectives through similar procedures?

Is every leader a pioneer and every pioneer a leader?

Can just anyone be a pioneer?

Since numerous leadership studies have been conducted in the last one hundred or so years, situating pioneering traits and concepts against the backdrop of research-based models may assist us in providing answers to some of these questions.

Modern leadership as a scholarly discipline is a rather recent development in human history. The word *leadership* made its appearance in English vocabulary in the 1820s, pointing merely to a "position of a leader, command." It wasn't until late in the nineteenth century that this definition was expanded to its modern understanding of "characteristics necessary to be a leader, [having the] capacity to lead."[8] From then until the present time, the number of helpful studies on the topic and related literature have greatly expanded our understanding.

Peter G. Northouse has done extensive work in leadership and communications theory. He defines leadership as a "process whereby an individual influences a group of individuals to achieve a common goal." Northouse explains that leaders impact followers, and without this persuasive effect, any sort of leadership would be nonexistent. The process by which followers and their leader interact also plays a role in the leadership equation, in that they influence one another over time. A significant outcome of this aspect of leadership is that "it is not a trait or characteristic that resides in the leader, but rather a transactional event that occurs between the leaders and the followers…. [It] becomes available to everyone. It is not restricted to the formally designated leader in the group."

Northouse rightly locates the practice of leadership within the context of groups. "Both leaders and followers are involved together in the leadership process. Leaders need followers and followers need leaders"[9] as they all focus on accomplishing a common purpose. Ethical leaders know that involving their followers in shaping desired outcomes creates not only team "buy-in" but also respects the contributions of the people in their care, and by whom they achieve their goals. As John Maxwell has famously stated, "Are you really leading, or are you just taking a walk?"[10] A true leader can see followers in the rearview mirror, or, better yet, they're seen with the leader's peripheral vision.

What about pioneers? Are they leading, or are they, as Maxwell has pointed out, just out for a ramble that might be just a bit more adventurous? Like Northouse's definition for a leader, there is a purpose to the forward motion of pioneers. Their walking around may result in mapping out new terrain on which no human had yet laid eyes, and it may result in unanticipated discoveries. Yet, there are some qualities that appear to be indispensable when it comes to defining the true nature of the pioneer—traits that demonstrate tangible divergences between the pioneer and those who are traditional leaders.

Possibility-driven (risk-taker)

All pioneers are leaders in one form or another, but not all leaders are cut from pioneering cloth. Many leaders in the business sector, for example, are content to function in a context of continual operation, advancing a team through status quo practice in known industry territory. In other words, the next year's bottom line may be better than last year's, which shows advancement, but it is not due to any innovative practice, just to status quo procedures. Of course, the financial gains may also be attributable to a wide range of causes, from deliberate enhancements through best practices to unwittingly making beneficial decisions (dumb luck, anyone?). The status quo practice is preserved, the leader continues to lead, and the organization is still viable. Everyone is happy. In fact, there are very detailed procedures involved in assessing and managing risk that are designed to minimize the threat of adverse developments. Risk management plays an important role in preserving financial viability and maintaining organizational integrity. It may even save lives when it comes to evaluating the functionality of new devices that assist human beings in mobility or exploration.

In its extreme, however, risk management has been made into an art form, as some leaders seek to minimize as much risk as possible. In this case, fear keeps leadership from adopting new, or even novel, practices. Pioneers find this sort of reality unacceptable. In fact, the status quo or "the known" may be the very barrier beckoning them to surmount it. In a desire to advance the mission and realize greater outcomes, pioneers dare to dream of a better reality, and they are willing to risk rocking the boat, perhaps to the point of capsizing it.

The world is full of leaders who are risk adverse, but the pioneering leader is not one of them.

Probing (curious/inquisitive)

A second quality that appears to set the pioneer apart from leaders in general is a spirit of inquiry. James Cameron, pilot of the Deepsea Challenger and currently holding the record for the deepest dive into the Mariana Trench, has stated: "Imagination feeds exploration. You have to imagine the possible before you go and do it. We have to go because we don't know what's there."[11] Inquisitiveness is the fountainhead of imagining the possible.

In pioneers, curiosity seems to be stoked by a burning irritant—an issue that will not leave their mind. The pioneer must find out what secrets the wilderness holds. Or she must determine a sustainable way to bring food and water to a group of remote, malnourished people. Or the pioneering group must find a way to move autism into obsolescence. Such focused determination in mission requires thinking that exceeds the current bounds of human knowledge. The pioneer must leap into the realm of imagination in order to create the means of accomplishing what has not yet been realized. This task holds the potential of becoming a complicated yet thrilling game of "What if?" through scenario playing, building upon the scaffolding of human knowledge, and then having the guts to leap from the top of the rickety known into the abyss of the unknown. The pioneer is willing to risk the known for the unknown in order to create a better future reality. Her need to imagine and then to know drives her into constructing that possible future. Not every soul—even if a leader—has the stomach for this trek, even after a good breakfast.

Persistent

In her bestselling book, *Grit*, psychologist Angela Duckworth explores the trait that combines passion and perseverance. She described it to a business student this way: "Grit is about working on something you care about so much that you're willing to stay loyal to it.... It's doing what you love, but not just falling in love—[it's] staying in love."[12] True, leaders may be in love, passionate even. But what is the object of their affection? It may be the organizational mission or their team members. In truth, it may be any number of things, but in the end, if innovative change is frowned upon by the organization, even fine leaders may cease and desist. This is not to say that these leaders are no longer fulfilling an important role; the mission of the organization may still remain a good one, and teams still need competent people to provide direction. In contrast, however, pioneering souls have difficulty continuing down the well-worn path under such circumstances, and they may deeply struggle with discouragement and disengagement, even if their paycheck is robust.

This struggle, though uncomfortable, may be the birth of something new as pioneers turn their attention to problem-solving through innovative trains of thought. Like a dog gnawing on a bone, they keep grinding at the problem and may bite and growl at the hand that tries to pry it away from them before they're finished with it. Peers may struggle to understand why the pioneer cannot just "let it go," citing a fine line between finding a solution and going rogue. Some might shake their heads and say the pioneer is obsessed. The stereotype of the mad scientist is well known, but where would we be without the stick-to-it-iveness of botanist George Washington Carver who developed methods to improve depleted soil by alternating crops? Or what about Nikola Tesla, inventor of numerous electrical devices, including the first alternating current (AC) motor? Or Marie Curie, a pioneer in understanding radioactivity? Or what of the social pioneers who helped correct societal errors, such as Rosa Parks on civil rights, Charles Colson on prison reform, William Wilberforce on the abolition of slavery, and Dorothea Dix on the care of the mentally unstable? The ability to stay with a project despite naysaying and setbacks is a trait that pioneers, though not all leaders, seem to share.

Peau-mance (skin in the game)

"Staying in love" with a cause or a challenge is the other element that comprises Duckworth's equation for grit. In the context of the pioneer, however, I'd like to borrow the French word for "skin" and call it "*peau*-mance" (rhymes with ro-mance). In essence, peau-mance is a romance with skin on it. There's an important nuance here that differs from Duckworth's definition in that there is not only a passion involved but also the pioneer's "skin in the game" in some form or another. Very often the risk and persistence needed to mount the pioneering effort involves some sort of loss: strained friendships, financial concerns, damage to one's reputation, or even a job loss in a traditional organizational setting. In extreme cases, it could even mean loss of life. The pioneer is willing to gamble some of these pitfalls, if not all of them, on hoped-for outcomes. She is not just content to strategize, but she shows a strong drive, at least at the onset, to be a part of the exploratory process.

Principled (conviction)

Pioneers have the conviction that their quest can be achieved if given enough time, resources, and effort. It's the sort of belief that one can almost taste. For them, the imagined reality is of such import that they must pursue it, and they cannot be dissuaded.

People can hold all sorts of beliefs and convictions, and not all are of equal value. This famous quote, which some have attributed to Mahatma Gandhi, traces the trajectory of conviction to outcomes: "Your beliefs become your thoughts, your thoughts become your words, your words become your actions, your actions become your habits, your habits become your values, your values become your destiny." The Bible offers similar guidance: "Guard your heart above all else, for it determines the course of your life."[13]

Sometimes pioneers have created far more harm than good. There have been pioneers in the not-so distant past (yesterday's newspaper?) who have embarked on ventures that have resulted in much human suffering due to ill-conceived convictions. While these elements exist and we can learn much from studying the history of such people and their efforts (so as not to repeat their mistakes), these instances will not be subjects explored in this book. For my purposes, this book will deal with pioneering journeys that have brought us benefits, not harm.

Persuasive

In order to enter a new space or uncover a novel discovery, the pioneer must build a base of supporters and resources from which the effort is erected and advanced. If the pioneer does not naturally have this skill, it must be developed in order to garner support. Persuasion is the pioneer's essential friend.

A pioneer's support must come in various forms, such as fellow believers in the pioneer's objectives and team members who will help achieve the pioneer's quest. Along with human resources, the pioneer may need material resources, such as funding. History is filled with those who believed in a pioneer's presentation and served as patrons, providing resources that made the quest possible. For example, early Antarctic explorer Ernest Shackleton named the three rescue boats taken from his crushed ship *Endurance* after three of his major patrons who helped fund the Imperial Transantarctic Expedition (1914–1916). These ships were the *James Caird*, named for Sir James Key Caird, a jute manufacturer and philanthropist; the *Dudley Docker*, named after the man who helped Shackleton complete the purchase of the *Endurance*; and the *Stancomb Wills*, named for Dame Janet Stancomb-Wills who helped outfit the ship and supported other needs of the expedition. Ultimately, these small boats carried his marooned crew from their icy home on the shrinking floes in the Weddell Sea to the solid ground of Elephant Island.[14]

More recently, two intrepid individuals, American Colin O'Brady and British Army Captain Lou Rudd, sought to capture the spirit of Shackleton and his *Endurance* team by completing the first unassisted trek across Antarctica. O'Brady, thirty-three, finished first, with Rudd, forty-nine, completing the journey slightly behind O'Brady and his team.[15] Both men benefited from corporate sponsors, and the world was able to share in the adventure and musings of both through posted pictures and blogs. Watching the progress of these men was none other than Alexandra Shackleton, granddaughter of the great explorer. Upon the two men reaching the South Pole, she shared these thoughts with fellow countryman Rudd:

Dear Capt. Rudd. It is an enormous pleasure to follow your journey, I'm utterly transfixed. My grandfather would have been extremely impressed by what you have achieved so far and proud that the expedition has been named in the spirit of our family motto and everything he represented—'*Fortitudine Vincimus*, By Endurance We Conquer'. Huge congratulations for reaching the significant milestone of the South Pole. I wish you all the very best for the second part of the crossing and I'll be following your progress with great interest. Good luck, Lou.[16]

At the end of the day, without the proverbial signature on the check, some pioneers, quite simply, wouldn't be.

Definition and Direction

Given these qualities, we might then define a pioneer as *a persistent, risk-taking individual who ventures into new territory in order to accomplish a goal and, in so doing, influences others to participate in realizing and expanding this goal.*

This is a bold definition, so it might be tempting to believe that pioneering is just for the brainy, courageous, or elite. After all, these are the sorts of people who typically mounted frontiering exploration and scientific breakthroughs. In turn, they have enabled other pioneering spirits to realize human dreams of flight, moonshot, and deep dives. However, there's good news for even the less techy and resourced among us. With a little help, more of us are capable of pioneering than we might think. We just need to know the way forward and what it might cost, and that's good information for anyone starting a fresh trip to a place not yet visited.

For example, when I entered my doctoral program several years back, I glanced around the rather large university classroom and was thrilled to see others who were also excited to get started. The room was full of chatter, people quickly getting to know one another and exchanging dreams of why they wanted further study and what they might do with the degree. As the orientation got started, the room hushed. Two directors of the program greeted us "candidates," as we would be known until our doctoral conferral. Our excitement was met with a more tempered—dare I say it?—*mundane, even tedious* view of what the next few years of life would be like. To be sure, we received affirmation for our desire to learn, but what I took away from the session was much more humdrum, and it sounded something like this: "This is a research degree and will be hard work. It will be marked by long periods of solitude filled with reading and thinking and writing, and when you think you've had your fill of it, there will be more. There will be times when you must set aside needful tasks like dusting (dust *will* collect on your furniture) to meet assignment deadlines, and to manage the rest of your professional and personal life that you have built for yourself. Ultimately, what you are trying to do with your work is to add *just a bit more* to the pool of human knowledge. And yes, in the end, we guarantee it will be worth it." That was it. No lights, no applause, just the truth. And the doctoral pursuit was just as they said it would be.

The day I walked across the stage to receive my hood and diploma, I was a long way from Horgan Elementary School. However, in some sense, I had become a pioneer again. I had added something new to the human experience. It was my contribution, my "little bit." Did it make a difference? To some individuals it did, but mostly the world continued to rattle on the way it had the day before. But it bears repeating: *to some, it did!* Most academics don't leave their place of study on a marbled podium, delivering groundbreaking and earth-shaking research to the world. Most are advancing human thought a little at a time, and it is upon this foundation that beneficial groundbreaking research happens. It's all needed.

This should give us hope. All sorts of pioneers are needed to envision the possible, not just the first manned flight to Mars or an end to cancer, though that would be incredible! There is still a need to improve human relationships, cultivate and protect our environment, and advance the overall common good. If people did not confront challenges by imagining best outcomes in all disciplines of life, along with the means by which to get there, the work to effect helpful change in the world might never happen.

It is my hope that, in devoting the balance of this book to the journey of everyday pioneers, those who have received the call of the pioneer might be encouraged and equipped to do their little bit—or more—for the common good. While we're on this path together, we'll have the opportunity to learn from those who have already made the trip, helping to set realistic expectations for our own journey. We will observe how pioneers in different fields, both past and present, have navigated the pioneering process. We will walk with them from conceptual development to creating needed tools and building a team. We will learn from them as they are on the journey and are faced with navigating the unknown while dealing with conflict. Finally, we'll see how successful pioneers make provisions to keep their pioneering work alive by handing it over to others capable of sustaining it. Along the way, there will be lessons in the "Points for Your Compass" section that we may apply as we begin our own pioneering process to bring needed change.

It's a big universe, with seemingly infinite challenges—enough for us all to take them on as pioneers. Are you ready?

LEG ONE

The Quest

The Irritant

"I gotta get out of this place!"

THE SCREAMS HOUNDED HIM. THEY FOLLOWED HIM EVERYWHERE, like stray dogs scuttling in and out of shadows. As if that were not enough, the shrieking voices were paired with images of contorted faces: muscles pulled tight from pain under blood-engorged skin stained with tears. The sights, sounds, and smells of human suffering gnawed at the edges of his mind like ravenous rats. Men, women, and children—they were all there. How he wished it were only a bad dream, but the voices and pictures were not fabrications. They were his own memories of real events.

Horace Wells was a wreck, and he knew it. As a dentist practicing in Hartford, Connecticut in the 1840s, there were days, even weeks, that he regretted his decision to practice dentistry. He vacillated with continuing, even though he had already made his mark on the profession at a young age. In 1838 at the age of twenty-three, he had already published *An Essay on Teeth* in which he described how teeth formed, how various ailments and diseases affected them, and perhaps most importantly, how to prevent dental degeneration. His purpose in writing the essay was not that it serve as a "systematic work" but that it "impart...information respecting the human teeth, which should be familiar to the mind of every individual."[1]

Wells wanted to share his knowledge. He wanted to help people preserve their pearly whites and avoid the pain that accompanied dental disease. He advocated for a healthy diet and, for habitual oral care, the use of the toothbrush. At that time, people commonly cleaned their teeth using "chew sticks"—twigs with a frayed end on one side and a pointed end on the other. Although it was not a new concept, toothbrushes made with boar hair would not be mass-produced in the United States until the mid-1880s. Wells even came up with a motto to help people remember to take care of their teeth: "The clean tooth does not decay!"

Despite his love of dentistry and growing success in the field, Wells could not separate his ability to heal from the need to inflict pain. It was why he both loved and hated his profession. As a man of compassion and deep Christian faith, he was unable to overcome the trauma both he and his patients experienced as he treated them. Powerless to offer anything to offset pain, his patients bore the full sensation of tooth extractions. This led him to question his ability to continue his practice. He even stopped taking patients for short periods after especially dreadful procedures. *There had to be another way*, he thought.

Unacceptable

Horace Wells encountered what all pioneers face: an unacceptable status quo. Out of compassion, he could not turn away from his suffering patients any more than he could continue to carry out the methods that the science at the time taught as "best practices." He was at an impasse with an intolerable scenario, an irritant so debilitating that it pushed him to consider the unimaginable—quitting.

By their very nature, irritants are no fun. While largely used to describe physical pain like inflammation, an irritant, by definition, can extend to causing mental or emotional aggravation or, in Wells's case, torment. As human beings designed to self-protect, we naturally move away from an irritant, or, if unable to avoid it, we search for ways to relieve it. If we can neither move away from it nor mitigate the pain it causes, we find ways to cope with it. Part of that coping is to begin to imagine a different reality and the ways we might remove or overcome the things that greatly pain us. We begin to think, with increasing determination, *Someday, if I had my way, I'd _____*, and we fill in the blank.

Consider the reasons some may give for a career choice or a career change. A girl grows up watching her younger sister battle cancer and stays by her side as she undergoes chemotherapy with the subsequent nausea and hair and weight loss. She later decides to pursue a career in cancer research, in hopes of helping to provide a cure for all she has seen, heard, and suffered alongside her sister. Or, a young person dreams of the security that a career in criminal law would provide. He attains his goal, yet as he matures, he begins to find his particular life course void of meaning. While he enjoys the latest gadgets, cars, and a fine home that his career affords him, he reconsiders his path. He then chooses to become a teacher, so he can invest in the lives of young people before they find they are in need of a lawyer.

Haley Wilk is a pioneer in process. The eldest child of two, what might have been a typical life trajectory altered when her younger brother, Derek, was born. In some ways, Derek was ahead of his time. At birth, the bones of his skull had already fused together—a condition called craniosynostosis. Skull bone fusion is a process that does not normally conclude until adolescence. For an infant, this condition is very serious. In that little body, the brain continues to develop and grow in size until about the age of two.[2] In Derek, with his skull bones already fused at the age of six months, the brain's growth would push against the inflexibility of his skull, creating a dangerous situation. As a result, Derek's prematurely fused skull bones needed to be separated through surgery.

Most children with craniosynostosis are born with a malformed skull, but cognitive development can proceed normally, and corrective measures are taken to reshape the skull. His mother Laurie recalls: "Haley and Derek would play as children often do at a very young age, but one day, Derek's interaction with Haley just stopped. As a family, we knew that something had changed."[3] Derek became more withdrawn. He began to experience frequent seizures. His speech did not develop. Testing placed him on the autistic scale, but questions remained. What were the root causes that troubled Derek?

Over two decades later, the Wilk family was offered the diagnosis of Lennox-Gastaut Syndrome (LGS) for Derek. While Laurie claims Derek does not fit every element of the profile, she believes that it is the best descriptor for his condition. As an epileptic disorder, it can leave children with learning, development, and behavioral problems. All seem to apply to Derek. After years of experimenting with different interventions, Laurie's fatigue is evident as she describes the ongoing failure to find a solution for her son.

> He can read a little bit. He likes being social, but he doesn't talk. He still has the seizures. His EEGs have always been erratic. His brain is firing all over the place. Whether it is due to his craniosynostosis, I don't know. You're living with a lot of ambiguity when you go for all these tests and a cause is never found. We just got the Lennox-Gastaut Syndrome diagnosis last fall…. I don't think anyone knows, but they have to label it something.[4]

Haley's experience watching her brother Derek struggle played a significant role in her own development. She recalls how difficult it was to watch Derek have seizures. As therapists came in and out of their home, her childlike curiosity caused her to wonder how the differing qualities of each helper influenced her brother's situation. Haley recalls:

> [As] I saw people work with him, I saw the theories and practices they brought to the table. It was fascinating to watch to see if they had a positive, negative, or neutral outcome. You could never tell what factors were at play. Was it the gender of the therapist? The pitch of the voice? The type of behavioral intervention used? Was there a change and what caused it? That was a driver for me because it fascinated me.[5]

Like many with a mentally challenged sibling, she became involved in Derek's care as she matured. These efforts, however, are never without emotion, and Haley experienced them alongside her parents: hope, disappointment, determination, and frustration. Out of their love for Derek, the Wilks refused to give up hope that something might be found to help improve his condition.

"But Derek never got better," Haley recalled. "He still had seizures. [That] was my irritant. So...my childhood experiences [eventually led] to...a psychology degree. When you're a student in this field, you're constantly studying the impact that different approaches have for people."

At one point in her academic career, Haley's curiosity and compassion ignited into a determined passion. If her own brother suffered without a solution, she reasoned, there were others like him. "When I opened my scope beyond my own personal lens and I looked past Derek, I saw an entire population of people who had some type of mental health challenge or issue who needed help. I also believed that pharmaceuticals aren't always the answer."[6] But if not traditional interventions, what then?

Beyond the Possible

On December 10, 1844, Gardner Quincy Colton arrived in Hartford, Connecticut to offer a presentation on the effects of nitrous oxide, known today as laughing gas. It was a demonstration that was part science, part entertainment. Once a crowd had gathered, Colton would offer the gas to a local participant:

> The gas used in these lectures by Dr. Colton was contained in a rubber bag, and was administered through a horrible wooden faucet, similar to the contraptions used in country cider barrels. It was given in quantities only sufficient to exhilarate or stimulate the subjects, and reacted upon them in divers and sundry ways. Some danced, some sang, others made impassioned orations, or indulged in serious arguments

with imaginary opponents, while in many instances the freaks of the subjects were amazing.[7]

On this particular evening in December, Horace Wells had come with his wife, Elizabeth, not so much for amusement but out of curiosity. A local clerk agreed to take the nitrous oxide and began to hallucinate to the delight of the crowd. He then imagined that a member of the crowd was an adversary. He sprang off the platform and began to run toward the man. Frightened at the sudden turn of events, the attendee jumped from his seat, hoping for safety with the clerk in pursuit. Around the auditorium they went until the effects of the gas wore off, leaving the frazzled spectator out of breath, the newly sobered clerk confused, and the crowd in hysterics. Upon taking his seat, the clerk curiously raised his pant leg, revealing a bloody gash in his leg inflicted while running under the influence. Horace Wells noticed. He wondered, if nitrous oxide could render the clerk unaware as he incurred that kind of injury, could it possibly be used to help his patients endure oral surgery without pain?

The only way he could be sure was to put it to the test at once—on himself. And why not? He had a bothersome wisdom tooth that he could do without. The next day, Wells arranged for an associate, Dr. Riggs, to extract the tooth, while Colton was to apply the gas. The trio realized that surgery required a greater amount of nitrous oxide to be effective. It wasn't enough for a patient to be intoxicated. He or she needed to be knocked out. No one knew what impact the larger dose would have. Riggs and Colton were hesitant, but Wells was adamant about proceeding. The surgery went forward and was successful, energizing Wells. Perhaps he had found the long sought-after answer for his impossible situation. Perhaps dental surgery and pain need not go together after all.

Exploring New Frontiers

As part of Haley Wilk's undergraduate studies, she took an internship at an equine assisted therapy center. There she learned the benefits that people received as they worked to offset some of their physical challenges through working with horses: "Therapeutic riding is usually done mounted, and it was found that it was closely related to physical therapy. They found that the horse's gait closely relates to the human gait. For veterans, if there was any type of physical injury therapy that happened, they would put them on the horse and the horse would act as an agent for their rehabilitation."[8]

In fact, this is just what happened for Lis Hartel. A Danish pioneer in her own right, she contracted polio at age twenty-three while expecting her second child. Despite almost complete paralysis, Lis was determined to do what she could to regain her strength and resume horseback riding. With the encouragement of her husband and mother, she recovered enough to be able to ride again, though she remained paralyzed from the knees down and had to be lifted onto her horse. Her efforts paid off. Only three years after her illness, she was competing again. In the 1952 Olympics held in Helsinki, Lis was one of three who, for the first time, were allowed to compete as women and civilians alongside military men in dressage. She received the silver medal for Denmark and revealed how horseback riding helped her in her recovery from polio.

Lis went on to place in more competitions, including earning another silver medal in the 1956 Olympics, but as her renown increased, so did awareness of hippotherapy, or therapy with horses. Lis went on to help create the first therapeutic riding center in Europe when early principles of modern-age hippotherapy began to develop. This form of care would finally arrive in North America in the late 1980s.[9]

Today, Haley Wilk works at a facility called Gaits of Harmony in Ashaway, Rhode Island. Though she currently supports herself full-time as an intake coordinator at a counseling center, she eventually hopes to serve full-time in the field, blazing a pioneering trail as a certified equine specialist in mental health and learning (ESMHL). Already she is making her mark in the southeastern New England area, a region that has yet to experience a fuller spectrum of horse-assisted therapy for those with mental health challenges. Haley reflects:

The mental health branches of equine therapy are [still] more limited, more recent; maybe over the last couple of decades. Just to show you how narrow equine mental health therapy is, in Rhode Island there are only two women who have the ESMHL certification that I do that would allow a mental health branch to flourish. Today, a program offering equine therapy for mental health would be a first at GAIT.[10]

Developing a Vision

Like many mission-driven pioneers, simply to be the first or an early adopter of something is not enough. A stream of passion courses through them to benefit the larger good. Horace Wells desperately wanted his patients to experience the benefits of healthy oral hygiene, and when they needed dental work done, he envisioned a future in which it could be done as comfortably as possible. This is the definition of "vision": an imagined future that has yet to be achieved. Furthermore, facets of the vision must be "attractive, realistic and believable," even though the vision's full attainment has not yet been realized.[11] These components continue to fuel the fire of the pioneer's passion, especially when outward circumstances suggest the fulfillment of the vision may prove unlikely. It is important that pioneers begin to shape and define their visions as concretely as possible, so that in seeking them, they will know when the vision succeeds in actually becoming a reality. The clearer and more well defined the vision, the easier it will be to communicate and pass along the excitement for it to others.

Even at a young age, Haley has thought much about her involvement in a preferred future: how she would get there, and whom the primary and secondary beneficiaries in society might be.

My dream is definitely to run my own farm someday. Own it, run it, staff it, make it a corporation. I'd love to see these types of equine therapeutic centers across the country, but I would want them to be research-based, with best practices. I would like to see it taken seriously so that there is backing and support behind it. In general, I would want others to realize the positive impact, and that it could offer a cheaper and quicker option for people than traditional therapy.

Spreading awareness of more effective techniques also would have a positive effect on other areas of a person's life. In the end, this means that you are freeing up resources for other issues in the culture that need funding. For example, there would be more money freed up to help cancer patients: more money, more time. In addition, we cannot ignore that when you're improving the mental health of an entire segment, that they are capable of becoming more effective members of society in other areas.[12]

All of this found its nascence in the heart of a little girl who had suffered alongside her brother and felt incapable of helping him find relief.

Defining a vision to overcome an irritant is the first step in pioneering. It is an important beginning in advancing toward undiscovered country.

Points for Your Compass

→ An irritant, or unacceptable status quo, can drive an emerging pioneer to envision an improved future, beckoning her to become the leading agent who will overcome the irritant.

→ Hope and passion fuel the pioneer's efforts, as resisting forces (including personal emotions like disappointment, doubt, and frustration) battle the positive change the pioneer is trying to create.

→ A pioneer's applied determination creates efforts, some risky, that further advance and define his vision, even when outward circumstances suggest the fulfillment of the vision may prove unlikely (such as when Dr. Wells tested nitrous oxide on himself).

➔ Once clarified, the pioneer's vision must be easily, realistically, and attractively communicated so as to draw and involve others to participate in the new reality.

The Trajectory
"Where do I go from here?"

WHEN I WAS SEVEN, MY MOTHER ASKED ME A LIFE-DEFINING QUEStion: "Jennifer, do you want to join Girl Scout Brownies or 4-H? You can't attend both, so you will need to choose." Mom and I decided that I would attend a meeting of each and then make up my mind.

I hardly came to a scientific decision based on any sort of in-depth study. Yet, it was one of the earliest times I was given an opportunity to choose my own path. Furthermore, the proposal came from an authority figure who was showing me that with certain decisions came select opportunities. Simply by saying yes to one option, I was closing the door on another and the potential prospects that came with it.

During my first scouting meeting, I remember gathering into a group of girls my own age. We sat on a cold, uneven, darkly painted concrete floor in a dank nineteenth-century church basement. An adult leader gave us instructions on making something called a "sit-upon" with colorful woven paper strips in a plastic square sleeve.

Though feeling awkward at the new social setting, real energy ignited when I heard about the opportunities girl scouting would offer me. Among them were taking hikes and earning badges, which piqued my competitive interest and kept me engaged.

Then there was 4-H. Girls and boys participated together in sewing, public speaking, and square dance contests. There were opportunities to work in community service, with animals, or in crafts.

In the end, I chose 4-H largely because I wanted to take part in a context that included both boys and girls (an interesting decision since I later attended an all-women's college, but that's another story). In the mid-1970s and at that young age, I had already become familiar with a social concept that funneled boys toward certain activities and girls to others. I recall wanting to be a part of a context that offered similar opportunities to both genders, though I wasn't mature enough at the time to express it. Regardless of whether an activity was a boy's hobby or a girl's pastime, I had a drive that motivated me to ask, "Can I try that?" Whether it was cooking or woodcarving, hiking or gardening, I was eager to get my hands dirty. With encouragement from my parents, I attempted all of these activities and more. The exception was when my father declared certain power tools off limits when I began to show an interest and aptitude in flute playing. Dad realized that advancement on the instrument required that all of my fingers remain attached to my hands.

After vacillating between the two groups, I announced my decision to my mom. With the decision to join 4-H, I remember experiencing a new sensation. It was a pain associated with loss, a sort of "pre-regret." This feeling would become more familiar as I matured. I realized that the first brownie meeting I had would be my last, and perhaps I would never see the leaders or the other girls again. By saying yes to 4-H, I was saying no to all of the possibilities I had just been offered in scouting: outdoor trekking, collecting badges, developing friendships with that special group of people. I wouldn't even need the sit-upon I had just made. I felt sadness and occasional remorse as I realized my choice's limitations. It was a valuable lesson to learn since life is full of decisions. Emotions we feel at the loss of a potential future are part of the package. It is part of the experience we undergo as we choose one path in favor of another. Subsequently, we must learn to enjoy the scenery of the route we have chosen, while living with the knowledge that we may never experience the vistas offered by another.

Setting a Course

A pioneer learns to understand the impact of choice as he or she begins to plot a course away from the irritant's impact. In the case of Dr. Wells, the agony associated with dental surgery in his day caused such personal debilitation that he found it nearly impossible to continue. Irritants, especially those that cause suffering, can be so distasteful and of such a magnitude that the aspirational pioneer gives up seeking a solution. Adding further stress is the social isolation that results from walking a different path than others. Withdrawing from seeking a solution to the irritant seems to be the best means of coping with a seemingly unresolvable issue. Trying something new and failing is tiring, especially if little to no progress has resulted. The haggard pioneer may have a crowd of family, friends, and associates watching at this point—onlookers who, out of apprehension, encourage leaving the matter behind altogether. Their concern is genuine. "Just let it go," they may advise. Abandonment appears to offer the hope of restored sanity.

Yet the irritant persists, and the pioneer squirms.

Somehow, in the arduous process of seeking a resolution to the irritation, a few of these innovators are able to gather some small, glowing embers of hope, and along with hope, strength to continue to persist in finding a solution. Learning along the way, they are able to engage the irritant and then put some distance between it and them. They return to it, pick it up again, and study it from different angles. They begin to scenario-play and ask, "What if?" As hard as it may be, they dial down negative chatter and turn up the volume on encouragement. They imagine the results of a future success, while grappling daily with the friction created by the achievable chafing against the implausible. They frame failed efforts in light of future success. In his quest to find an economical, practical filament for a light bulb in a competitive environment, inventor Thomas Edison famously noted: "I have not failed. I have just found 10,000 ways that will not work." Thomas Edison was unwilling to live in the dark.

Out of the Shadows

Prudence Crandall contended with another type of darkness. Born in 1803 to a Quaker family in Hopkinton, Rhode Island, she experienced more equality between the genders than many of her peers did. As a curious young woman, she was thrilled at the opportunity to attend the Friends' Boarding School (today known as Moses Brown) in Providence, Rhode Island. Both boys and girls studied there. She had access to subjects that very few females of the day had occasion to learn, including Latin, philosophy, "political economy," and religion.[1] The advanced scholarship she received was in preparation to become a teacher, which was her aspiration. It was one of the few professions open to women of her day, most of whom typically only had an education through grammar school.

Despite some of these progressive occasions, Prudence also remembered events that drew her ire, especially when it came to gender limitations. Decades after the event, she would retell the story to her great-grandnieces of her ten-year-old self overhearing a conversation her father, Pardon Crandall, had with their neighbor, Mr. Arnold. The year was 1813. The discussion first addressed difficulties created by the war with the British, and then it turned to business matters. Seeing his daughter nearby, her father stopped the discourse and told her to go back into the house. Defiantly, she responded, "I won't!" Her father then took her by her ear, brought her to the doorway, and called for his wife, Esther. When questioned by her mother, Prudence explained that she wanted to hear the conversation and protested that her older brother often got to listen. Her mother explained that her brother would "soon be a man. He needs to know about business, but that is not necessary for [you]. Now, sit down and do a stint on [your] sampler."[2]

Prudence also observed that her mother had limited input. This included the decision to move the family from southern Rhode Island to Canterbury, Connecticut, in July of 1813. Her mother was unhappy about the move because it took them away from family. Her restrictions also extended to the purchase of a new cooking stove and house cleaning. Unable to tolerate spring-cleaning, Pardon Crandall issued a mandate that it was off limits. Esther could not accept this, so she would wait until her husband took one of his semi-annual business trips. Once he was gone, she unleashed a force of female neighbors, including her daughters, to clean the whole house. Though Pardon never seemed to notice the more sanitary environment, Esther was satisfied. Prudence, however, "resented her father's dictation in matters which seemingly might be left for Esther."[3] Such events stoked her sense of justice, and she built upon them later in her life, though at the time she didn't realize the course her life would take.

Pre-Flight Trepidation

Likewise, I had no idea the trajectory that my 4-H career would lead to. In fact, I saw it less as an investment in my future than I did an opportunity to try fun things and do them with the young friends who were members of my club. Under the guidance of my parents, I tried my hand at cooking, a little bit of sewing, and some wood burning. During one summer, my sister and I even cared for broiler chickens. We kids were excited about the fuzzy, yellow chicks that my mother brought home one day, but the excitement soon wore off as spring turned to summer and the maturing chickens demanded more effort. In the heat and humidity, the chickens' comfort was deemed more important than our own, as there was a financial investment in them. With the work and financial investment came a hoped-for outcome (chicken salad sandwiches, anyone?). So the birds got the luxury of enjoying the family box fan during those hot summer days while the rest of us melted under the heat.

Especially valuable were the 4-H lessons in leadership and community service, but it was in the area of public speaking where I found success. My earliest speaking effort involved a demonstration of how to build a homemade, diamond-shaped kite, complete with a bow-tied tail and decorated with brightly colored tissue paper. I soon graduated to the more challenging illustrated talks, which were presentations that relied less on partially completed props and described a topic more with words and with the visual technology at the time, which in my case meant my own artistry on poster board. My 4-H public speaking career culminated in advancement from the county contest to the state finals, a nerve-wracking but exhilarating evening of presenting a speech on American slang. At the end of the evening, I walked away as the state winner. Yes, Rhode Island is a tiny state, and it did not present the stiff competition that perhaps Texas or California or Illinois would proffer. Nonetheless, it was my home, and I was proud to represent it in public speaking at the National 4-H Congress in Chicago, Illinois.

That Chicago trip would be my first experience as an airline passenger. I remember having a wild flutter in my stomach as the whine of the jet engines lifted the heavy metal bird away from the earth. It would prove to be a familiar experience over the years. As I racked up frequent flyer miles, I also leapt from the public speaking platform into the unknown country of the pioneer.

A Pleasant Surprise

One never knows at a ship's celebratory christening on what types of seas the vessel will eventually sail. So it was with Prudence Crandall as she launched out on her own journey—diploma in hand—from Providence back to Connecticut to teach in Plainville. There she became accomplished and recognized as an educator. This, along with the economic growth of the area, resulted in some of the more prosperous families showing interest in educating their daughters as well as their sons. The conditions were right to create an interest in establishing a school for women in Canterbury, Connecticut.

By late 1831, Principal Crandall received her first students at the new Canterbury Female Boarding School. More would arrive in the months that followed. Along with them came Marcia Davis from Boston, though she did not matriculate as a student. Instead she came to work, preparing and serving meals and attending to housekeeping. Life in the little town of Canterbury must have seemed awkward at first in contrast to Marcia's previous existence in busy Boston. But she was committed to her new path, as she was joining her fiancé, and his family lived in the area. Further cementing her "outsider" status was her appearance, for Marcia Davis was black.

In its early stages, the school was full of activity. The young students were occupied with various subjects, including mathematics, philosophy, history, geography, English grammar, reading, and writing. French, music, and painting were also offered, as were various forms of recreation, which included walks to the store, post office, or along the river, listening to theological talks by some of the local pastors, playing games such as dominoes, and putting puzzles together.[4] Marcia Davis was part of the bustle. She served breakfast in the morning and tea to the school's visitors, in addition to keeping up with the housekeeping. This industrious woman also took up some borrowed books when she completed her work in order to join some of the classes. Outside of class, as she worked alongside the principal and her instructors (two of whom were Prudence Crandall's sisters), she asked questions about the things she was learning.

The new school attracted many guests. Of course, there were the families checking in on the progress of the students. From time to time members of the "Board of Visitors" stopped in to assess the status of the school, and various clergy came to give devotional messages. Members of the Crandall family were also counted among the visitors. Now that she had moved to the area to be closer to her intended husband, Marcia Davis also had friends stopping by, and this included Sarah Harris, sister of her fiancé, Charles.

At seventeen, Sarah had reached the end of her educational options. Like Prudence, she had a strong desire to become a teacher but realized that she needed more education to obtain that goal. However, as a free, young, black female, her ability to find a learning opportunity in a segregated society was nil. Or was it? Would Prudence Crandall's new school accept her as a student? Could she be trained there to become a teacher? It seemed a possible solution. However, her request to join the school took Principal Crandall by surprise.

On the (Air)Waves

"Jen, have you met Eleanor from the radio station?" My mother's inquiry was offered more out of politeness than anything else. She knew I hadn't met the public affairs director of the small AM facility in Warwick. Apparently, Mom had made the acquaintance when she purchased advertising for the church concert we were attending, and the station public affairs director had decided to attend. My mom's simple question, followed by an introduction, served as an entrée to an unanticipated interview with the station operations manager. I thought I was making a visit to tour the station, when, in fact, I was walking into an interview.

I left the interview with a part-time job. Though a surprise, it suited me fine since I was finishing my last year of undergraduate studies. The position was the humblest of radio beginnings: an announcing position at a local 5,000-watt daytime station. This meant that I was usually taking shifts in the late afternoons and weekends and signing the station off at sunset.

Just because a beginning is simple doesn't mean it is easy. Most challenging for me was learning to speak in a General American dialect. Think: Southern New Englander trying to sound like a Midwest native. It was an uphill climb. I was told at work to find an "R," then questioned at home as to why I was "tawkin' funny." To add insult to injury, there was an "R" in the call letters (WARV), the city of license (Warwick), and, of course, at the end of my name.

Eventually, the practice paid off. The thick Rhode Island accent on the air began to fade, and I flourished in the setting. I was eager to try anything in addition to my announcing and board operation duties, be that copy writing, recording, or scheduling airtime (called radio traffic). I loved the whole radio environment. Even hosing down the icy satellite dishes in the winter to get a signal just added to the spectrum of my experiences.

When I received my undergraduate degree, I was hired full time, appointed traffic director, and eventually promoted to music director. It all seemed so easy. I had simply fallen into the career for which I was made, and I was receiving a promotion every other year or so. My career path began with a simple introduction by my mother, but I had to say yes to the next steps.

Then came the day when I went from being a peer to a supervisor. It was a valuable experience upon which I would build. I learned immediately that not everyone celebrates your promotion. There was another lesson intimately tied to it: Some people get ornery when your new assignment is unexpected. In my case, a lack of acceptance might have had something to do with the big hair, spandex pants, and Stryper T-shirt I often sported, but it likely had more to do with my age (twenty-four years) and gender. No female had served as an operations manager up to that point. Pioneers do not always receive praise when life's path takes them off-roading.

Some of the comments were hard to hear, such as "She shouldn't be a manager" or "She's going to be a tough one to work with." Some of the men argued with me, and one woman in particular would occasionally fly into a rage, as she held a longer tenure than I did but had not advanced as far. On the other hand, my supervisors believed in me and assured me, "You can do it, Jennifer." Their encouragement cemented their belief in offering me the position. However, I was a new leader and had a lot to learn about the business. I also had a lot to learn about responding to others when they openly questioned my ability to lead, or, more discreetly, displayed disapproval through their body language. Though unspoken, it wasn't hard for me to pick up on the negativity. These occasions were like insidious erosion that would wear me down, eventually causing a devastating effect.

Simple Questions, Complicated Solutions

"Might I join your class?" Today it seems like a straightforward question. In fact, many instructors would be thrilled to find a student who wanted to study with them. However, it wasn't so simple in the 1830s, especially when it was a darker-skinned young lady expressing a desire to enter an affluent, all-white context. It took real courage to make such a request.

Though the actual conversation between Sarah Harris and Prudence Crandall is left to the imagination, there is evidence that the ground for this encounter was prepared ahead of time. As a Quaker, Prudence was familiar with the theological concept of *imago dei*, that humanity was created in the image of God. Christian theologian John Piper explains, "man is in the image of God means that man as a whole person, both physically and spiritually, is in some sense like his Maker."[5]

While a modern understanding of justice and equality cannot be superimposed over an early-to-mid eighteenth-century context, it is known that Prudence Crandall and her sisters became increasingly aware of how difficult it was to be African American. Biographer Marvis Welch explained: "Brought up among Quakers whose teachings propounded the divine in all men, Prudence knew that slavery was an evil, but it seemed to be an evil far removed from Canterbury. It was disturbing to her to learn from Marcia that the attitudes of northerners resulted in a great hardship for [black] people."[6]

Marcia also loaned her employer copies of the *Liberator*, a paper published in Boston by abolitionist William Lloyd Garrison. Articles in the paper contended for an end to injustice based on race and the termination of slavery, messages that resonated well with Prudence Crandall. It also documented the nightmarish abuse inflicted on subjugated people, which no doubt jarred the sensibilities of the sheltered instructor.

As Prudence Crandall's awareness of racism and its effects grew, so did her sensibilities toward the African American situation. Sarah Harris's request to join her student body sent her into deep reflection. Prudence quietly retired and turned to the Bible, seeking guidance.

Coming upon the Old Testament book of Ecclesiastes, she read, "So I returned, and considered all the oppressions that are done under the sun: and behold the tears of such as were oppressed, and they had no comforter; and on the side of their oppressors there was power; but they had no comforter."[7]

Action and Reaction

"What can I do?" Pioneers often find such questions swirling around their minds at pivotal moments. Like nagging mosquitos on a hot summer evening, very often these kinds of questions follow the sort of outrage that drive declarative statements like "This *has* to stop!" They motivate a person to take action. Pioneers press into the situation, feel the pain of the irritant, and then may waver at the implications of their desire to effect change. As for Prudence Crandall, she wasn't merely swatting at a few hungry mosquitos. For her, change meant overcoming a mammoth irritant that manifested itself in the blight of human slavery. What could one young woman do against such a global force that was driven by power and greed? It was enough to deter even the bravest of souls.

When the evening was spent and Prudence returned to the classroom, a new student quietly slipped in to join the ranks of Canterbury School's pupils. In saying yes to Sarah, Prudence may not have solved the global slavery problem, but, in her mind, she was helping to educate one young black woman who, in turn, was eager to continue educating others like herself. Truly, does anyone know the enduring impact that one good act might beget? Very often the act is done, and we move on.

But even one virtuous act, such as the choice to allow Sarah Harris to become a permanent student in the Canterbury Female Boarding School, created an unfolding trajectory for Prudence Crandall that would eventually be reinforced by other decisions she would have to make. In choosing one path over another, her options narrowed over time and her course was set.

As the pioneer forges forward, choices have to be made. One direction is taken over another. The impact of individual decision-making is felt as the pioneer lives out the consequences. Does the pioneer feel any pangs of regret as the path unfolds? Is there remorse over the loss of potential futures that peel away as each choice is made? The impact of choice, whether positive or negative, is intimately felt by the pioneer, especially as others in proximity to him also bear the consequences of decisions that were made. Even ethically grounded decisions have the potential to not only impact the decision-maker but to ripple out to those around him for whom he deeply cares. Prudence Crandall was no different. No one, however, could have anticipated the sort of reverberating backlash the courage of Sarah Harris and the kindness of Prudence Crandall would cause in the village of Canterbury, the state of Connecticut, and across time.

Points for Your Compass

→ Changing life circumstances, coupled with personal conviction, may create a pioneering fork-in-the-road opportunity worth exploring.

→ Awareness of others' condition motivates pioneering personalities to take on giants (such as disease, racism, hunger, and a lack of education), solving for these issues within their own sphere of influence.

→ In saying yes to the difficult path of pioneering, the agent of change may find it difficult, if not nearly impossible, to return to the well-worn easier way. In fact, her convictions may keep her from doing so.

The Way Forward
"Follow the yellow brick road?"

My mother once shared with me a very sobering saying: "Once you know the truth, Dahlin', you can't unknow it." In her case, the context was cancer. Like so many, she heard the words that would change her life forever. At the time, she was a stay-at-home, thirty-nine-year-old mom, occupied with three young children. Surprisingly, she discovered her own breast cancer during a monthly self-exam. Friends and family couldn't believe it. Surely, someone so young couldn't have cancer, they reasoned, but testing proved that she did. The disease would ultimately bring her down an uncertain medical path, hopefully toward recovery.

Though modern oncologists have proven protocols in place to treat the disease, a person new to any sort of experience doesn't know what to expect. Physicians, family members, and friends, especially those who have experience with a certain challenge, step up to form a support team to walk through the medical treatment plan with the patient. This is how it should be. No one should have to walk through life's difficulties alone.

However, what of the pioneer? If a truth cannot "be unknown" and the only option is to press forward, how does a pioneer navigate new territory? There is no map or GPS signal, and there is no blueprint. And what if there are only a few individuals willing to form a support team to help ease the rough patches along the journey? For the pioneer, the situation can seem like she's standing on the edge of the world—alone.

The Trouble with Transplants

As a young radio professional, I had the benefit of being located in a context conducive to growth. My early years in the industry were much like a greenhouse environment: I had a lot of supervision, correction, and encouragement. Mistakes on the air were embarrassing enough, so my supervisors didn't need to hammer many points home. True, I dreaded hearing the owner's voice on the other end of the line when I picked up the phone during odd hour shifts, but he always prefaced his corrective comments with the all-important *we*. In other words, when I made a bad call about on-air content, he would say, "Jennifer, *we* probably don't need to mention that on the air."

When I was appointed as operations manager, it was the first time I was placed in a supervisory role. I liken the experience to transferring a growing plant into a larger pot. Anyone who has gardened knows that plants don't always thrive when they're transplanted. There is a period of time after the transfer when they need more attention. Trauma may have occurred, such as some of the roots being cut or left behind, or some of the more fragile branches may have broken and need pruning. The plant may even look like it's dying before it stabilizes.

The same is true of people when they transfer into different organizational roles, especially when these roles carry more responsibility. One factor that helped me make the transition was remaining in territory I already knew. My roots were in familiar soil, even though

I was moved into a larger context. Any wobble I felt in my new role was offset by being "staked" to the mentorship of leaders and peers who believed in my ability to succeed in the new job. Another factor that helped my growth was that I had been through periods of success and failure. My trunk had begun to harden through experience. With reference to plants, this is called getting established. In radio, one gains experience in a public context. Failure, of course, is publicly embarrassing, while success merely sounds like "business as usual," which includes fluid, pleasing vocal delivery, interesting and entertaining content, smooth transitions between program elements, and an uninterrupted signal. This recipe should result in a connection with the listeners on the receiving end of the radio. So the sum of these experiences were the proverbial sun, rain, and soil that contributed to my belief that I could, in fact, accomplish the task I had received.

Like any young plant, I still had to contend with factors that worked against my growth. I had to deal with the friction of those who were disappointed at my new appointment as well as the skeptics who wondered if I would last. What I didn't realize at the time was that the stake supporting me would be removed. Eventually I would have to bear the full force of the wind as I made the relocation out of my comfy little houseplant life into the wild outdoors.

The Nagging Truth

Like my mother and many others who have faced unthinkable life challenges, Prudence Crandall could not "unknow the truth" of the African American condition in the early-to-mid nineteenth-century. Thanks to the accounts of personal friends and abolitionist literature, she could not ignore what was happening to people brought into the country to a future that made them the property of others. As a native of southern New England, she knew many black men and women were free. Still, Prudence learned that even these individuals suffered harsh treatment from those of her own skin tone.

Within the month of accepting Sarah Harris, the young head-master began to receive her own group of visitors. The first was a member from the local Episcopal church, the wife of the pastor. The second was a deacon who was one of her school's Board of Visitors, or board of directors in modern-speak. While the minister's wife shared her displeasure with Prudence's inclusion of Sarah, the visit was informal, and the rebuke reserved. The deacon's arrival, on the other hand, was official. He told Prudence that her decision to admit Sarah was improper and, of all things, unjust. His thinking apparently reflected that of the larger board and its members. That his family name was Frost is an example of the amusing irony that history sometimes hands us.

We don't know if Prudence Crandall was expecting any sort of resistance when she took Sarah under her scholastic wing. Chances are she knew there might be some repercussion after having spent time reading *The Liberator* and reflecting on what she had learned from her own experiences. She had come to know the Harrises personally and found them to be hardworking, God-fearing people, like many of her own family. It's likely that she took all of this and processed it through her theological and philosophical convictions. This alignment of knowledge, experience, and conviction creates a strong magnetic pull in a person's internal compass. It also prepares a pioneer to take the desired path while under emotional stress. It was a direction that Prudence Crandall would increasingly need to survive and to protect the students who had been given into her care.

Though she hadn't fully known the way to obtain equal treatment for all, she had begun to walk the path toward it. Taking the verses from Ecclesiastes as her own mandate, she likely consulted the Bible further for comfort, strength, and direction in subsequent days. Like a compass pointing the way were guiding principles such as those found in the book of Proverbs, including "Withhold not good from them to whom it is due, *when it is in the power of thine hand to do it*," as well as a companion verse in the New Testament, "Therefore, to him that knoweth to do good, and doeth it not, to him it is sin."[1] Though she had not sought this path, the direction became clearer as her principles hardened the shifting ground underfoot. Her own developing convictions were pointing the way, and she would face each challenge as it came.

Running on Empty

"We're fixing it finally!" This was the joke among the leadership that ran the small daytime radio facility in southern Connecticut. Part of the joke was that the statement fit the call letters of the station, WFIF-AM. The other part was that the facility was in such rough shape that the owner teasingly threatened to send me there for punishment if I gave him grief. Now he really *was* sending me there— and with a mandate to turn it around. I was twenty-nine years old, finishing a masters in broadcast management, and on my own, hours away from familiar turf. Furthermore, I had been granted a shiny new title: station manager. I was proud of that role and the work that would come with it. No matter that the station was a small AM daytimer, which meant that it legally had to be signed off at sunset. It was now under my care and that's what mattered. I would work hard to make it the best it could be.

After I arrived at the station and surveyed it, I ordered two dumpsters. I found a lot to trash. And stuff to fix! I pushed Brillo pads into holes in the transmitter building, because squirrels had nested in the insulation, making it look like a war zone. I found a crab skeleton under some of the copper grounding in the basement where the tidal marsh near the building had flooded the lower level.

The station also floundered operationally. Programming and paperwork were in disarray.

The small staff was discouraged. The station's reputation had taken some blows as a result of drifting local leadership and lack of communication with community partners.

All of this had to change, and it came with a price. Fix it finally, indeed!

It didn't take long for me to discover that I didn't fit the expected profile of a radio station manager. I was young, female, and assertive. Simply put, I was unexpected. Trips to broadcaster association meetings found me in a sea of dark blue and gray suits and ties. It became quite obvious to me that I was a rare bird. I was, however, taken aback when the birds of another feather asked me what I was doing up in the tree. This took various forms, like being asked if I was misdirected when I attended meetings for management. Event registration personnel inquired which trip I might like to go on with attendee wives: Would I like to go on the shopping trip or take the tour around Amish country?

Back in my own community, reactions varied as well. A clergyman-client told me that I was "nothing but a secretary" when a request required a check-in with the station's owner. His lack of respect was especially surprising to me given his vocation and his own standing as an ethnic minority. He wasn't treating me as he would want to be treated. Guests entering the radio station looking for the manager gravitated to one of my staff members who looked more mature (in fact, he was about five years my senior) and had a stature that exceeded six feet tall. When my staffer directed the visitor to me, it was hard to ignore the visitor's sheepish expression. After all, this was the mid-to-late 1990s and fewer women were involved in media management than there are now. Personally, I didn't know many like me. While there were a few of us at the time, they were many miles away from me and decades older than me. At that juncture, I hadn't met them, and I hadn't even thought about connecting with them to benefit from their support and experience. Looking back, I wish I had reached out to them, but it didn't occur to me or to my supervisors at the time.

At the radio station, I was challenged by some of the station personnel, and my methods were questioned. I assured these staffers that I knew what I was doing, but more often I let my actions tell the story. Eagerness to excel in my position was the side A of the record I was playing. Side B rehearsed the blues of what failure might bring. I blended a toxic cocktail of overwork and isolation (morning show duties required an early-to-bed, early-to-rise mandate, which limited social interaction) and drank it down each weekday. My mother's advancing cancer led me to spend my weekends with her one hundred miles away rather than putting roots down in the community where I lived. It was a slow creep of resource depletion, and the more I felt depleted, the harder I felt I needed to work.

Into Rocky Waters

It didn't take long for the next wave of visitors to make their way to the Canterbury Female Boarding School. The report from Deacon Frost stirred the board to send more representatives to reason with its leader. According to what was known about the encounter, the board members reflected on the school's fine reputation—a reputation that Prudence had worked hard to build—and how the opinion of the school's parents might be negatively altered if the mixing of races in the student body continued. Having thought through the issues, Prudence referenced the book of Exodus, noting that Moses, one of the great fathers of the faith, had married a black woman. Frustrated with her unyielding responses, the board retreated to allow several of the students' mothers to persuade Prudence Crandall to turn Sarah out of the classroom.

If there was a "meeting before the meeting," no one knows. However, it did appear from all accounts that the parents who met with Prudence Crandall that day were of one mind when it came to ejecting Sarah from her seat among their daughters. While warming themselves before the fireplace, the women received tea served by Marcia Harris, who was completely privy to all that was being said. Without concern for their server, the visiting women made their minds known. Marvis Welch, in her wonderfully researched book, *Prudence Crandall: A Biography*, records the exchange:

> "Miss Harris must be dismissed. We will not have our girls in a school with [her]. If you do not send her away, we will withdraw our daughters and your school will sink."
>
> "Then sink it must! I shall not dismiss her," came Prudence Crandall's clear reply.[2]

Taking on Water

It was a hard day when I found myself sobbing at work yet again, curled underneath the radio console in tears. When the station program was over, I crawled out from under "the board" and pulled myself up to the microphone, wiping away the tears. I rubbed my neck, swallowed, clearing my throat to steady the vocal muscles before I cracked the microphone for the station ID along with the warm invitation to the listeners to stay tuned. I expended the little energy I had for the cheerful station break. When it was over, I slid back under the console for the cycle to begin again. What was happening to me?

Something I had heard on the air triggered my reaction, but my response was beyond the amount of sorrow and despair that I was feeling. Cognitively, I knew this, but I could no longer corral my emotions back into the barn. The gate was open, and they were on the loose, running wild on their own course. Unable to grab the reins, I cycled between fatigue, despair, and anger. I slept longer and became bitter at the conditions my new position—one that I loved—imposed on my life. Against my personal nature, my schedule required long hours in solitude; early station sign-on necessitated that I turn in early, limiting any time I might have spent in social settings. Time spent tangling with my emotions drained any energy I had to manage the station. Feelings of guilt and failure grew, and it became increasingly difficult to keep my eyes laser-focused on the mandate of "fixing it finally."

Looking back, I understand that I naively omitted some vital principles that anyone on a different path must consider, the first being self-care. As a thirty-year-old thrust into a new leadership position, the last thing on my mind was physical, mental, and emotional depletion. Day after day I would report to work and plow through my tasks, while roiling emotions continued to gnaw at my soul until it felt as if all that was left was a pulpy, throbbing nerve. I couldn't go on. I told trusted friends about what was happening to me. As this was the mid-1990s, some kindly listened, some offered suggestions, and some chided me. Very few people in my circle identified what we now readily recognize as a free-fall into depression. Suicidal thoughts assaulted me, but like lucid dreaming, I cognitively rejected them with all that was in me, knowing that taking my life was no solution. I had one other option—to get help. I had come to the end of my own resources.

While I was navigating my own emotional wilderness, I was also stumbling in my attempts to stimulate healthy directional shift within an organization. While some of the efforts I implemented produced immediate improvements, others seemed to yield none. And in some cases, what I received in return was resistance from a handful of staff. My lack of experience attributed to some of the failures and hostility. Yet, my attempts at using various methods and experiencing outcomes that produced no results or poor results worked together to create feedback that I parlayed into personal learning. If an effort didn't work, I learned the hard lesson and didn't repeat it. About that same time, a helpful resource on the topic of organizational improvement hit the bookstores: John Kotter's *Leading Change*. A 1996 release, it was the sort of well-researched guide that would have helped me avoid some heartburn, to be sure. Still, I wouldn't learn to add his resource or similar ones to my handyman's bag until a later time.

However, another important resource *did* catch my attention. It was in the form of a motivational story, a real-life history lesson in which the protagonist displayed conviction and resolve despite an overwhelming challenge. Leading a just cause and driven by a fiery spirit, the lead character made a difference, and not only in the lives of those who lived concurrently. Her leadership ended up having an impact that rippled through history. As I rehearsed the hopeful story, it continued to keep a small ember lit in my soul. I loved it. Short of inspiration myself, I was desperate to take it in whatever form I could. I'm referring to the story of Prudence Crandall. I discovered it sitting on a branch in my family tree. Prudence Crandall is a cousin of mine, related through two Crandall brothers who fought in the Revolutionary War. While separated through time and circumstances, I took away valuable lessons from her life, and I wondered if I could find my way forward on my own path as she had on hers.

A Breach in the Hull

It is one thing to stand on principle. It is entirely another to find that your principles are the deck planks of a ship rapidly taking on water. Most leaders don't think of abandoning ship as a first option, and Prudence Crandall was no different. Rather than conceding defeat, her ultimatum to the group of women warning her to dismiss Sarah Harris on that day was a declaration of how far she was willing to go before heading for the lifeboats. It wasn't long after that fateful meeting that the breach in the ship's hull grew larger and wider, as the families of each student withdrew their girls *and* their funding from Prudence Crandall's school. The school ship was sinking—and quickly! What would Captain Prudence do? She had the support of her family, including that of her sisters, along with the Harris family. But all of this wouldn't be enough. She had to do something more, and time wasn't on her side.

There's an old saying, "Desperate times require desperate measures." In those situations, all kinds of leaders, including pioneers, can become desperate under intense pressure. These are conditions under which even good leaders can make poor decisions. This kind of stress can sometimes cause the taxed soul to call up all of its resources, throwing whatever it can—creativity, experience, physical strength, fierceness of spirit—into the breach just to survive. Though the way forward may appear fuzzy and forbidding (even a GPS will tell a driver when she or he is entering an unmapped area), there are some helps to steady forward steps. The first is to remember what's been learned from the map available to you before off-roading. Relying on experience and training before entering the unmapped territory may often be helpful in addressing what is ahead. For example, I observed how my mentors at work wisely handled conflict with others, and I learned from them before I was called on to do it myself. Some of the same types of conflicts they faced reappeared in my dealings with others.

In addition, pioneers must maintain the direction set by their own internal compass. A functioning compass always points due north, unless there is interference by a strong magnet nearby. Likewise,

Prudence Crandall refused to allow others to dissuade her from her personal conviction that Sarah Harris should join her classroom. She took a great risk to persevere, acting on her convictions, though the town brought social and legal pressures to bear, along with very real threats of imprisonment and bodily harm.

Stress has a way of increasing when individuals are faced with unfamiliar circumstances. Even thick branches can be stripped from a tree trunk when they are layered by assaulting snow, ice, and freezing rain. So no matter how mature or experienced, every pioneer must take time for self-care if there is to be any hope in long-term pioneering. Though many can't be bothered with self while on the job, there is a time when the body tells the mind, *I've put up with your abuse long enough. No more.* This is what happened to me as I put in long working hours, and it amounted to a mental and physical setback that was even more frustrating. I had to learn that a "staking" technique wasn't just for young plants that needed to get established. It was also used for wounded plants—and I had wounded myself. I needed time to recover, rest, and stake myself to those I could trust to support me in recovery. This included exposure to healthy contexts, such as spending time with a mentor and friends as well as being aware of habits, such as negative thinking, that dragged me downward.

As for Prudence Crandall, she had to cobble together a solution to her dilemma with few resources. Her board had turned against her, as well as some members of the clergy and many of her neighbors. What would she do? The pressure had caused her to dig deep, to tap into resources she didn't even know were there when she set out to found her own school. She had wanted to be a teacher. Where did those sunny days go when she could offer instruction without all the drama? They were gone, and now new days and new ways were ahead. She hadn't gone looking for them; they had come to her. Now she was in uncharted territory. Her creativity handed her a plan, her convictions set her face like flint, and her determination allowed her to put one foot in front of the other. She entered the realm of the pioneer, and once she did, she refused to look back.

Points for Your Compass

→ Being staked to a wise mentor allows the emerging pioneer to become established in a new role.

→ While a pioneer might not have a way forward completely mapped out in his mind, he can at least prepare for what he anticipates he might encounter and begin taking the steps that he knows will move him in the right direction.

→ An ethical pioneer allows her strong internal compass to guide her.

→ As the pioneer ventures into new territory, navigating difficult, unforeseen challenges may take a toll on personal resources, leading to individual depletion.

→ Self-care plays an important role in allowing the pioneer to continue pioneering.

The Equipment
"Use the right tools for the right job"

In many ways, my mother's father typified an old-fashioned Southern New England character known in that part of the country as a "Swamp Yankee." Plaid was his favorite color, done in cotton during the summers and wool in cooler weather. Every now and then, an odd solid-color chamois shirt was thrown into the mix for good measure. Grampy, as I called him, had twinkling blue eyes, tempered by a booming, gruff voice, one that required his holding the phone receiver a distance from his mouth. That voice both comforted and terrified me, often reminding me that if I needed an opinion, its owner would be happy to give me one.

Grampy was a gifted machinist by trade. He worked at Browne and Sharpe, a firm with a history of producing precise measurement tools. It was a natural fit for him; he came from a long line of industrialists. His great grandfather, Arnold Moffett Jr., for whom he was named, had purchased a wooden mill that was said to be built around 1812. Nestled tightly along the Moshassuck River in

Lincoln, Rhode Island, it would become one of the earliest industrial mills in the nation, possibly second to the Slater Mill in Pawtucket. Though surprisingly small in size, its intricate rusting gears, thick, hanging, leather drive belts, internal water wheel, and raceway no doubt became a boyhood fascination as his father recounted the mill's glory days when it sang with productivity. By the time Grampy was born, it sat silently, having long succumbed to larger, more modern industrial mills in New England. But to Grampy, the leaning, wooden edifice and its contents continued to whisper of an innovative, pioneering past. For him it was the place where the men of his clan—uncles, grandfather, and great grandfather—pored and brooded over yellowed ledgers filled with completed jobs for community members, mathematics solving for efficiency, and new inventions. The now-mute mill had become larger than life as innovation entwined itself with family lore.

Given this propensity, it's easy to see that very little could land a person in hot water faster than picking up a rake when a pitchfork would accomplish a task more proficiently. If picking up a rake was an unwise choice, selecting one that further complicated the job was worse. Woe to the one who chose a bow rake instead of a leaf rake! He chose poorly.

"For crying out loud, use the right tool for the right job!" Grampy might bellow if he caught you. These were tough ways for a youngster to learn best practices in tool usage, but lest we be too hard on Grampy, it helps to remember that he was a man of his time. He could recall when having the right tool was a necessity and creating those tools was an art. He could also reminisce that having the correct, well-crafted tool might save the owner time in efficiency, provide money to fill hungry mouths, and guard a person from a sore, injured back that might prevent the worker from returning to the job the next day. This was an era when all three resources were at a premium, and a broken tool might prove ruinous to forward progress. God help the sinner who left his tools out overnight! If Grampy had been a Catholic, this kind of neglect would have been regarded as a cardinal sin. But for a Protestant of his nature, he saw the owner who mistreated his tools as one firmly in need of reformation, and he was not one to hold back from preaching this to the wayward soul. Under the right circumstances and with no exaggeration, in Grampy's day and that of his forefathers, having the right tool for the right job might mean the difference between life and death.

This lesson is one that many pioneers learn through the difficult task of anticipating need and the subsequent effort required to fill that need. Often, the way real-life challenges play out proves that the original preparation was not nearly enough. Lack of experience creates gaps in knowledge that might prove detrimental to the pioneer and the mission. That is why there is always risk involved. For example, were there enough of the right kinds of supplies purchased? Inasmuch as is known, are the proper techniques being used? Are resources being distributed wisely? Is this the best strategy? Do we need a course check and subsequent correction? Are there other experts who should be consulted? Lessons learned and applied from this sort of inquiry by the pioneer bring refinement over the course of time, so that those who follow after might be more successful in their effort. However, the question remains: If one is a pioneer, how then is it possible to anticipate needs if a task has never been accomplished or a goal has not yet been reached? If one is going to aim for a new target, how can the right equipment be identified or, in my grandfather's words, the right tools be anticipated for the job to come?

A New Tool for a New Need

Imagine what it might be like to be a young adult from the countryside, entering a nineteenth-century industrialized city for the first time. The sights, smells, and pace of city life were altogether new. Writing in 1835, Charles Dickens described central London as "streets and courts [that] dart in all directions, until they are lost in the unwholesome vapor which hangs over the house-tops and renders the dirty perspective uncertain and confined."[1] Making sense of such an "uncertain and confined," roiling and depressive setting would overwhelm the visitor since he had no previous context in which to put the experiences. Less than a decade later, in the same setting, George Williams would establish the Young Men's Christian Association so that rural men who were drawn to the city in search of work would have an oasis from "the bleak landscape of tenement houses and dangerous influences" that were part of London at that time. The organization started simply, offering a place for Bible study and prayer, yet it uniquely began "to meet social need in the community…and its openness to members crossed the rigid lines separating English social classes." [2] By the 1890s, the Y, as it is currently known, had spread beyond English borders to other European countries as well as to the United States. It offered skill development tracks and athletic training as well as a spiritual component in keeping with its intent to provide support for sustaining the body, spirit, and mind of an individual.

Late in 1891, the season was changing, with the trees having long cast off their leaves in the northeastern part of the United States. It was time for winter to step up and cross the seasonal threshold, pushing people inside and limiting leisurely outdoor activity. As they always have, the population obliged reluctantly. Clocks appeared to slow, grinding forward more hesitantly through another icy, inclement season. It was one of those times when every parent has heard exclaimed "I'm bored" by their children, who give little thought that perhaps their own parents might be bored too.

Outdoor activities, especially sports, more easily fell prey to the change of weather. While skiing and ice-skating have long been favorites, team sports such as football, baseball, and track all came to a standstill. For those who were training young men, like instructors at the Y, this proved problematic as "there was little for [them] to do except work in the gymnasium…[and they] quickly became bored with gymnastics, calisthenics, and other similar activities." [3] Physical activity that is boring does little to generate enthusiasm, so there was an awareness that combining athleticism with play activity, even for adults, increased engagement. Seasonal doldrums combined with indoor monotony was precisely the dilemma the athletic faculty of the Springfield, Massachusetts, YMCA faced in the latter months of 1891.

Dr. Luther Gulick, the young superintendent of the physical education program at the facility, summed up the need to create a new indoor game that would both exercise and entertain:

> We need a new game, a competitive game like football or lacrosse, but it must be a game that can be played indoors. It [requires] skill and sportsmanship, providing exercise for the whole body and yet it must be one which can be played without extreme roughness or damage to players or equipment.[4]

Gulick had a tool in mind, but it was not yet defined well enough to be a workable solution for the problem that the Springfield Y's teachers sensed was a "growing unease" among the students. For this task, he called upon James Naismith, a faculty member who had a heart for the Y's mission as well as for its physical education program. Naismith frowned as he was given the assignment, for it targeted a particular group of nearly twenty young men who were especially disinterested. One of their previous instructors had even resorted to playing a children's game of potato races to drum up some enthusiasm. He gave up on the group of young men as did another instructor after him. Now Gulick was assigning this bored gang to Naismith as well as the invention of a new indoor game. He also put a clock on the creation of the new game; he gave Naismith two weeks to develop it. Naismith recoiled from this double duty and tried unsuccessfully to worm his way out of it. He recalls an exchange he had during which Gulick

> saw a vision of some project, and I suggested that the thing to do was to begin in a remote way to reach the point. Gulick said, "Naismith, you are nothing but an obstructionist." I understood his attitude and answered, "I am not an obstructionist, but a pathfinder." At this remark, we both laughed.[5]

Naismith's self-assessment was correct. He *was* a pathfinder, and this latest, most undesirable challenge would press him into the untouched court of the pioneer, catapulting him onto the international sports scene.

Digging around in the Toolbox

Anyone who has needed a straight slot screwdriver and has only been able to find a Phillips head in the tool chest knows the frustration of having a simple task put on hold by the lack of a common implement. Frustration may drive the one in need to try different objects to get the screw to turn (a dime? fingernail file? fingernail?) or return to the hunt for the missing screwdriver. But what if your task requires a tool that's a little more complex than a straight slot or a Phillips head? Let's take this one step further. What if you had a job to do and you found that *none* of the items in your tool chest were suitable for the work you were about to undertake?

This was the situation that faced Carol Estwing Ferrans. As she began her graduate work in nursing, she connected with Dr. Marjorie Powers, who became her advisor in graduate school. Powers had been involved in nursing during the days when kidney dialysis was a new procedure. Though the ability to provide dialysis was a true breakthrough, changing the status of kidney failure from a fatal condition to a chronic disease, the technology brought with it complex challenges for healthcare professionals and patients needing dialysis.

In the early days of kidney dialysis, the need for dialysis machines outpaced their availability. Furthermore, these machines were often placed in hospitals. People who needed the life-saving treatment were lining up, but the hospitals couldn't keep up with the number of patients and the amount of time they needed to spend on the machines. This resulted in the formation of committees that would evaluate each applicant to decide who would be dialyzed. Carol Ferrans recounts the process:

> Each hospital…committee would meet to decide when they had an opening, who of the candidates would get that opening. And so they were deciding, who would live and who would die. And when they would die, they would die of uremic poisoning, which was a terrible way to go. And [Marjorie Powers] was a part of that decision-making. I know that [for] everyone who was part of those committees, it was just soul-scarring.[6]

In the 1960s and early 1970s, people with kidney failure lived in a kind of anguished tension. On the one hand, the development of dialysis gave these people hope that others in their condition had never had; kidney failure was no longer a death sentence. On the other hand, gaining access to a dialysis machine was another matter. It is hard to imagine going through the application process only to be denied dialysis. Any hope of a prolonged life would be crushed, with the reality of it worsened by the knowledge that death would come after a progressive, painful process.

The individuals choosing the dialysis recipients were guided by national protocols, but the protocols didn't seem humane. In sum, these procedures objectively focused in on certain qualities of the patient. As Ferrans summarizes:

> Typically the way it would work is a man who was supporting a family would get precedence over a teenager, even though the teenager was young. If the man was old, of course, that would go against him. A woman who was raising many children, then she would have a fighting chance to be selected. A woman with no children, and particularly no job, forget it. It's over for her. So, the [committees] interviewed these people, they looked in their eyes, and they knew what decisions they were making. It was horrible.[7]

Assigning value to a life based on work status and the number of dependents took a dehumanizing, nightmarish toll on all those who were on the panels making these decisions.

In 1972, the struggle over who would receive dialysis and who would be denied came to an end. The federal government stepped in and created a law that would provide funding for dialysis for all Americans with kidney failure. Called the End Stage Renal Disease (ESRD) legislation, treatment was provided through Medicare. "It was, and continues to be, the only categorical coverage for any disease in the United States."[8] With the passing of this new law, resources became available to increase the number of dialysis machines. In time, every person who needed dialysis received it, but some unintended consequences surfaced. As patients who spanned the range of health began making their way to receive dialysis, healthcare professionals began to wonder, "Have we gone too far? Are we dialyzing people who are too old or too sick to benefit? Are we keeping people alive who really should not be?"[9] In other words, was life being prolonged just because it could be? Were some who were gravely ill having life extended and suffering needlessly as a result?

The time had come to step back and look at the situation from a different perspective, an ethical one. Compassion and science joined to give birth to a new concept: quality of life. But how does a medical professional, who works with objective metrics such as body temperature, pulse rate, respiration, and so forth, measure a subjective concept like a patient's quality of life? A new tool was needed to help guide the medical world, the patients, and their loved ones to make the best decisions humanly possible, and it couldn't come quickly enough.

A Tool Is Forged

The job wasn't an easy one: James Naismith was tasked to develop a new game in two weeks that could be enjoyed indoors by grown men, but it had to be designed in a such a way that the gym wouldn't be torn up when honest-to-goodness competition kicked in. As a self-declared pathfinder, Naismith got to work to meet the parameters his supervisor had set for him. He also tried to think of a way to channel the antsy behavior of the guys in his gym class. Actually, he didn't blame them. This particular group of men was learning secretarial and administrative skills. Unlike other students at the YMCA, they were not training to be physical education directors, so they had little interest in the physical requirements of their coursework. In relating to them, Naismith also found that his empathy motivated him. Even though he didn't want to deal with the group in the first place, he reflected, "I learned to appreciate the attitude of the class that I had been given. They were older men, and I felt that if I were in their place, I would probably have done all I could to get rid of the obnoxious requirements."[10]

Naismith first experimented with some tried-and-true tools—popular games that he knew were a low risk, first crack at his experiment. Initially, "these games relieved the men of the drudgery of which, they complained; but fifteen minutes of a game like 'three deep' became more monotonous than work on the parallel bars." Naismith then turned to outdoor games he might adapt to an indoor context. He tried first to adjust football by changing the way that the tackle was delivered, but this failed to win player support. "To ask these men to handle their opponents gently was to make their favorite sport a laughingstock and they would have none of it," Naismith discovered.[11]

He then tried an indoor version of soccer, followed by lacrosse. During both attempts, the more moderate versions still produced smashed windows, equipment dislodged from wall racks, and sundry injuries among the players. Days passed, and Naismith would soon have to report back to his supervisor on his progress, or lack of it. With only a day or two left before he was to give an account, he was still at a loss:

> So far they had all been failures, and it seemed to me that I had exhausted all my resources. The prospect before me was, to say the least, discouraging. How I hated the thought of going back to the group and admitting that, after all my theories, I too had failed to hold the interest of the class. It was worse than losing a game. All the stubbornness of my Scot[tish] ancestry was aroused, all my pride of achievement urged me on; I would not go back and admit that I had failed.[12]

Crushed, Naismith had one more class before his deadline. He had nothing new to try, so he gave no instructions to the class. When the last player left the gym for the locker room, his hopes went out the door with them. What did he feel? Failure? Loss? Humiliation seasoned with shame? Visions of his upcoming report to his supervisor and peers attacked him as he entered his office. "Hi, I'm James Naismith and I failed." Then, something very curious happened. From his office perch above the locker room, he could hear the men laughing, and in his own words, "having a good time; they were giving expression to the very spirit I had tried so hard to evoke."[13]

There's an old expression: "Laugh and the whole world laughs with you." The expression is true, and the reason is based in science. Laughter is most often found in groups of people, and it's hardwired into us. When we're with others, we're thirty times more likely to laugh, and it is contagious. We may find ourselves laughing with someone else or with a whole crowd of people. Something else happens too. We feel better. Spirits lift and muscles relax. People intrinsically know that laughter helps the whole person, which is why it's often said that it is the best medicine. No hangovers, no blackouts, no tremors, but you just might need a box of Kleenex to cleanup.

The laughing class knocked Naismith out of his funk. In fact, it infused him with enough energy to review why the tools he had proposed hadn't quite fit the job.

Initially, he realized that changing well-loved team sports like football was problematic. There was a reason these games were popular, and people resisted fiddling with them. No, he needed a fresh concept. Then, he began looking at the situation holistically. What did he need this new tool to do? The first step was to define and then refine the objective: create a game that would engage the spirit while exercising the body. A team sport would also stimulate the mind, but in order not to take the fun out of it, it should be easy to learn. The playing field needed to be indoors so it could not be overly rough. Objectives, check.

Now, onto the tools that would fit this task. What was needed to play a game with these types of parameters? Naismith went through his own needs assessment that fit the task at hand. It went something like this: Team sports usually handle a ball. What kind of ball should it be? Larger balls seemed easy to handle, and most players could throw and catch one easily. Naismith reasoned that small balls are easily hidden, so he opted for a bigger ball. At the time, larger balls were either round or oval, like a rugby ball or football. He eventually settled on a round ball.

He then thought about which of the outdoor team sports was the most interesting, and his thoughts brought him back to rugby again. Rugby, of course, was simply out of the question for an indoor game. As a contact sport, it can get pretty rough. However, when Naismith drilled down on the reason for the roughness, he saw the whole "chase drive" in motion: the one carrying the ball is pursued by a band of men trying to stop him from scoring. Furthermore, the ball carrier also has his own team in pursuit to keep opposing team members from interfering with a potential goal. Naismith had his answer. "I can still recall how I snapped my fingers and shouted, 'I've got it! If he can't run with the ball, we don't have to tackle; and if we don't have to tackle, the roughness will be eliminated.'"[14]

It's one thing to find a solution; it's another thing entirely to successfully apply the solution. Naismith now had to work out the objective of the game (what would it look like to score points?), the rules of play (how would the game be played?), and the equipment (what would be needed to play the game, besides the ball?). Naismith searched every angle, evaluating successful team games, turning them this way and that in his own mind the way a fine jeweler would examine a multifaceted diamond. From there, he developed a kind of needs assessment for each area of his new game and filled them with solutions. In the end, he had worked out "the basic framework for the whole game, [which] seemed entertaining and competitive and had an objective."[15]

Naismith woke the next morning feeling confident about his concept. He crossed paths with the building superintendent and asked if he had any boxes. He intended to use these as goals. The reply came back, "No, I haven't any boxes, but I have two old peach baskets down in the storeroom if they'll do you any good."[16] Baskets in hand, Naismith nailed each onto the lower railing of the balcony on either side of the gym. Before he was ready to play, he knew he had better write up some rules. He came up with thirteen in all. Then, with rules in hand, it was time to test his idea with the arrival of the next class.

The first student arrived and walked out onto the floor. Eyeing Naismith, his ball, and his baskets, he cynically said, "Huh! Another new game." When the rest of the class gathered, Naismith announced that he did have another new experiment, but promised if this one failed, there would be no more. However, inside he felt confident. He knew that his tool needed tweaking, but he believed the refining would come as he put it to work.

At first the execution of the game was sloppy, and there were many fouls, but everything soon started working together. In Naismith's estimation, "The game was a success from the time that the first ball was tossed up. The players were interested and seemed to enjoy the game.... It was the start of the first basketball game, and the finish of the trouble with that class."[17]

Taking the Tools from Hardware to Software

Much of medicine is hard science. As it relates to the human body, there are ranges of acceptable metrics that indicate whether a person is healthy, moving into a danger zone, or just plain sick. Body temperature is easily relatable. An elevated temperature is a sure sign that the body is fighting an unwanted invader in the form of a virus or bacterial infection, and it is a warning to its owner to help the body heal. These signals, whatever they measure, are neglected at your own risk. Too much sugar? Hello diabetes (and/or tooth decay; reread chapter 2 for instructions from Horace Wells). Elevated cholesterol? Higher risk of stroke or cardiac issues. Not enough fiber in the diet?...Well, you get the idea. No human is exempt. We live and move and have our being in organic machines, and it's a beautiful thing.

But what is it like for each one of us to live in our own "machines," especially when going through treatment for a serious illness? And what if that treatment compounds the misery we're already experiencing? This is the question that haunted Carol Ferrans as she began to learn about the trauma experienced by people who were passed over for dialysis treatment as well as those who suffered needlessly, who were "over dialyzed" simply because the treatment *was* available. She knew there had to be a better way.

Quality of life as a concept was a fresh idea in the twentieth century. Part of Ferrans's research necessitated study in bioethics and the development of quality of life concepts. "If you look back at [its] history, one of the earliest uses of [quality of life] was during the Nazi era in World War II with the idea that there was a life that was not worth living and therefore you were morally justified in either letting that life die, or making that life die quickly in murdering them." Clearly, without moral parameters, an ideal like quality of life could disastrously wander far afield with horrific consequences.

Other areas where quality of life issues began to emerge were in fields relating to cancer research and treatment. With the development of chemotherapy, physicians began to wonder if those receiving it would survive, much less benefit from it. There had to be a way to determine who might get the most out of the treatment. In the 1940s, Dr. David Karnofsky and some associates developed the Karnofsky Performance Status Scale, a tool designed to standardize the measurement of a cancer patient's ability to carry on with his or her life. "The Karnofsky Performance Status scores range from 0 to 100. A higher score means the patient is better able to carry out daily activities. [It] may be used to determine a patient's prognosis, measure changes in a patient's ability to function, or decide if a patient could be included in a clinical trial."[18] This early assessment was not designed to measure quality of life, though it was one of the first tests designed to take patient feedback under consideration before administering treatment.

While medical professionals were deemed experts with the final answer earlier in the twentieth century, shifts in societal views toward authority in the latter decades revealed a glaring gap: the patient's voice was nearly absent in the quality of life conversation. Then PhD candidate Carol Ferrans and her advisor Marjorie Powers set out to correct this oversight, and in so doing, they pioneered the Ferrans and Powers Quality of Life Index. Ferrans remembers some of the challenges she faced:

> Though we had measured quality of life before on [a] single scale, the problem with that single scale was [a] total number, but you couldn't unpackage it, investigate what contributed to it. You also couldn't compare this person to that person because you didn't

> know what went into it. You couldn't measure it
> over time to see how it changed for a person, so we
> thought what we really needed was a measure that
> would allow us to understand what went into this
> person's evaluation of their own quality of life.[19]

Armed with knowledge of how other pioneers had previously measured quality of life while carrying a highly magnetized personal ethical compass and a burning passion to help medical care providers and their patients make more informed quality-of-life decisions, Ferrans prepared herself to forge her way up to the furnace to craft her new tool.

From the onset, Ferrans was adamant that the patient would inform the results. The results would represent a holistic view of the individual, which would include how health impacted an individual's ability to function (much like Karnofsky did), as well as the person's social and family components, financial assessment, and psychological and spiritual well-being. Furthermore, Ferrans realized that results showing how satisfied a person was with these aspects of their lives didn't necessarily relay how important they were to the individual. So, she mirrored the satisfaction portion of the test and created a second part, in order to score how much people valued these various parts of their lives. Then she hit a snag. As she tried to work her scoring system, she found that the formula she was using wasn't getting the job done. With frustration mounting, she needed a fresh perspective. Right about that time, it walked through her front door.

> I was working on it all day long, trying to figure
> out different mathematical combinations, and
> my husband Jim having been a math major as an
> undergrad came home and said, "How about if you
> do this?" And it worked. It was innovative. Nobody
> had a scoring system like ours, and the beauty of it
> was that it captured conceptually what we wanted, to
> give that best representation of quality of life in terms
> of your satisfaction with the things that are [most]
> important to you.[20]

Since the creation of the Ferrans and Powers Quality of Life Index, Carol Ferrans has seen tremendous growth in both the adoption and adaptation of her tool. Now in over twenty-one languages and cited in more than four hundred publications of which she's aware, Ferrans has seen her assessment mature into illness-specific surveys that help others beyond those with kidney failure, including those suffering from arthritis, cancer, cardiac issues, chronic fatigue syndrome, and diabetes, to name just a few. She has made all of these surveys available at no cost. Rather than profit from her tool, she continues her medical research work in other areas that concern the well-being of others.

Most recently she has been involved in studies that have revealed that "cultural beliefs contribute directly to later-stage diagnosis of breast cancer in African-American and Latina women in Chicago."[21] As a result, the findings and recommendations of the team Ferrans led, called the Metropolitan Chicago Breast Cancer Task Force (MCBCTF), were influential in passing the Illinois Reducing Breast Cancer Disparities Act. This legislation assures better access to screening, improved quality of mammograms, and subsequent treatment for African Americans and Latinas. "The Chicago black/white disparity in breast cancer deaths has decreased by 35% since MCBCTF first released its report." In relaying this story to me, Ferrans beamed. "These are lives, real lives that have been saved!" Ferrans is an excellent example of a pioneer who continues to pioneer.

Founded in Fire

Instructor, athlete, and pathfinder James Naismith was aiming for a new target, and without realizing it, he created an enduring sport. Having come to the end of his ideas, he was close to quitting when the spirit of his own students revived him. Not long after basketball's creation in 1891, the sport began to take off, and, gladly for Naismith, he would live to see it.

After the first few games, word got out that some of the men were playing something new. Curious, others came to watch, and within a couple of short weeks, there were as many as two hundred spectators who had filled the gym gallery. Basketball was appealing to many and attracted some of the women teachers at a nearby school. When they expressed their desire to try playing the game, Naismith open-mindedly said he didn't see any reason they couldn't. "One of the reasons Naismith was so pleased with the invention of basketball was the game's popularity among women, who he thought could play the game as well as men.... [Naismith's] wife, Maud...participated in one of the first women's games ever played."[22]

As some of the students from the Y went home on break, they took the game with them, spreading it across the United States and Canada. Missionaries who had been students at the Y traveled to other countries and introduced the game to their new friends, contributing to the spread of basketball internationally. The first game in Japan was played in 1915, a country that was one of the early adopters. Though James Naismith died in 1939, he no doubt would have been pleased to know that his game was adapted to meet the needs of people in wheelchairs. Wheelchair basketball was created in the mid-1940s both in England and the United States. Disabled World War II veterans were among the first to play, with the National Wheelchair Basketball association formed in 1948.[23] Women's wheelchair basketball followed in the 1960s. Today, basketball is an Olympic sport, for both abled and disabled people, not to mention a multimillion-dollar pastime in the world of professional sports.

Though part of James Naismith's story includes the pressure to develop basketball on a fast-track timeline, many pathfinders discover that their race is more of a marathon. Carol Ferrans's story is a case in point. Despite the often frustrating and onerous work it takes to create a tool like the Ferrans and Powers Quality of Life Index, pioneers often seem to be drawn back to the grindstone like a farrier is drawn to the furnace. I asked Ferrans what it felt like to be a pioneer. She responded: "Slogging. My work has always felt like slogging. Just working. Working, working, working, but it's actually probably true of all pioneers. Going back is never an option. Press forward. You keep going. You can't quit." She then became thoughtful and wanted to share some advice to future toolmakers, knowing full well some of the barriers they would encounter:

> If you find out that you have hit a wall, gone in the wrong direction, or hit a dead end, learn everything you can about it. Ask, "How did we get into this cul-de-sac and how do we get out of it?" Then you should ask, "Does this mean that the direction I was in was completely wrong? Or what is it that I can pull out of this that can help us?"
>
> What I mean by that is some of the most interesting things that we have found in our work are the things that we didn't expect. At first, they looked like maybe they're mistakes, and you look really hard and sometimes when you peel back the layers, you uncover something that gives you much better insights than you could have ever imagined in the beginning. But you never would have gotten there if you hadn't been plowing through the snow, and hit the wall, and then backed up, and reassessed. So I think that's probably the definition of the essence of a pioneer. I think that's it.[24]

As a machinist, Grampy knew that he had to get his measurements just right. Close enough wouldn't cut it. Even an error of a thousandth of an inch might cause him to cast a piece away. (Incidentally, on average, a human hair is roughly three thousandths of an inch in diameter.) He knew that, in the end, if he didn't get it right, it wouldn't work. In this way, pioneers are sometimes called upon to be master toolmakers. When presented with a problem or an obstacle that must be resolved to enable them to fulfill their pioneering mission, they set about to address the gap, creating what is needed to give them the necessary knowledge to provide a resolution. In James Naismith's case, he was given a class of secretarial students who resisted boring but mandatory physical exercises. Naismith addressed not only the physical component of the situation but the motivational one as well. He provided a fun, heart-pumping game that his class of young men, and, as it turns out, many others, wanted to be involved with. Likewise, Carol Ferrans found herself grieved that people were not involved in their own healthcare decisions. So she developed a tool for the primary segment she was serving (dialysis patients), and her assessment was adapted for many other ailments and translated into many different languages. As Naismith and Ferrans kept their eyes fixed on their mission, they were able to push through frustration when initial attempts of designing a solution weren't quite right. The world is better off as a result of their pioneering persistence.

Points for Your Compass

➜ Sometimes pioneers must create their own tools in order to realize their vision.

➜ Forging a tool is not an easy process, and it may take a number of efforts to create one that is just right for the job at hand.

➜ Pioneers may use negative motivators to propel them forward in the tool-making process ("I don't want to fail"), but largely the positive motivators are more fruitful (examples: a new team sport that is fun *and* stimulates the mind, or a resource that can help medical patients assess their own quality of life).

➜ Partnering with others when reaching an impasse may offer valuable insight to help create a breakthrough in the tool-making process.

➜ Pioneers frequently can imagine how the tool they developed for a specific purpose might be adapted to meet other needs (examples: Naismith believed basketball would also be an excellent sport for women; Ferrans saw that her Quality of Life Index could be used for other ailments).

The Team

"It's what you know and who you know"

THEY WERE HIT BY ANOTHER FRIGID WAVE. TRULY, EACH MAN WON-
dered how long he could continue to work under such conditions.
But to give up was to invite death, and not just one's own demise
but also that of the other five men in the lifeboat. As a small rescue
team battling the fury of the Scotia Sea, they were fighting not
only to save their own lives but the remainder of the shipwrecked
crew of the *Endurance*. They were left behind to carve out a temporary home on a cold, rocky shore, reluctantly loaned to them
by the inhospitable Elephant Island. If they failed to succeed, no
one would know. It was highly unlikely that the crew would ever
be discovered in such a remote and isolated part of the world. In
fact, if asked what they believed about Ernest Shackleton and his
courageous crew, most realists back in England would likely say
that the group had perished on their quest to cross the continent of
Antarctica by way of the South Pole.

Shackleton himself was one of the six souls working their way toward what they hoped would be their salvation on South Georgia Island. He gave himself no special treatment, taking his turn at the hard labor to move the little skiff forward. In 1914, it was an era long before satellite navigation and cell phone communication. At the time, they were on the edge of the known earth with no means to call for help.

As the sea grew more furious, the way forward was exceedingly hard, testing every muscle and every fiber of mental determination. Even worse was the question worming its way to the forefront of each crew member's consciousness: Were they heading in the right direction to reach a whaling station at South Georgia Island where they might find help? In the inclement weather, getting a good navigational reading was a crapshoot. Taking measurements with a sextant was dicey as the sun was a recalcitrant friend in the stormy southern sky. The boat's balance became a concern as ice crystalized around it. The hardened seawater had to be carefully chiseled off by skillfully eking out on a tossing deck, working the ice free with frostbitten fingers. One miscalculation would send a crew member sliding off the little wooden skiff into the hungry, sapphire sea. Ballast in the form of rocks taken from Elephant Island's beach had to be strategically moved about the hull of the *James Caird* by hands that were constantly frigid and wet. It was backbreaking work for cramped bodies, continually kept in a hunched-over position by the confines of the boat. The crew had already incurred physical punishment from having to live months in the extreme climate. Basic refreshment in the form of food and sleep were scarce. There was no rest, no relief. There was only the obligation to will one's self to press on.

He Didn't Start the Fire

Shackleton was no newbie to the Antarctic region. As a young man he was drawn to some of the earth's most extreme climates. In 1901, he was handpicked by Robert Scott to join him and Dr. Edward Wilson in an attempt to reach the South Pole, an accomplishment that had not yet been achieved. Though the effort was ultimately a failure, due in part to Shackleton falling ill during the journey, it did result in new discoveries in meteorology, geology, zoology, and the earth's magnetism, and the team had come closer to reaching the pole than anyone had previously. Furthermore, it also stoked the pioneering flame in Shackleton's soul. He was hooked.

When Shackleton returned to England, he was determined to return to Antarctica and be the first to reach the South Pole, this time leading his own team. He gathered his sponsors, chose his team members, and sailed south in the *Nimrod*, much to the dismay of his former leader Robert Scott. Shackleton and his colleagues then pressed further into the inhospitable Antarctic wilderness than anyone had previously, but then "The Boss," as Shackleton was known, made the hard decision to abandon the trek after the harsh environment began to wear his team down. "Barely a hundred miles short of the Pole, he took the decision to turn back, after planting the Union Jack at 88° 23'. Had he been prepared to sacrifice the lives of his team, Shackleton would have claimed the Pole."[1]

History records that the race to the South Pole would be claimed by another. Norwegian explorer Roald Amundsen reached the South Pole with four other men and sixteen dogs on December 14, 1911. A little more than a month later, Shackleton's colleague-competitor Robert Scott arrived at the pole with his team, only to meet with exhaustion, hunger, and eventually death on their return trek. And now, with this prize having passed him by, Shackleton set his sights on another "first": to cross the Antarctic continent.

Now here they were, in a Hail Mary attempt to make their way to the whaling station on South Georgia Island on the open sea after having survived in the Antarctic for four seasons and then some. Due to Shackleton's leadership (along with the group's willingness to follow him), they defied the odds by stretching their supplies, avoiding mortal accidents, and keeping their spirits up. Their perseverance and sense of mission (albeit altered from crossing the Antarctic continent to merely surviving the botched expedition) pulled them through the most boring of the long southern days of sunshine and slush, to the most frightful of long howling winter nights and even a harrowing lion seal pursuit. Time seemed to slog through the sunny, mushy, twenty-three-hour southern summer days and lumber through the biting, inky, twenty-three-hour winter darkness. With each day that passed, supplies diminished, bodies craved respite, and frayed emotions longed for rescue. At times the crew amused themselves by reciting poetry and imagining the food they would eat once they returned home. In reality, back in the British Isles, only the most optimistic nursed any hope that Shackleton and his team would be seen again.

Another Race against Time

Far from the tumultuous waters of the Ross Sea, about a decade later, an icy rescue of a different sort was mounted. Dr. Curtis Welch, the sole physician in Nome, Alaska, reached for his supply of antitoxin serum, and, to his horror, he found it had expired. Several children had fallen prey to diphtheria, with two Inupiaq children having already died. He knew it would not be long before all of the residents were exposed to the toxin-producing bacteria. It was an insidious illness. Transmitted through coughing and sneezing or touching an infected item, diphtheria leaves the victim struggling to breathe as the tissues in the respiratory system are poisoned and die. Children and those with fragile health were especially vulnerable. Dr. Welch feared an epidemic that would not be stopped without the life-saving serum. Nome was put under quarantine.

Dr. Welch had another problem. In 1925, the New Year had bitten hard. The January chill had iced up the harbor and made flight to Nome impossible. Desperate, he took to sending a wire to the Alaskan territory's governor, Scott Bone: "An epidemic of diphtheria is almost inevitable here STOP I am in urgent need of one million units of diphtheria antitoxin STOP Mail is only form of transportation STOP."[2]

Delivering mail in Alaska in the 1920s was not the usual affair one might see in the lower states. It was not uncommon for the territory's mushers to become involved, exchanging the horses of the Pony

Express with doggies. With the nearest serum in Anchorage (about one thousand miles away from Nome), Governor Bone arranged for a train to bring the precious cargo closer to the languishing city, dropping it off in Nenana, which was 674 miles away. And then came the great, historic "Great Race of Mercy," accomplishing what had not been done before.

Fur protectively swaddled the antitoxin as it was carefully handed to "Wild Bill" Shannon, who secured it to his sled. Putting his dogs in drive, he began the first leg of the non-stop trek to Nome. Musher after musher received the package as the paws of hardworking dogs hit the ice and snow, bringing the much-needed solution closer to the diphtheria victims. At times, the temperature dropped to sixty degrees below Fahrenheit, forcing some mushers to run alongside the dogs just to keep warm. At one point, a storm blew up while musher Gunnar Kaasen was on his leg of the journey. His lead dog, Balto, well out in front of the team, couldn't be seen though the blinding snow. Balto also had difficulty seeing in the blizzard and took to sniffing his way up the trail. "Suddenly, a massive gust upwards of 80 miles per hour flipped the sled and launched the antidote into a snowbank. Panic coursed through Kaasen's frostbitten body as he tore off his mitts and rummaged through the snow with his numb hands before locating the serum."[3]

Early on February 2, Kaasen and his thirteen-dog team arrived in Port Safety. The weary and storm-beaten group arrived only to find that the team that would take the final stretch of the delivery wasn't ready to go. Rather than delay, Kaasen got back on the trail to Nome. What a welcome sight they must have been to the worried citizens of Nome as they drove to find Dr. Welch and place the serum in the hands of the one who would administer the much-needed medication.

Pioneering People and Paws

The end of the journey to put an end to the epidemic in Nome became the inspiration for a celebratory race that would serve as a remembrance of the unbelievable teamwork of over 20 mushers and

150 dogs that was accomplished over the course of the 674-mile Great Race of Mercy. What normally took about a week and a half to finish was completed in just over five days from late January to early February of 1925 as the courageous mushers and their dogs forged forward with a precious package that would save many lives. Alaskans continue to commemorate this historic act of teamwork today through the Iditarod Sled Dog Race, or the "Last Great Race." The origin story of the race continues to inspire many from around the world to participate in the dog sled challenge and keep the memory of the pioneering mushers and their dogs alive.

One such Alaskan native and Iditarod participant, Karl Clauson, describes the thrill the race evoked in his own heart, and how ultimately that excitement moved him from being a spectator to a contestant to an unwitting pioneer. He recalled the first time he heard the race broadcast on the radio:

> It was only the fourth year of the race and I got a little AM radio and I'm listening to this scratchy [program].... I had a vision I had in my mind's eye of traveling 1,100 miles by dog team, and crossing under the Burled Arch (the finish line) in Nome, Alaska to commemorate this great race that celebrates the saving of an entire village from a diphtheria epidemic and that I could somehow run that trail with a team of my own dogs. The fact that Nome was saved by a relay of like-minded people in a shared passion to save someone from dying; that's a pretty cool thing. I don't even know who the winner of the race was that year. All I know is when I heard the winner come across the finish line, I looked up into the heavens and I said, "I don't know how, but I *am* going to do this."

Though Karl had a clear vision of finishing the Iditarod, he was a long way even from the starting line. At the time, he had a small team of only three dogs. Furthermore, he was a teen, and at the time, no one eighteen-years-old had completed the Iditarod. How would he get from where he was to where he could actually experience flying past the Burled Arch? Thinking back on his experience he recalled,

"What's weird is, I was more compelled by being in the Iditarod, than to necessarily complete it. I think that getting to the starting line was my goal, and then [thought], 'How in the world am I going to get a team that's worthy of running that thing?'"[4] He had a thing or two to learn about how to build a team and how to discern character, not only in dogs, but in other people as well as himself.

Shackleton's Picks

To say that Ernest Shackleton's method of filling positions for his Imperial Trans-Antarctic expedition was different is an understatement. He had a nose for sniffing out talent and an ability to determine a man's appetite to secure a position. After all, he wasn't hiring for banker's hours; he was hiring for the adventure of a lifetime that would be hard won. To be selected as part of a pioneering expedition at the dawn of the twentieth century was a lot like being a rock star. Before the ship raised its sails, team members had the proverbial red carpet rolled out and were fawned on in popular society. Shackleton, however, knew firsthand the unforgiving reality of the earth's most southern region. He had to see past the glamorous aspirations in his applicants and ascertain a requisite gut of steel.

One sure way to bypass the sparkly allure was to hire those who already had experience in the region. Theirs would be a practiced perspective at having already been exposed to the harsh environment of the Antarctic, yet they had come out of the experience with a willingness to return. To that end, Shackleton engaged known entities like Frank Wild and Tom Crean, who had been with him on previous expeditions. Wild had experienced the harsh realities of the Antarctic alongside Shackleton in a previous effort to reach the South Pole in 1908 and 1909. A mutual affection and respect had developed between them. "The two men, in fact, formed a well-matched team. Wild's loyalty to Shackleton was beyond question. And his quiet somewhat unimaginative disposition was a perfect balance for Shackleton's often whimsical and occasionally explosive nature."[5] To Wild, Shackleton granted the position of second in command. Crean received an appointment as the second officer on the *Endurance,* and had been put through the paces in past polar explorations that included two with explorer Robert Falcon Scott. He was among the *Terra Nova* crew when Scott finally reached the South Pole but perished on his return trip.

As to his unusual means of interviewing, Shackleton espoused somewhat eccentric methods that winnowed out those who would have been an ill fit for his team. For example, during interviews he commented on an applicant's appearance, inquired about their singing ability, and asked rapid, unrelated, unexpected questions. "There is no record of any interview Shackleton conducted with a prospective expedition member lasting much more than five minutes…. [But] despite the instantaneous nature of these decisions, Shackleton's intuition for selecting compatible men rarely failed."[6]

Shackleton chose geologist Raymond Priestley, who had joined the explorer on his previous *Nimrod* expedition (1907–1909). Priestley recalled his interview: "He asked me if I could sing and I said I couldn't; and he asked me if I would know gold if I saw it, and again I said No! He must have asked me other questions but I remember these because they were bizarre."[7] Reginald James, who was chosen as *Endurance*'s physicist, was also asked about his crooning ability, along with his own assessment of his temperament and if he had varicose veins and good circulation. Leonard Hussey had virtually no qualifications as a meteorologist yet was chosen for the position after much pacing by The Boss. He was later told that he was picked because he "looked funny."[8] Hussey himself was a good pick, especially when it came to his banjo playing, which served to cheer the team over the many months they were stranded. Shackleton seemed to know that music lifted morale after long days of hard work. Overall, when it came to putting together a team who would pioneer the trip Shackleton was envisioning, biographers Morrell and Capparell aptly observed that "The Boss was listening for enthusiasm and for subtle indications of their ability to be part of a team."[9]

For such a venture, it would appear that success depended on talent, individual temperament, tenacity, and team spirit. By virtue of its nature, a polar exploration creates an isolated work environment.

Any sort of maverick or behavioral bravado could send the delicate balance of the *Endurance's* culture a-kilter, placing the expedition in jeopardy. It was no easy thing to log months upon the seas with the same small lot of people working together hour by hour to realize a goal in one of the earth's harshest climates. Morrell and Capparell further note that "Shackleton wanted men who contributed to *esprit de corps*, those with a passion for the life of an explorer, and confidence in success. One thing Shackleton looked for was a happy person."[10] No doubt this optimistic attitude was a major contributor to the survival of every team member through the harrowing ordeal they would later face.

You're Only as Fast as Your Slowest Dog

Young musher Karl Clauson was learning his own lessons about how to build a team in his quest to run the Iditarod. He credits George Attla, an Alaskan legend in mushing, with teaching him how to identify talent in young pups even when they were only a few months old. Clauson reflected:

> Talent is an amazing thing, but there's no substitute for the ability to run fast for a husky. George Attla would determine talent and drive in a certain way. He would take a litter of puppies about 4 to 6 months old, and then he would tell his wife, "Honey, when I get out of the dog lot about one hundred meters, let this litter of puppies go from their pen. They will follow me," and he would go out on the trail ten straight miles. Then he would turn that team [of older dogs] around and head back in. And as he was heading back in, the first puppy he would run into? The pick of the litter. The second one? Second pick of the litter. And so on and so forth. Because the ones that showed the drive and ability to be furthest out on the trail trying to find this team? Dead ringer, quality talented dogs. So, you got to have talent, no doubt about it.

The type of dog that runs the Iditarod is not the typical house pet. Rather, it is a helpful blend of breeds that is able to withstand harsh climates while enjoying the work of pulling a sled long distances. These dogs love to run. "The Alaskan husky that runs the Iditarod is a unique animal. I think a lot of people would imagine a very stout, sturdy, thick kind of a dog, but they're light. They're fast and can keep it up for a very long time. So, it's a mixed breed. It's not a pure bred: a whole lot of husky, a lot of Siberian, a little bit of Labrador. All kinds of breeds."[11]

Sometimes pioneers have to start with what they have, and, as a young man who had just been introduced to mushing, Karl started with the three dogs that he already owned. The memory of his meager beginnings brought out a wry grin. "These three dogs I had couldn't run down the block let alone run 1,100 miles. I got my first dog out of the dog pound. I didn't even know how old she was. She was probably ten. She had no clue what a harness was. She was a husky who hadn't learned how to run. I had a ragtag group. We had no business even dreaming this way!"

Many pioneers begin this way. Living a reality far from that which has the potential to launch them to great heights, the weight of their actual circumstances binds them fast to terra firma. This doesn't stop the dreaming or the vision from taking shape in their mind. As Clauson pressed into his imagined future as an Iditarod participant, he gradually learned how to throw off the hindering weight of his present by learning and acting on his new knowledge to shape a fresh reality. Even though he hadn't yet reached the starting line, he was slowly developing into the profile of a serious contestant.

Sometimes, the refining process cuts deeply. In Clauson's case, the weight holding him back was a favorite dog. He reflected on how love and the need for performance don't always align:

> Your team is only as fast as your slowest dog. The interesting thing about development for the team I would take to Nome is that we would continue to improve, improve, improve, but with each improvement, we had dogs that either had to get better by training on the side, or they weren't going to make

the cut. When you're doing a high stakes thing like running the Iditarod, no matter how much you love a dog, sometimes they can't take the trip. It's hard. One of my favorite dogs on the Iditarod was Target. She was one of the first dogs I ever had. I loved her. She was an amazing girl, [and] she ran because she loved me. And one day, heading into McGrath, about 350 miles into the race, she looked back at me from about the middle of the team and it was as if she said, "Hey, Friend, I can't do it anymore. Can't you see that I'm lagging a bit?" I stopped the dog team, put her in the sled, and as we were heading down the trail, started petting her. When we got to [the next checkpoint at] McGrath, I looked at her and said, "Target, this race is over for you, girl. We can't go any further." So, for the sake of the team, I had to let her go, and she understood it.[12]

Shackleton himself had to make his own cuts to his personnel. After sending the *Endurance* on ahead to finalize details, he arrived in Buenos Aires, Argentina to find that some of the discipline aboard the ship had slacked off. He found the cook drunk, so he was immediately invited to ply his culinary arts elsewhere. A couple of seamen also found themselves staff casualties as a result of their combative behavior.

Serious about succeeding, pioneers won't risk the mission and will make the cuts necessary to align team members to the task ahead of them.

The Right Dog in the Right Harness

In his book *Good to Great*, author Jim Collins popularized a phrase that describes the organizational process of getting talented people into the positions that are best suited for the organization *and* for them: getting the right people on the right seats on the bus. In an organization's pursuit of greatness, Collins noted:

The executives who ignited the transformations from good to great did not first figure out where to drive the bus and then get people to take it there. No, they *first* got the right people on the bus (and the wrong people off the bus) and *then* figured out where to drive it. They said in essence, "Look, I don't really know where we should take this bus. But I know this much: If we get the right people on the bus, the right people in the right seats, and the wrong people off the bus, then we'll figure out how to take it someplace great."[13]

Pioneering leaders have no less need for this sort of discernment, though sometimes they know right where they want to take the bus, ship, deep-sea craft, or spaceship. They know that the venture on which they've embarked will depend on having the right sort of competencies available in their people (or pups) when needed.

In an Iditarod contestant's world, the course is already set: be the first sled under the Burled Arch. For Karl Clauson, the challenge was a bit more compounded: it was to be the youngest musher under that arch in his time. But there's much more needed to win the race than putting the fastest huskies you can find into your harness. Once a musher has selected dogs with drive and speed, he or she must decide which dogs will fill the positions needed to swiftly pull the sled. In effect, they've got to get the right dog in the right position on the team, and this takes knowing the capabilities of your dogs. Clauson describes the process:

> [There's a] way you do role selection for different positions on a dog team, and I'll start from the back and go to the front. The wheel dogs are right in front of the sled. They handle a lot of the stress, strain, and weight more than any of the other dogs in the team. If the sled is catching up to the team too fast, they're the ones who feel that slack and have to take that slack out. If there's excess weight or the musher falls off the sled, they feel it first. So their tug lines are most directly related to that sled. It's a dangerous position, because if that sled were to run up on the back legs of

the dog, they're going to get clipped first. That's why we're very careful about how we handle wheel dogs. They're strong. They don't have to be really brilliant. They just gotta be tough![14]

Team dogs follow the wheel dogs, and from the sound of it, they don't appear to play a vital role other than to provide more horsepower (more accurately, dog power) in moving the sled forward. A seasoned musher, however, knows better. These team members can be anywhere between two to six sets of two and they are relied upon to keep up the pace and a rhythmic flow.

Next come the swing dogs that are positioned right behind the leaders of the team. Clauson describes them as anticipatory: "Those dogs almost need to expect what's coming around the corner. They carry a lot of the brunt of fast sweeping turns." But the swing dogs may also be serving another role. As Clauson explains: "If you're training [for] lead dogs, you put [the swing dogs] right behind the lead dogs. Then you get up to the front and then you have the lead dogs. And my two sharpest lead dogs that I had were born in the same litter. They lived together, trained together, raced together, and died together."[15]

Trust...under Pressure

Loyalty to The Boss, a passion for the ongoing mission, and team spirit also contributed to the willingness of Shackleton's team members to switch roles when needed. After the crushed *Endurance* succumbed to the grip of its icy predator, several original work assignments associated with the ship evaporated, necessitating an evolving agility and flexibility under stress. This required extreme learning skills under duress. Without *Endurance*, a harsh, new reality forced its way into the lives of the expedition personnel. Flexibility became a requisite: Medics also served as mushers, seamen became seal hunters, and every hand was needed to haul the remaining lifeboats and supplies as life on the ice became a daily affair. One of the men described the sledging stint this way: "It's a hard, rough, jolly life, this marching and camping, no washing of self or dishes, no undressing, no changing of clothes. We have our food anyhow, and always impregnated with blubber-smoke; sleeping almost on the bare snow and working as hard as the human physique is capable of doing on a minimum of food."[16] The needs of the moment dictated the role to be played.

When pioneers are out on their own, pressing their way through new territory, victories are hard won, and the quality of their personnel decisions is borne out. Every team member may hold the potential solution to a sticky situation, and the team member has got to have the temperament and doggedness to give that extra when called upon. Musher Clauson remembers having a life-saving discussion with one of his huskies as they were stopped in a storm on the Alaskan icy trail:

> I remember I didn't have a lead dog that had the physical stamina to lead anymore. It's a mentally fatiguing role to be the lead dog hour after hour. I went back to a dog that was in wheel [position], and I looked at her and I said, "Hey, girl. I got a problem. I got no one leading this team right now. You've seen me try a bunch of leaders up there, and [we're stopped] on the river ice. Now, we have a choice: we can die out here, or you can lead us. Now, you've never led before. You've never wanted to, but I'm going to try you. Would you do it?" And I grabbed her up out of that wheel position, and I walked her to the very front of the team and I walked back to the sled, and I [clicks tongue], "Hey girl, ready to go?" She jumped into that harness and led the team all the way to the next checkpoint because I asked her to.[17]

Love Them Forward

Clauson's observation, "She led because I asked her to," illustrates the profound loyalty that can develop between a pioneering leader and the team if there's a knowledge that the pioneer values and even loves the group who is moving his or her vision forward. That loyalty can extend between a musher and his dog team. "Dogs are not fooled for long by misleading cues and stop responding to people who have proven unreliable.... They are very socially aware, both of humans and of each other. Many studies have reported that they can sense human emotions. Recent research has found that they can tell the difference between happy and angry faces, and even show jealousy."[18]

While the love that exists between a human and a canine companion differs from human-to-human love, dogs seem to sense when human love and affection are directed toward them. When asked how a musher creates a team dynamic among the sled dog pack, Clauson did not hesitate:

> Love. Sadly there's two different kinds of dog teams out there. There are some dog teams that are "motivated," and I use that word very loosely, through fear. This was more prominent when I was a young musher. A dog team motivated by fear will never win the Iditarod trail sled dog race. Happy teams win the Iditarod. Loved teams win the Iditarod. See, when the chips are down and it's 20 degrees Fahrenheit below zero, a dog that's been yelled at doesn't have the motivation to get through that storm. The dog that's been loved on, when the musher says, "Can you give me a little more? Can we get through this?" They'll say, "You got it. Let's go."[19]

Testing, time, and trust are all part of the loyalty equation. In Shackleton's case, he had already exhibited behavior that spoke of the value he had for each member of his team. He was not so single-minded as to risk the lives and well-being of his crew for success. Rather, he "focused on making sure every man had the strength to pull through the ordeal ahead.... He shouldered the entire burden of the dilemma, leaving his men free to focus on the work at hand." And there was plenty of work to do when the *Endurance* had to be abandoned and supplies needed to be collected. Then there were long, boring days of camping on the ice, waiting for something, anything, to happen. Ennui was its own type of challenge. "[Shackleton] worked to maintain the established routine and structure so the crew felt secure....

Ultimately, he won the crew's unwavering loyalty with his extraordinary ability to communicate and connect personally. His contact with his men was constant, friendly, instructive, and often fun."[20]

You Never Do It Alone

In twenty-one days, twelve hours, eight minutes, and twenty-nine seconds, Iditarod rookie Karl Clauson crossed under the Burled Arch, and in so doing, became one of the first eighteen-year-olds to have completed the race. Though placing thirty-eighth and receiving no prize money, Karl realized his dream. However, he didn't forget that it took the help of others—his own team—to get him there. He received inspiration and instruction through the efforts of others, and his own family provided him with encouragement and resourcing. When Clauson reflected on his accomplishment, he quickly recalled the feeling he had, though nearly four decades had passed when I interviewed him: "Yeah, when I got across that finish line that was an adrenaline rush. I was almost happier for my dad than I was for myself. Isn't that weird? Because my dad was there and he was so proud of his son, because my dad had sacrificed a lot for me to be out there."[21]

And what of the furry friends that had carried him over a thousand miles from Anchorage to Nome? Clauson made sure each dog received custom canine expressions of gratitude from their musher:

> Different dogs love different things even as far as affection. I mean some dogs don't want to be hugged and others want to lick you to death, and some want to be challenged to go harder, some want to be encouraged to go harder.... When I got done with that race, the [dogs] that loved fish, got more fish than they could handle. The ones who loved beaver, got more beaver...the ones who loved butter, got more cubes than they've ever seen in their life! So, did I reward my team? You better believe it. I let them know, we're done. We're not going any further. Some

were happy. Some were disappointed because these
dogs were born to run. It's funny. There are a lot of
parallels between dogs and people.

Clauson's reflection draws out an important principle: A pioneer's
team not only wants to experience the thrill of a realized adventure,
but they deeply crave individualized, expressed appreciation of their
personal contributions from the pioneering leader. Shackleton was
a master at this. According to Morrell and Capparell, "his conver-
sations never seemed contrived or staged to the men.... No praise
or condemnation was ever done through a middleman or in a circu-
itous way. Shackleton spoke with the highest and lowest on his crew,
finding some common ground on which to meet."[22] Shackleton even
wanted to be seen taking his fair share of the tasks, despite his moniker of "The Boss." Instead of using his position to avoid interaction
with his team, he "wanted to appear familiar with the men. He even
worked on it, insisting on having exactly the same treatment, food,
and clothing. He went out of his way to demonstrate his willingness to do the menial chores."[23] In the final pages of his book *South*,
Shackleton honors his team for the advances and contributions they
made to science, even though the larger mission of the expedition
was never realized. He noted: "To the credit side of the Expedition,
one can safely say that the comradeship and resource of the members of the Expedition was worthy of the highest traditions of Polar
Service; and it was a privilege to me to have had under my command
men who, through dark days and the stress and strain of continuous
danger, kept up their spirits and carried out their work regardless of
themselves and heedless of the limelight."[24]

After the sweet taste of success hits the pioneer's palette, it is
tempting to claim accolades for one's self. However, the wise leader
will not forget to look back and commend his or her team. When
asked about the importance of others' contributions in helping to
develop fresh treatment ideas, Dr. Carol Ferrans, innovator of the
Quality of Life Index, becomes emphatic: "It's never just one person
who wins. Never just one. I know that from being older now, and
working in the realm of health care and science. There's lots of room
at the [pioneering] table and it's not just that one person wins. And

if anyone ever says, 'It's just me, I did it, it's my work,' they're lying! They're forgetting that nobody succeeds alone. Nobody. Nobody accomplished anything of importance alone. Nobody."

Pioneers, choose your team well, love them forward, and thank them for a job well done.

Points for Your Compass

➔ When attempting something that has never been attained, it is wise for pioneers to engage team members who have previous experience within the pioneering context but may also have expertise to supplement those of the pioneer. (For example, Shackleton chose Frank Wild as his second in command, who had polar experience and possessed a complementary temperament. Likewise, Shackleton chose Tom Crean as second officer on the Endurance; he had previous experience as a crewman on Robert Falcon Scott's South Pole *Terra Nova* expedition.)

➔ Pioneers must sometimes make tough calls when team members can no longer function well in the venture. It may mean leaving a well-loved dog behind or cutting a fighter from the pioneer's roster in order to achieve the mission.

➔ Role selection is as important as choosing the right team members. Progress with a great team may be slowed if individual members are not largely functioning in their areas of giftedness.

➔ Team members who know that their pioneering leader loves them will perform at a higher capacity than those who are motivated by negative goading or punishment. Correction may be needed at some points, but it is reserved for rebellious behavior.

➔ Wise pioneers will reward their team members appropriately, depending on the penchant of the individual member. These pioneers will always publicly point to the talent and hard work of their members as the reason for their success.

LEG TWO

On the Trail

"Thrival" as a Mindset
"Failure is not an option"

IT STARTED OUT AS A TYPICAL FLEET-FOOTED ZIP DOWN MY DRIVEWAY
to retrieve the mail. It was a scalding summer day, one that made me
eager to get back into the house. While flipping through the assort-
ment of envelopes and paper of the day, I spotted a hot pink flash
with my peripheral vision. Its location was an anomaly, enough to
bring my stride to a halt and make me do a double take. At first, I
thought it was a piece of trash on the patio landing. When I looked
again, I saw a single, blooming moss rose plant growing up through
a tiny crack in the concrete. The sun was beating down on it mercilessly, and due to its location, it endured that condition most of the
day. Granted, this type of flower has desert-like, succulent durabil-
ity. It can withstand bright, dry conditions that would make others
wither. So there was nothing out of the ordinary about its growth
under a burning, summer sun. Yet, there was something about seeing this beautiful soldier standing erect—a fragile beauty fixed in
hot concrete. For me, it became a visual metaphor for the coura-

geous and the pioneering: those who work in unlikely and hostile surroundings. It brought a smile to my face. The flower was thriving where it shouldn't, bringing to mind exceptional people who have persevered despite where they have been planted.

Seeing beyond the Visible

Stuff happens. Sometimes really unfortunate stuff happens, like getting hit in the eye with a rock as a kid, at about the same time you discover that you're really into art. Throw profound astigmatism into the mix, along with a pronouncement of being legally blind, and you have a cocktail of circumstances stiff enough to make anyone want to hang up the smock and ask for another drink. End of story, right? Maybe. Most people would have given up, or maybe taken the whole set of circumstances and chalked it up to a series of signs that becoming an artist was not a viable option. But I'm not talking about just anyone. I'm referring to Charles R. Knight. Not only was he an exceptional artist, but through his work he brought to life animals that no human had ever laid eyes on. His artistry had huge repercussions, of mammoth proportions you might say, and along the way, he became a pioneer.

At about six years old, Charles Knight came to rely on his left eye. His right cornea became irreparably damaged by the stone-throwing incident. Thick lenses in his glasses allowed him to see through the remaining astigmatic eye. Later commenting on the accident, he said, "For me, of course, it was a catastrophe for in my chosen line as an artist, I naturally needed two good eyes and here I was attempting to do difficult and intricate work with only one poor organ at the best." The impact also left some emotional scarring. Knight added, "I have no doubt that the accident contributed a great deal to my later nervous condition as my vision was always under a strain which reacted upon my entire nervous system."[1]

As he progressed artistically, he continued to lose more of his vision. He would hover closely over his work in order to ensure that he was obtaining the results he desired. Having spent much time outdoors, he loved nature, choosing animals as his subject matter, and like many children, he began drawing what he saw in his books. As he matured, he developed a conviction that art should be drawn from real life. The disciplines he developed because of this conviction would lead to the work for which he is best known.

Fortunately for young Charles, his parents nurtured his growing interest in art. He matured in an environment where his twin passions of nature and art were cultivated. He attended the Metropolitan Art Institute, expanding his adeptness with various mediums, such as painting (watercolor and oil), along with crayon, pencil, and charcoal. While a teen, Charles Knight would frequent the zoo at Central Park in the morning, capturing the creatures for all time in his art. He observed the uniqueness of species, carefully replicating fur, scales, or skin. He noted structural differences in various animals, perceiving how muscles, bones, and tendons worked together to help the animal leap, pose, and relax. His fastidiousness allowed him to not only capture an individual's likeness but also convey character, much like a radio announcer is able to send a smile through imageless airwaves.

Before he turned twenty, Charles lost both of his parents. He was a young man now on his own: a legally blind artist seeking work in bustling, late nineteenth-century New York City. Much like my moss rose plant's "thrival" (surviving and thriving!), Charles persevered in his passion, driving his roots down deeper where he landed. He secured a job illustrating books and then obtained work at a popular periodical, which drew greater attention to his work. However, he never lost sight of what he really loved: expressing animal anatomy through art. Knight pressed himself beyond his Central Zoo sittings to frequent The American Museum of Natural History's taxidermy collection daily. There he scrupulously studied the animals on display, refining his observational skills and expressing their distinctiveness through art.

When passion pushes you into a certain space every day, you cannot help but attract the attention of others who share your passion, increasing the likelihood of creating synergistic relationships. Such was the case for Knight, as those in the museum discovered his presence, his passion, and his product. A colleague put him in touch with Dr. Jacob Wortman in the fossil department. Dr. Wortman had a problem. He had the bones of a huge hippo-piggish sort of animal, and he had a name for it: elotherium (or entelodont), but he couldn't quite picture what this thing might have looked like. Furthermore, he had the bones on display and wanted to bring them to life through a picture for the public. He needed the giftedness of an artist—someone with an unusual ability to see what had never been seen.

Since the late nineteenth century, much has been unearthed in the area of paleontology. Some of these animals are better left in our imaginations (or nightmares?), and with much gratitude, we don't contend with them today, save in movie theaters. Such a beast was the entelodont. A writer for the *Scientific American* describes them collectively as "the giant killer pigs from hell [that really] aren't pigs."[2] A brief excerpt from the *Scientific American* illustrates Dr. Jacob Wortman's conundrum:

> The postcranial morphology of entelodonts is remarked upon less often than their skull anatomy. Even giant forms had a surprisingly gracile, slender neck. Large neural spines on the anterior thoracic vertebrae show that very large nuchal ligaments were present: the anterior thoracic neural spines of *Daeodon* are almost on par with those of bison and other tall-spined ungulates. Entelodonts were strongly cursorial, with elongate and slender limbs where the radius and ulna, and tibia and fibula, are often fused together. Unlike pigs, entelodonts were didactyl. Not only were they nasty and with a frightening dentition, they were also fast![3]

For the typical reader (I include myself), this contorted mess of anatomical verbiage is confusing and frightening. Granted, I am no paleontologist (thought I wanted to be one when I was a kid and would gladly play one on TV), so I have a hard time picturing a slender-necked, hoof-footed, pig/bison/hippo-concoction that could run like the wind and would count me as a tasty morsel on a bed of palm tree salad (they were omnivores). The creature sounds more jacked up than the modern platypus. Yet, for someone like Charles Knight, restoring or rendering an extinct animal with only its bones as a reference was the challenge of a lifetime. It required the studied accuracy and observational skills of a scientist, along with the imagination and skill of an artist, to create a believable, informed rendering of the animal. Of the task, Knight remembered, "I completed the drawing satisfactorily in black and white watercolor.... The date is 1894. Thus without realizing it I had stumbled on a kind of work that was to occupy much of my time for the next forty years or more.... To many of us, very important things in our career occur quite casually, and I was no exception."[4]

When Knight unveiled his work, Wortman was enthralled and quickly put the likeness on display for the public. Visitors to the museum were also filled with wonder at this new animal that had never been seen wrapped in flesh. Wortman quickly engaged the artist to create more such renderings, and that's just what he did, but Charles Knight's greatest work was yet to come.

Grow with the Flow

At high elevations, strange things can happen to plants, animals, and even people. Oxygen levels are lower, which can cause high altitude illness (HAI)—also called mountain illness—in people who are not used to it. This largely happens at elevations over eight thousand feet. If one moves to high elevations slowly, the process allows the body to get used to the new climate, which can help one avoid HAI.[5] It's one thing to visit these pristine environments (highly recommended if you're into seeing different types of plants and animals), but it's another to make your permanent home there.

While some species of plants and animals differ at high altitudes, others are familiar, though they look different because of how the environment has forced them to adapt. An example of this are alpine krummholz trees. These trees live in harsh conditions higher than 3,500 feet above sea level and have been warped and twisted by ice, years of continuous wind, and a lack of water, to name a few challenges. They can be various types of trees, like birch, balsam fir, or spruce, but have been given the name "krummholz" (meaning "crooked wood" in German) to describe the effect the harsh environment has had on them. These trees can also be called "knieholz" or knee wood. Having less resources on which to thrive, a krummholz tree may never grow very high, giving it a dwarfed, bonsaied effect. The tree is also painfully slow growing. "The factors impacting krummholz trees are complex, and can include latitude, geography, elevation, location, temperature, soil, growing season, wind, snow cover, ice, exposure, and moisture."[6]

Another effect of living in a more inhospitable mountainous environment is that some krummholz trees can experience "flagging." The winds may blow so relentlessly in one direction that the branches of the tree only grow on one side, making it look like a flapping blanket attached to a pole. Even though the tree may send out limbs on all sides of its trunk, the continual force of the wind from a certain direction, along with frost, wears down any new growth. The effect is comical, but the lesson learned from the tree is a sober one: Life's icy winds can either spur us on in successful pioneering or influence us to call off the adventure far too soon. Growth during adversity may be slow, and it may force us to adapt by bending for a time, but growth can continue nonetheless. In Charles Knight's case, he "somehow persevered, refused to call attention to his handicap, and produced some of his greatest murals when he could barely see at all—a feat of astounding courage and dedication."[7] While experiences may scar and twist us, they need not destroy us. In fact, if we let them, they give us strength to find our own path, while fiercely gripping onto what most anchors us.

A Tangible Presence of Hope

Juni Felix is a fledgling pioneer who has had every reason to call off her own gig. Yet no matter what life has handed her, she continues to press forward, holding firm to that which anchors her. She exhibits a peculiar type of resilience that many pioneers demonstrate is a vital ingredient that leads to the fruition of their dreams.

For starters, Juni's life was planted high up on the mountain of adversity. The winds began to blow as soon as she made her entry into the world. Her mother was suicidal, and having Juni was her way of giving herself another chance at life. Juni relates:

> I was born into a whirlwind, into the kind of soil that is left [by a storm, like the footprint] of a tornado. My birth father was a drug addict, an alcoholic, and was very abusive. He would beat my mother bloody with beer bottles and whatever else he could find. My parents were just so unwell. I have cigarette burns on my body from the time I was six months old. According to my medical records, I started trauma therapy [since I was] four. I have been trying to make sense of the madness since [that time].
>
> [My parents] were two orphans who found each other. My dad is African American. He used to say he was Puerto Rican. He was unfaithful, wild, and hurting. My mother was orphaned at age four in Japan, and she never healed from that. I have memories, even as early as age five, of my mom passed out on the bathroom floor from a suicide attempt. I [came] to the realization that nobody loved her and she needed someone to take care of her. So I did everything I could…to start taking care of her, being there for her. I noticed even as a five-year-old that my father never told her that she was beautiful, and I thought she was beautiful.

Noticing beauty in life, having an awareness of others' needs, and all the while enduring hardship have become major hallmarks of Juni's life. Like a tree overshadowed by others, she has believed that "there is always some way to find the light, no matter how hard it is, or how dark it looks." Plants naturally reach for the light when they sense it. Even houseplants will turn toward a window to increase their exposure to the life-giving source. But for Juni, merely reaching toward the light, or the "goodness in a situation" as she says, is not enough. She has a firm belief that goodness and hope always have a presence, and it is part of her personal mission to point it out to others. "For as long as I can remember, I was the kind of child who felt like I was supposed to help anyone around me to look on the bright side in the situation because it's always there."[8]

Juni reached a particular milepost in her life at twelve years old during a school field trip. Her stepfather was in the US Army, which brought the family to Germany. Her seventh-grade class was taken to Dachau, the infamous concentration camp, where over 200,000 persons from all over Europe were imprisoned and 41,500 lives were snuffed out.[9] She especially recalls a particular event that day. After touring the gas chamber, ovens, and crematoriums, the group of students was brought to a roughly built chapel. Juni thought about all the people who may have been there and what it may have meant to them. Though they may have come from different backgrounds, she identified one trait that unified them all:

> They were all unwanted people. I really connected with that because I felt unwanted in my life. So I [learned] about these people who were executed, exterminated in the camps. Before we entered the chapel, I felt the tangible presence of evil, but in that chapel, I felt the tangible presence of hope. When you feel the tangible presence of hope, even in a concentration camp at age twelve-and-a-half, you don't forget it. And I decided right then and there for the rest of my life that I would be a part of the good in this world. I knew full well that there was enough hurt, neglect, harm, abuse, and unfiltered evil, and I decided that I would be a part of the good.[10]

Giving Life to Dry Bones

It is hard to imagine large natural museums void of fossilized creatures. As patrons, we have come to expect that any collection would house some sort of skeletal remains of extinct, prehistoric animals. What is a natural museum without its dinosaurs and youthful patrons agape as they get their first glimpse of what these terrible lizards might have looked like?

In reality, we moderns have had this luxury for a relatively brief time in history. As dinosaur bones were unearthed in the nineteenth and twentieth centuries, some made their way into museums. Precious few museums received the whole skeleton of an animal. Reflecting back on his early years as a prehistoric artist, Knight described the paucity of specimens:

> Indeed, very few museums in the world at the time could boast of more than a very few fossil creatures actually set up in approximately natural position. For the most part, collections consisted of separated bones, very interesting to specialists, but totally lacking in popular appeal. Also, not even an experienced scientist could properly visualize the finished effect of an accurately mounted skeleton. Indeed, the collecting of prehistoric animals in the US was still in a very primitive state, and the wonderful technique which has since been so successfully employed was then unknown in field operations.[11]

Knight made the acquaintance of Henry Fairfield Osborn, who was assuming the senior position in the Department of Paleontology at Columbia. He was also the first curator at the American Museum of Natural History overseeing the vertebrate paleontology department. Osborn eventually became president of the museum.

Osborn had a vision for the museum's natural displays, and it included Knight. Osborn imagined a place where patrons could not only see restored animals but also place them in displays in which they were accurately mounted in natural surroundings. Having been chosen to work with the museum's paleontologists, these scientists often reflected that Knight's artistic renderings were an extension of their own work. Together, they not only stretched the imaginations and knowledge of the patrons, they also served up a clever marketing technique to bring the curious into the museum to see what had never before been seen.

Knight was to restore many ancient animal likenesses between the turn of the century and the 1920s. He continued to dominate the field for many years and placed the bar of his craft at a very high level for any newcomer who might have entertained a passing thought of getting a spot in Knight's artistic space. "Although his primary artistic interest continued to be portraying living animals, Knight had become—almost inadvertently—America's premier 'reconstructor' of prehistoric animals."[12] Knight was not just prolific. The breadth of his art spanned various forms of media.

In 1896 Osborne wrote an article about some big-boned discoveries that had been dug out of the western United States. He asked Knight to provide some pictures of what these animals might have looked like. With its publication, Knight's artistic renderings caught the public's attention in a big way.

Under Osborn's further direction, Knight's portfolio expanded even more. Osborn began discussions with Knight to create huge, hall-sized murals that would be mounted in tandem with the museum's fossil collections. The endeavor was stressful to Knight in several ways. Among them were Osborn's continual efforts to draw Knight onto the museum's payroll as part of its staff. This Knight staunchly refused time and again, preferring to work on a contractual basis so that he was able to take other commissions and preserve his artistic process without interference. Another added stress was the toll the tedious process took on Knight's eyesight. Painting murals was demanding, so much so that eventually when mounted they were intolerably out of focus. Over time, he was forced to downsize his efforts by adopting a method of painting on a smaller canvas and having them copied by others onto the larger canvases. Knight would finalize the murals by adding his own detailed final touches, but it had to have been painful to his sense of self-sufficiency to resort to this process, even though it allowed him to continue working. Soon, other museums, not to be outdone, would be knocking on his door to include the distinct Knight "paleo-art."

A Parallel Track

Sometimes pioneers venture down a path unaware how the experiences gained will weave together to create a more complete picture at a later time.

After completing high school, Juni married her sweetheart, escaping her stormy childhood home. She was grateful to put "homeless days" behind her. Tired of sleeping in public restrooms, people's garages, and shelters, she looked forward to a new life with her husband and a new baby. This self-described "minimalist" notes that she came out of this period of her life with "scarcity as a mindset."

Her husband had joined the army, so Juni was off to live in a military community at Fort Polk in Louisiana. It wasn't long before she met new people in this new place, and many of them had plenty of needs. So, she did what most nineteen-year-olds would *not* do in the situation: *She ran for mayor!*

> I thought, *I made so many wonderful friends, I have this great baby, and we're doing well. I'd like to do something.* So I ran for community mayor. I don't even know where this idea came from! I saw so much need.... At this point my son is a year old and I had him with me all the time [while] I'm campaigning for mayor. It was a real campaign! There were three others running against me, and long story short, I won.[13]

While Juni was leading the community, she was also applying herself as a student in one of her favorite disciplines: technology. At age nine, she had developed a fascination with computers, and in tenth grade, she took her first class in computer programming, the same class in which she met her future husband. While at the military base, she sought to keep up with the subject of technology through correspondence courses and did her testing at a local university near Fort Polk.

> I was studying independently because I had a baby and a community to run.... I fell in love with [computer] programming and systems. It teaches you how your

mind works. I believe that. And so, I stuck with it as
a hobby, because after I ran for mayor, my life started
getting very complicated.[14]

Life in a complex environment often places unanticipated obstacles in the pioneer's path. It can make growth in a certain direction
very difficult, if not impossible. Like the krummholz tree, the pioneer may strive to branch out in a different direction, only to have
any new growth blown or frozen off. It twists the trunk and branches,
turns them in a different direction, and sometimes the inhospitable
elements bring several different areas of growth together in an unanticipated, fruitful way.

Juni's life took various twists and turns as she adapted to new
demands in her life, and one of those unanticipated turns was the
need to balance work with home life. When her husband left the military, she worked as a director of sales in the hospitality industry, then
did a stint in banking as a manager in branch support, helping with
branch operations, technical issues, and customer service. Knowing
that her future was not in banking, Juni made a leap into radio, eventually scoring a morning show cohost position in a major market. Her
enthusiastic voice, energetic delivery, and positive outlook made her
a favorite to many listeners in the area. Throughout her various occupational changes, however, Juni never lost her twin desires to assist
those who needed help by meeting their needs through technology.

For the pioneer who is ahead of her time, perseverance yields
fruit as ideas, coupled with technology, await the maturity of the pioneer's skills and vision to apprehend them. Persistence, while painful,
ends up being the pioneer's friend. The passage of time allows certain areas of an industry to mature and develop, meeting the bud-
ding pioneer at an innovative intersection when she is able to use
the inventive ingredients at the right time. Sometimes pioneers are
naturally drawn to each other, leading to bursts of innovation.

In Juni Felix's case, she stumbled across the work of Dr. B. J.
Fogg, a behavior scientist at Stanford University. Dr. Fogg is considered the father of Behavior Design, a new systematic way to think
clearly about human behavior and design for lasting change. He also
created the Tiny Habits method. In Dr. Fogg's words, "I teach good

people how behavior works, so they can create products & services that benefit everyday people around the world."[15] Early in her journey into the field, Juni read Fogg's work and made observations when she saw the principles being applied. She developed her own ideas and concepts for application and then bravely shared her thoughts with Behavior Design's founder through an email. A phone call soon followed. She excitedly recalls her first conversation with her techy hero:

> He called me and we talked, for exactly eighteen minutes, because I was watching the whole time because I'm thinking he'll give me ten, fifteen minutes; no, it was eighteen minutes. He invited me to come and study with him in person. [Soon] I was flying to California, and gaining my certification in behavior design and studying with one of my favorite innovators on the planet.[16]

As her investment in learning this new area unfolds, Juni has taken some bold steps in the direction of her dreams to unite human need synergistically with technology. As she has increased her knowledge in behavior design from a technical perspective, she is quick to emphasize the importance of working in concert with our own construction as human beings to realize the biggest impact.

> I have walked through an open door of opportunity to start my own tech consulting company, Mastermind Behavior Design. If you think about mastering your mind, it's something very important…because I feel like our minds are a gift. If we don't understand how our minds work, we spend our lives battling against our design.
>
> What I do in the tech community is a kind of user experience (UX). I advise tech teams on UX in a way that is rooted in behavior design, and it's unique in that it gives you this amazing compassion for people. It's all about caring for people, and when you come from that direction, you can really create things that

are helpful and good. In the tech community, there aren't a whole lot of people who can do this.

A lot of these helpful and good creations Juni mentions have yet to be developed. They are waiting for innovators like B. J. Fogg, Juni Felix, and others to call them into reality. Just like the images of the terrible lizards that Charles Knight brought to life as he pondered their construction from their skeletal remains, Juni's dreams may seem as remote as the dinosaurs' existence: a long time ago, on a planet not too far away. A reality that may seem distant to us is paved with the pioneer's dreams that may seem just out of reach but are still close enough to be pursued until they become apprehended and realized. However, sometimes, the dream also knocks on the door of the pioneer. When that happens, the pioneer must open the door. Juni recounts:

> Not long after I left my major market [radio] morning show gig to open up my tech consulting company, I got a message from Professor Agnis Stibe, founder of Transforms.me. He is an MIT professor of sociotech.... We began working on a presentation that we were going to pitch to the 2018 Persuasive Technology convention in Waterloo, Canada, for what we call the "caring, feeling, and understanding cities of the future." This is a comprehensive plan to design cities or integrate into the design of existing cities ways to not only get to know your residents, but to find out what their needs are and get them in touch with resources to meet those needs.[17]

When Life Passes By

Time passes, not only for dinosaurs but for people. With the sweeping hands of the clock, things change, and it is up to the living to adapt—or not.

Charles Knight's paleo-art has been described as "romantic realism."[18] It became jeopardized as the twentieth century rolled into its second decade. Artistic tastes were changing. Impressionism was now in the shadow of post-impression, and many were gravitating toward the swelling popularity of the bolder European strokes of Gauguin, Matisse, and Picasso.

Knight was not impressed. He made little bones about describing the new movement as a fad buoyed by marketing efforts. As an artist skilled in detailed observation of the world around him, it is little wonder that any artistic styles that were less representational in nature would grate on his sensibilities. This shift in artistic preference was even more injurious to Knight in that art buyers displayed less interest in the subject matter in which he excelled. People were not as interested in his animal pictures. "During the peak of his powers, no artist, no matter how excellent, could make a living selling wildlife art. Too artistic to be counted among scientists, and too scientific to be embraced whole-heartedly by the art cognoscenti, Knight became his own man and went his own way."

Knight's tension with Osborn and the museum also continued. "An utterly inept and indifferent businessman, Knight was perpetually broke and in debt. Far from being a tenured employee with a secure income at the museum, he remained a fiercely independent artist."[19] The stress from the pressure to remain independent yet solvent took its toll on the Knight family and on Knight's own health. He suffered through times of illness, depression, a lack of concentration and inspiration, as well as the temptation to put off until the future what he could have accomplished in the present. Another stressor was his failing eyesight. He struggled through multiple surgeries. Unable to face the mounting professional tensions, he began to depend on help from his wife and daughter to keep relations between him and his patrons well-oiled and moving forward.

Eventually, after a full career of capturing prehistoric and modern animal life on canvas, Charles Knight finally lost his ability to see, along with his ability to invest his soul in any new creations. However, he did leave behind a myriad of paintings, sculptures, and even advice for people to enjoy. In the final summary of his 1947 guide, *Animal Drawing: Anatomy and Action for Artists*, Knight advises:

> Remember too that above all it is *art* we are seeking
> to experience while we turn these pages, that our own

individualities are being consulted at all times, and that the better artists we strive to become the finer will be our productions in the field of art expression. Indeed, all the things that I have told you in this book are merely guides along the path that you have elected to follow.[20]

Like a true pioneer, Knight points the way for others. Having painfully cut an original path for himself, he beckons others to join him in excellence and perseverance but not in imitation. Rather, he encourages developing artists to dynamically build upon the counsel he has offered, so that at some point in their own journey, the joy of artistic creation will bring them to a land of their own.

In 2014, I made the move from West Palm Beach, Florida to the Chicago area. One of the attractions I was most eager to see in the area was Sue the T-Rex. Owned by the Field Museum in Chicago, Sue is one of the most complete skeletons of its kind. To see her size and take in those formerly powerful jaws and imagine the speed of those massive legs bounding across the land after its prey were terrifically horrifying while frightfully awesome. While still cherishing my first date with Sue, I had little foresight as to what awaited me as I reluctantly left Sue's side. Next on my agenda was to see what was in the hall of the dinosaurs. As I turned the corner and cast my eyes across all of the erected fossils, I was also welcomed in by rolling, gentle colors portraying scenes that were strangely familiar and welcoming. There on the walls of the hall were the grand larger-than-life pages of a favorite childhood book. Like a déjà vu torn from my own past, I was not only brought back to the time of the dinosaurs, but also taken back decades to my own childhood when I would spend hours poring over the pages of dinosaur books my parents had given me. These books were treasured possessions. My adult mind stuttered in an attempt to link the experiences. Then, it finally clicked. It was the Knight effect. It was Knight's visionary artwork that populated the pages of my books and gave this young child, and many others, a first glimpse into life past. I spent hours memorizing dinosaur names, descriptions, and even the visual details of each piece Knight had created.

And yes, just like the artist had done when he was a child, I copied his drawings from his books until I could create my own.

"Living in the Not Yet"

At present, Juni is continuing her work in behavior design, collaborating with others in technology who are working on a global scale to improve the quality of life for people. For Juni, getting people in touch with needed resources, whether they be for a person's physical, spiritual, or emotional health, is a no-brainer. However, it doesn't take much nudging to bring her back to the time when she was a wounded young woman much in need of her own resources. She developed an outlook of living in the "not yet," existing in the tension of a tough reality that she refused to allow to define her. In the process, she discovered and forged a brighter future of the realized potential of all she knew she had to offer.

Living in the "not yet," or with hope as some might say, is not for the feeble-hearted. It is a discipline in attitude, emotion, and soul. It is an ingredient that many pioneers seem to possess as they lean forward into icy, unforgiving winds, while being rooted in the inhospitable soil of circumstance. Juni describes what it is like to live this way:

> Don't trust your eyes. Seeing is not believing. You have to live by faith. Look at whatever situation is in front of you...and know that on a deeper level the reality is that you don't have all the pieces of the puzzle and [perhaps] unseen factors are what are going to be the determining factors. So, don't rely on your emotions or your feelings but you honor your emotions and your feelings. You honor what you're seeing and experiencing, but don't ever let it be the bottom line. Don't let it have the final say, because from my life experience, it's the unknown, the hidden factors, it's the wild cards that really determine the direction of anything. Whether it's a relationship or a

professional endeavor. It doesn't mean that you can't plan or be strategic, but you always remember that there is an unknown factor. And when things are at their worst, that unknown factor [can] give you hope. But you have to choose [hope], because unknowns can give you fear. And hope is a gift to humanity that never runs out and never fails, but you have to choose it—even in your anguish and in your tears, you have to choose it.

Fully understanding the frightful "scarcity as a mindset" reality, she continues to work so that others may never have to live this way. Consequently, fear has had an opposite effect on her. Rather than paralyzing her, it has given her motivation to continue her pioneering efforts. She whimsically reflected:

I think it's really neat that I went from being a homeless girl, sleeping in public restrooms, living in shelters, to helping to design "caring, feeling, understanding cities of the future." Oh my gosh. I don't know where I'm going or what I'm doing, but somehow, it always turns out awesome! [*Laughing*].[21]

A fragile flower pressing through concrete to bloom in unforgiving sunlight, a blind artist who paints hall-sized murals depicting life from skeletal remains, a formerly homeless girl who is helping to design cities of the future, and a dwarf, twisted tree sending out new growth while in an inhospitable mountain environment: all of these exhibit the hopeful qualities of the pioneer. They accept the present tense while persevering toward a better future.

Points for Your Compass

→ Adversity can serve as a motivator, pushing the pioneer to break through opposing circumstances in order to achieve the quest. Perseverance allows the pioneer to practice and hone needed skills in order to overachieve.

→ Suffering pioneers benefit by learning about others who, like them, have survived and succeeded in new ventures despite challenging circumstances. History offers many inspiring stories of hope that a pioneer's dreams are achievable despite handicaps and setbacks.

➔ Sometimes the pioneer is ahead of her time. Concepts and ideas may take a while to mature and take hold in society's collective thinking. In addition, technology may also need to evolve in order to make the pioneer's quest attainable. During this waiting period, the pioneer's passion helps her to keep her pioneering dream alive until ideology, technology, and opportunity converge to make her venture a possibility.

➔ An altruistic pioneer paves the way for others to share in the endeavor and will offer instruction and encouragement for those who come behind him to further and even improve the work he has started.

➔ Until the work is achieved, the hopeful venturer must continue to fuel the vision with hope while living in the not yet, else she may never attain pioneer status.

The Unknown
"We're not in Kansas anymore"

EARLY IN 1833, PRUDENCE CRANDALL, PRINCIPAL OF THE CANTERBURY Female Boarding School, sent out a distress call. With many in the community having turned against her because of her refusal to dismiss Sarah Harris, a young black student she had recently accepted, she needed reinforcements. Many of the parental threats made to her had already been carried out, with daughters removed from the school. She needed help in the form of fresh ideas, outside resources, and above all, new students to bolster her collapsing educational endeavor. But with the small Connecticut community having made their opinions on a racially integrated classroom clear, she would have to extend her plea beyond her immediate sphere of influence. Who would understand—no, not just understand, but empathize with her predicament enough to help?

William Lloyd Garrison of Boston, publisher of the *Liberator*, came to mind. It was a stretch to be sure. He didn't even know her. Yet, he had established himself as a vocal abolitionist journalist and would be sympathetic to her situation. Surely he must have some assets, connections, or at least some thoughts on how to resolve her tricky situation. She quickly sent off a letter to this public figure who was a celebrity in their day. She took a risk, exposing her plans and her heart to this man. Twice in the letter, she implored him not to reveal her intentions to refill her classroom, not with white but with female black students, with the hope and the determination to spend "the remaining part of my life benefiting the people of color."[1] She posted the letter and put her positive hopes into action. She made plans to travel to Boston.

Eleven days and a bumpy coach ride later, Prudence Crandall sent Garrison a brief note informing him that she had arrived in town and asked that he call on her. One can only imagine that she sent her request off with hopes, prayers, and tentative breath. Garrison responded amenably, and soon plans were in motion to gather "young misses of color" together for the purpose of learning at the Canterbury school. Garrison was well networked with the local abolitionist community. It would not be hard to imagine that during their meeting, these two quick minds cobbled together an itinerary for instructor Crandall to make the most of her remaining visit to Boston to bring success to her plan.

With Garrison's direction, Prudence visited African American families, black church pastors, and businesspeople, hopeful that these resourced people would send their daughters, sisters, and friends to receive an education in Canterbury. Her efforts drew fruit. Her first new recruit, Ann Eliza Hammond, came from her own home state of Rhode Island. She joined Sarah Harris, and so the school grew to two. It was a small step for these women, a giant leap for womankind. Prudence Crandall had created the first school for African American girls in a largely segregated United States. She had become a pioneer, but her journey was far from over.

As she crossed the pioneering threshold (or more accurately, was pushed across it), it's unlikely she would have detected any halo radiating from her head, had there been one. Under the circumstances, she wouldn't have had the time nor the inclination to take notice. Like my mother's discovery of cancer, Prudence Crandall couldn't unknow the truth as her neighbors' real feelings surfaced and emotions were put into action. Much like a swiftly spreading disease, her bad situation turned insufferable; she was too occupied with having to plot a new course each time the previous one became obsolete—something that would happen frequently.

Paying the Piper

Thomas Edison once said, "Our greatest weakness lies in giving up. The most certain way to succeed is always to try just one more time." For Edison, this meant relentlessly trying to find success with his light bulb.

Two years into my tenure as a station manager, I wanted to give up. While I had seen tangible improvements in the operations of the facility that had been placed in my care, other areas seemed stalled, and tension began to rise between a key staffer and me. The truth was, I couldn't afford to lose him. The skills and heart he brought to the job were needed, but no attempts I made to persuade, cajole, bribe (with food!), or threaten seemed to keep certain unacceptable behaviors from impacting the operations of the station. I was at a loss. Furthermore, my own personal resources were depleting, which, unknown to me, were leading me to a very dark place. I didn't know what was happening to me. I was becoming a person that I didn't know: fatigued, unimaginative, and miserable. My spirit felt flattened. There seemed to be no way out, save the unspeakable one. But I spoke up, and it saved my life.

At the time, I had adopted a mantra of "I love my job, but I hate my life." This came as a result of violating universal human principles, such as "All work and no play make Jack a dull boy." I had exceeded personal boundaries and was, as another proverb states, "paying the piper." As I am a piper (truly, I play the flute), I owed myself a great debt. My mind and body eventually said, "No more, amiga." My favorite pastime became sleep. I replaced the USDA food pyramid suggestions with a different carb in every category. Initially, I turned to those closest to me—mentors who had helped me grow in my profession—but they struggled to understand what was happening to me, just as I did. Some listened, some offered advice such as "you just get through it," and still others shook their heads and chided. These were people who cared but could not help. My situation just wasn't in their frame of reference. I needed another sort of mentor to walk me out of this dark place since no pulling up of my own bootstraps had any varying effect.

Tired of seeing her daughter chronically negative and deflated, my mother begged me to get some help—and not just any kind of help, mind you, but the sort of help that some people swear they'll never get for as long as they live. I was embarrassed. I made the phone call to a doctor I had met through the radio station.

When I walked through the door, the doctor said, "What's happened to you?" Had I really changed that much since we had met less than a year ago? Apparently, I had.

As I opened up through conversation, the causes for my illness unfolded as well: I revealed my schedule, my concerns, my fear of failing. With that, I shared my coping schemes to deal with those fears. He asked questions. I offered rationales and justifications. I wormed my way around his observations.

At the end of the appointment, he offered a diagnosis: simple clinical dysthymic depression. I responded by saying, "Well, that's depressing."

In a thick southeastern Massachusetts accent, he observed, "I can see you haven't lost your sense of hume-ah." He prescribed a return to his office to continue our discussion, along with medication. Sure, I'd come back to him to talk (he had said some helpful things). But put my brain on meds? No way.

As I left the office that day, I found I couldn't unknow the truth about myself. I had received a diagnosis, and in some ways, it provided relief. There *was* something wrong with me, and it had a name. It wasn't a pretty name, but it offered an explanation to my ugly, inexplicable behavior. In other ways, the diagnosis left me with a feeling of uneasiness and uncertainty. Would I ever feel better again? Could I ever find the way back to the person I was, or believed I was?

As I tried to digest what I had learned, I knew life would be different. The life I had tried to live to produce the results I wanted didn't work, and my methods wouldn't take me any further into the future. My path had taken me right up to the base of a high, brick wall.

The New Kids in Town

The once smiling faces who stoked her dreams of educating young women now scowled as they saw that Prudence Crandall had rotated one crop of students out for another. Like a tea bag plunged into scalding water, the contents in the bag infused the communal water, and it was pungent stuff that Crandall, her staff, and her new students were forced to drink. What the community didn't count on was Crandall's character and that of her new students. That was an equally strong brew.

While the state of Connecticut at present counts Prudence Crandall as its state heroine, enough cannot be said of the young black students who joined her. These women were adolescents, yet had the conviction and fortitude of souls more advanced in age. Likely these were developed out of their own adverse circumstances of being a different sort of bird made to sit in the same tree. Together they sat, and they sang. Then they lighted in a nest with Prudence Crandall and weathered the storm together.

When citizens of Canterbury saw that Sarah Harris remained a student in the school, their attention turned to dissuading the new scholar, Ann Eliza. One of the members of the school's board secured a warrant to have Eliza arrested for vagrancy, which included a penalty of $1.67 every week she remained in Canterbury. If a person had no funds to offset the fine, a "whipping on the naked body not to exceed ten stripes" would be imposed.[2] The sheriff was sent to deliver and read the warrant to Ann Eliza in person. Prudence sat with her as the officer saw to his duty and departed.

Now what? Would this happen every time a new student came to town? Ann Eliza and her family had the means to pay the fine, but was that fair after they had already invested so much to advance her education? Prudence could offer to pay the fine, but the cost might become prohibitive if she offered to underwrite the mounting fines of each out-of-town "vagrant" student. Eliza steadily shared her intention to stay and to take the whip if need be.

By April of 1833, the Canterbury school's student body had increased to three, but who would want to attend under such circumstances? Apparently, quite a few. With pressures mounting, new students arrived. At the end of April, there were seventeen students, from nine to eighteen years old. Some came from Connecticut, but others became boarders trekking from nearby Providence and as far away as Philadelphia. When the student body grew, so did the opposition, and the expressions grew baser. Due to the many farms in the area, manure was in great supply, and it was thickly spread on the school's steps. Local chickens provided the eggs that were pelted against the school's front door. All but one local grocer refused to sell any provisions to the school. It seemed that insurmountable circumstances blocked any progress that was made, but like mounting water retained by a dike, Prudence Crandall and her tribe would wind their way around the barrier to find provision in time of need.

The wall was buttressed in an attempt to meet the force of the rising tide. The state became involved and created legislation that outlawed, among other things, boarding black students: "[N]o person shall set up or establish in this state any school, academy or literary institution whatsoever in this state, or harbor or board, for the purpose of attending or being taught...any colored person who is not an inhabitant of any town in this state without the consent first obtained of a majority of the civil authority." According to the new act, a school such as the one Prudence Crandall ran "would tend to the great increase of the colored population of the state and thereby to the injury of the people."[3]

Prudence Crandall had already prepared herself for the possibility of being arrested. And she was, along with her sister Hannah Almyra. They accompanied the deputy sent to take them into custody, enduring taunting along the way. Back at the school, the young women left behind surely agonized over what might come next: an enforced trip home? the end of their education? an impossible fine? prison? a humiliating, nude, public whipping?

Beyond Self-Help

The day after seeing the doctor, I returned to work at the radio station just as I always had. The transmitter sat silently waiting for me to wake it to start the broadcast day. The sweeping red hand on the studio clock counted away the seconds before sign-on, when I would start the programming for the listeners. My desk was still littered with tasks I had left from the previous day. Nothing had changed around me. But I had. I had received new knowledge. And in this case, it was about myself. Even if I had wanted to, I couldn't turn back time and unknow the truth of what was haunting me. Still, I determined to try to overcome my condition myself—nothing new there. So my selective serotonin reuptake inhibitor (SSRI) prescription was left unfilled.

I continued to see the doctor to talk to him, which gave me hope that my adjusted outlook was helping, but I always had the feeling that there were still flies in the room, even though I couldn't always hear the buzzing. To those who have never experienced the specter of depression, I explain that it's like having a tear in the screen door in your house on a summer's evening. The bugs are naturally attracted to the light beaming from inside the house, and they land on the screen. Eventually they find their way to the tear in the material and steal inside the house, some more quickly than others. A healthy brain functions like an intact screen. The insects (or negative thoughts) land on the screen and are kept outside, unless of course, the homeowner chooses to open the door. While this may not be a flawless metaphor, it does portray how difficult it is for the mind of the depressed person to combat the humming negativity and hopeless feelings, even if they cognitively make no sense. Somehow, the screen door must be repaired if the person is to keep the insects from growing from simple intruders to an overwhelming infestation.

I pressed forward into the fog of the following months, tediously balancing on the fulcrum of my own emotions, and for a while, I continued in this manner. The highs never got very high, but if there was a slide toward one end of the emotional seesaw, it always seemed to veer downward until I hit the ground with a thud, such as what happens when a partner suddenly jumps off the high end of the seesaw while you sit on the other side. My diagnosis made me aware of the condition but did little to stave it off when I stumbled over a trigger.

One weekend evening while visiting my parents, I sequestered myself in a bedroom while I was experiencing one of these thud-like episodes. I looked out of the bedroom window at the glow of the moonlight on the open fields around the house, seeing the contrasting dark shadows that blended the stonewalled perimeter with the woods beyond. The crickets and katydids sounded through the open window. I looked up at the moon and, with tears streaming down my burning cheeks, uttered my desire to die. True to my own convictions, I took no action. Instead, I exhausted myself to sleep.

The next morning, I woke and thought with resignation, *Well, I'm still here. I guess I should take the meds.* I had spent the better part of a year groping my way through life using the same coping methods while hoping for different results. Some call this the definition of insanity. However, there is something to be said about a healthy fear of the unknown. This was my brain, after all, and despite helpful medical assurances, I would be the one living with the consequences. In the end, I was tired of dealing with the fallout from my own failing self-effort. I took the medication, not without some small fear of how it would affect my brain. It's one thing to receive assurances from a doctor; it's another to have to live it out yourself.

Refusing to take prescribed medication after receiving a professional medical recommendation to do so is a personal choice, and it is one that should be made soberly with the full understanding of the consequences, which sadly, in the case of depression, includes a potential loss of life. In my case, had I not refused to take the prescribed SSRIs, I would have forgone a wasted year needlessly mucking around in the slough of despond. However, it was a reality I had to come to grips with myself while having a small core of caring, very patient individuals around me: a close relative, my doctor, a mentor, a couple of coworkers, and friends. All of them allowed me to process my dilemma as I lived through it. I finally had been guided around the vast wall I had become used to staring at. It was new territory for me.

As the medication began to take effect, I had a sensation of a "return" or a coming back to myself, the way a car may return to operating on all four cylinders. I remember looking at myself in the mirror thinking, *Where have I been these past couple of years?* Sadly, I had become used to seeing myself with distant, sunken eyes, and what appeared to me to be a dull countenance and gray skin tone. Within a short time of taking the medication, I distinctly remember the return of a flood of creative energy and thinking. Perhaps others have a different experience. While none of my external tribulations went away, the ability to think through them and act decisively had been fortified with the help of the medication. The chemical bridge that allowed my brain cells to communicate had been restored, and as I like to explain, my brain leapt out of its time-out and was talking to itself again. This made all the difference in my world.

We're Off to See the Warden

They had come to study, not change history. Yet, the series of events that followed Prudence Crandall's welcoming of black scholars into a small Connecticut town set in motion a series of events that would have a profound impact beyond the lifetimes of any of those involved in the Canterbury conflict.

Now in custody for violating a law custom tailored to intimidate and deter the Crandall sisters, their partners, and the scholars from continuing their educational endeavors at the school, Prudence was prepared to spend the night in prison. The charges were read, and the $150 bond for release was intentionally not paid. It had already been decided that she would "permit herself to be taken to jail. This would show the public the real extent to which her enemies would go and it would lend propaganda value to the efforts of her friends in the Anti-Slavery movement." Her sister, Almira, was released due to being under twenty-one-years of age. When Justice Adams saw that no bond would appear, he announced that the sheriff would jail Prudence. Her simple reply was, "I am ready."[4]

Pioneers, Get Ready!

The pioneering life may seem glamourous: taking in that which the human eye has never seen, making sense of previously unsolvable problems, bringing new form of art or music to life. The applause and honor for such findings and creations are their own kind of reward. But going to jail for a human right? Many would say, "No thanks," especially if the experience entails a life disruption sending the pioneer into an unknown trajectory, which might end in professional or personal ruin. It is sobering to think, *If I make this decision, there's no turning back. There will be a permanent mark affixed next to my name. This could ruin my life!* Surprisingly, however, many individuals have chosen this course, not out of preference, but out of conviction. Family members and peers may have abandoned these courageous ones out of fear, pressure, or disappointment. And while historians have written about some of the pioneers who have impacted our lives, many everyday pioneers, the great impact of their efforts, and the convictions that drove them have gone unrecorded. Doubtless, however, the world would be different than it is now without them, and we would all experience that loss. Glamour and fame are fleeting, and they only come to a few. But a hunger and devotion to change even a small but significant part of our world no matter the cost? That's the pioneering spirit and drive the world needs, whether historians record and applaud those efforts or not.

And that requires grit. The grit necessary to overcome great obstacles does not spontaneously appear. For many, this sort of resolve builds over time as challenges come and they rise to meet them. Many pioneers tap into their own experiences and skill, anchored in their convictions to meet and surpass mounting pressure.

In his recounting of the battle between a young Israelite shepherd boy named David and a massive Philistine warrior named Goliath, Malcom Gladwell emphasizes that "when [David] tells [the Israelite King] Saul that he has killed bears and lions as a shepherd, he does so not just as a testimony to his courage but to make another point as well: that he intends to fight Goliath the same way he has learned to fight wild animals, as a projectile warrior."[5] The use of a slingshot was a skill that David and many in his day had rehearsed so frequently and accurately that they could strike a target almost without thinking, which is needful when those skills are tested under stress. David also was anchored in conviction. As a shepherd, David's job was the protection and prosperity of his flock. It was his livelihood. As frightening as either a bear or a lion might be on its own, running away is not an option when such animals are intent on taking the bread and butter off your table. The best choice might be escape if it's your own skin at stake, but when the enemy is intent on tearing apart your flock, there is little one can do but stand and face the predator.

On a deeper level, David's principles, along with Prudence Crandall's, reach even farther. At the core of their convictions was a need to demonstrate a very fundamental human trait to stand up for something that is transcendent, something that rings true in the human soul. In David's case, he was moved to action in defense of his own paralyzed people in the face of a taunting predator. Prudence Crandall tethered her courage to speaking up for the oppressed and powerless. Even in my own situation, I was forced to face the consequences of self-harm before I acted, and the possibility of erasing a future that might benefit others while bringing self-fulfillment and resonance for my own purpose.

The grinding cycle of conviction, practice, and increasing challenge refines the emerging pioneer until the day when he or she can say, like Prudence Crandall, "I am ready." It is a purpose of mind over time. This does not mean that there will be no fear or misgivings, but there will be a well-rehearsed ability to take the first step into thin air with a cat's innate confidence that it will likely land on its feet.

Waving the White Flag

True, there are worse experiences in life than Prudence Crandall's overnight stay in jail. She remained in a stuffy small room in the center of a two-storied, stone building. A bed was brought in for her, and the cell was freshly cleaned. Anna Benson, whose home had provided the bed, offered to stay with Prudence overnight, and this was granted. Having her bond paid the next morning, she was released.

Even after securing her freedom, eggs were hurled through an open window during a prayer service just two days later. Her own family members were drawn into the turmoil as threats were made to them and others associating with the school. Prudence Crandall's case went to court, and ultimately, she was spared a conviction. While she was greatly relieved, the decision had the immediate effect of beating her enemy's beehive, and they mobilized and reacted with even more ferocity in their stings. On September 9, 1834, a mob congregated and created a frightening display of yelling and vandalizing the school. Sounds of crashing glass and breaking wood were added to the whooping and calling. Those dwelling inside were terrified. Deeming the future too tenuous to continue and the safety of her students too precious, Prudence Crandall dissolved the school and sent the students back to their homes.

The pioneer's path forward may be filled with setbacks, switchbacks, and anticipated and unanticipated dead ends. History recounts the ultimate fate of "Prudence Crandall's school for young ladies and little misses of color." For the headmaster herself, the whole endeavor into which she thrust her heart, soul, mind, and strength appeared to be a complete failure. But the investment of the teacher is never without its mark upon her students, and students grow to make their positive contribution to others. Reflecting upon her final day at the Canterbury school, one student shared the profound impact her teacher and fellow students had on her:

> There is something in parting from those we love from which nature recoils; and when I thought of the distance that would be between us and contemplated the uncertainty of things, I could but acknowledge the

probability of never meeting again in the company of my school mates. I have found among them simple manners and intelligent minds; and there, if any where love was without dissimulation. My teacher was ever kind: with her I saw religion not merely adopted as an empty form but a living all-pervading principle of action. She lived like those who seek a better country; nor was her family devotion as a cold pile of hypocrisy, on which the fire of God never descends. No it was a place of communion with Heaven.[6]

This alignment of conviction with action was not lost on these students, and it would be a lesson they would carry with them into the future.

When the Smoke Cleared

The Prudence Crandall Museum in Canterbury, Connecticut, housed in the building that was formerly the Canterbury school, compiled a listing of the African American students who attended. While some of the stories of the young student scholars remain a mystery, history records some of the impactful trajectories of those who endured as they pursued their education:

- Sarah Harris, the first African American student at the school, married George Fayerweather in a double marriage ceremony with her brother Charles Harris and "Ann Mariah (Marcia) Davis, Prudence Crandall's former 'household assistant.' The wedding took place at the Westminster Congregational Church" very nearly across the street from the school. The couples chose Tuesday, September 9, 1834 as their wedding date, and it was that very evening that the school had been vandalized. Charles' father, William Harris, was the local agent for the *Liberator*. It appears that Sarah and Charles never forgot the lessons they learned from their father, the newspaper, and their interactions with the Canterbury school. Sarah and her husband, George, became very active in the abolitionist movement, serving as conductors on the Underground Railroad. This couple also hosted William Lloyd Garrison and Frederick Douglass in their Kingston, Rhode Island home. Sarah maintained her friendship with her teacher, exchanging letters and even visiting Prudence Crandall Philleo at her home in Kansas. (Before Prudence closed the Canterbury school, she married Baptist pastor Calvin Philleo.) Sarah and George named their first child Prudence Crandall Fayerweather.

- Mary Harris, who was Sarah and Charles' sister and also attended the school, married Pelluman Williams, a teacher in Norwich, Connecticut. The couple relocated to New Orleans and both taught African American students of every age. Their oldest son also became a teacher "with six teachers under him."[7]

- Harriet Rosetta Lanson was sent to the school from New Haven, where she lived as a ward of abolitionists Reverend Simeon Jocelyn and Harriet Starr Jocelyn. Reverend Jocelyn was the first pastor "of a black congregation at the 'Temple Street' church, which would later become Dixwell Ave. Congregational Church."[8] Reverend Jocelyn had made efforts of his own to found a school for African American men, but it never got off the ground. Upon hearing of the Canterbury school, he sent Harriet eastward for her education. Harriet worked part time at the school to offset her expenses. After the school's dissolution, she continued her own scholarly pursuits and taught Reverend Jocelyn's children. She died of tuberculosis at eighteen years old. Her obituary in the *Norwich Courier* read that she was known to "never utter an unkind word towards the people of Canterbury" and "prayed for the slaveholder—never uttering one revengeful sentiment towards them."[9]

- Elizabeth Smith was a native of Providence, Rhode Island, and she returned there after the Canterbury school closed.

She became a teacher and then the principal of a school that served black students. She was also a linguist and a piano teacher.

- Ann Eliza Hammond was Prudence Crandall's first out-of-state pupil. It was she who was ready to be "whipped on the naked body not exceeding ten stripes" rather than be sent home. She was joined by her sister, Sarah Lloyd Hammond, who was only age nine at the time. Their father Thomas died while the girls were still young, and it was their mother, Elizabeth Hammond, who introduced Prudence Crandall to the Benson family—a family who remained loyal supporters of Prudence and her actions at Canterbury. Although the details of Ann's life after the school closed are uncertain, it appears that she went to England and was still living in 1871 when Prudence Crandall referenced Ann in a letter to Sarah Harris Fayerweather. One fact is certain, however: The brave young woman Ann did not have to suffer the pain or indignity of the town whipping post.

- Massachusetts student Julia Williams continued her education after the Canterbury school closed and transferred to the Noyes Academy in New Canaan, New Hampshire, which was also dissolved in 1835. Nonetheless, she remained active as an advocate of abolition, representing the Boston area in the 1837 Anti-slavery Convention in New York City. Julia met her match in Henry Highland Garnet, also a prominent figure in the abolitionist effort. Henry was a fugitive slave as well as a minister, and the two married and traveled to Jamaica as missionaries. Julia led an industrial school for girls. Sometime later the two moved to Washington, DC, due to Henry's health, and he took a pastorate at the Fifteenth Street Presbyterian Church. After the Civil War, Julia worked with former slaves. She died on January 7, 1870.

As for Prudence Crandall, history was much kinder to her than her neighbors were. Today she is recognized for her pioneering work for operating what may arguably be the first integrated school classroom in the United States and establishing the first school for African American girls. In 1886, Connecticut reversed its posture toward Crandall in offering her an annual pension. While not a great sum of money given all of the suffering she endured by the will of the state, it was, nonetheless, a token admission that the state had wronged one of its own. She died in Elk Falls, Kansas on January 28, 1890. She was eighty-six.

In her closing remarks titled "Prudence in Perspective," biographer Marvis Olive Welch stated:

> The ramifications of Prudence's trials did not end with her demise. The stand that she took in attempting to integrate her school was vindicated 120 years later. Thurgood Marshall, the National Association for the Advancement for Colored People counsel, before the US Supreme Court drew from the briefs of her counsel in 1834. The principles for which she sacrificed so much became the law of the land by the Supreme Court decision of 1954 [in *Brown v. Board of Education*].[10]

One of the more painful pioneering lessons that can be drawn from Prudence Crandall's life is that there may be occasions when the pioneer's efforts are not appreciated during her lifetime, let alone supported. In this way, Prudence, and others like her, live life ahead of their time. In Crandall's case, it would take years for her community and even society at large to fully realize the ramifications of her stand against racism and the price she paid for pioneering. Prudence and her students, along with many other abolitionist associates, would go to their graves without a full realization of how their sacrifices positively impacted the treatment of others far into the future.

Points for Your Compass

→ When entering unknown territory, sometimes all that can be done is to continue walking forward in the direction that the pioneer knows is right. (For example: When Prudence Crandall had decided to admit her first black student and the response was the loss of her white students, she continued to teach, while gaining help in the abolitionist community to populate her classroom with black students who wanted to learn.)

→ When attempting something new, it is crucial for the pioneer to find a few supporters who act as ballast, grounding the pioneer in reality, while supporting him individually as well as his mission.

→ While a pioneer may not have dreamed up every scenario awaiting him in new territory, to a degree, he has anticipated possible outcomes: positive or negative. Prudence Crandall realized that she might be punished for her decision to welcome African American students. As a result, she was mentally and emotionally ready to go to jail.

→ Agility in learning while pioneering is vital, creating an ever-deepening pool of experience from which to draw. Experience produces internal strength.

→ Virtuous pioneering does not end with the pioneer herself, but creates a beaten pathway beckoning others like her to follow and expand on and refine her work. As such, her courageous effort creates positive ripples throughout her community and time.

The Scenic Overlook
"Let's pull over for awhile"

As I begin this chapter, I just wrapped up a rewarding trip to Nigeria. I was part of a five-member team invited to offer training to radio professionals in Abia state. The fun for me is not just being in an environment far away from my own work-day setting but being in a different culture with those who also love doing what I do. We learn from each other, and each one comes away enriched by having gone through the process. Don't get me wrong; it's hard work to listen through heavily accented exchanges. I also have to remember to speak more slowly than I am used to, even though we speak the same language. Nigerian participants find Americans hard to understand too—imagine that? We work through the communication hindrances, though, and laughter is as much a tension reliever as acetaminophen, and without any negative side effects.

Nigeria was new to me. Though I'd been to Africa multiple times, this was the first occasion in which I would have a Nigerian immigration stamp in my passport. I was on my own pioneering trip of sorts; there were new people to meet, new customs, unseen terrain, even a different national history to learn about. With three flights behind me, I found myself in a van with the newly assembled team, bumping along a crater-riven road on the way to the radio station. We zig-zagged our way along the route as the driver attempted to avoid the canyon-like holes, saving what little he could of the weary suspension system. The seats in which we were planted had also experienced much use, with bouncing human hind ends having pounded the stuffing mercilessly into crepe-like submission.

Anyone with motion sickness knows that a back-and-forth approach to reaching the destination is not optimal for sustaining a satisfied stomach. A medical doctor along on a concurrent trip told me that the human brain gets confused when it cannot see the horizon, and that the best thing to do to maintain intestinal equilibrium is to look forward as far as the eyes will see. For the life of me, I don't know why the brain feels that it must punish the stomach because of its own addled state, but it does, and for that reason I experienced some mental relief when I remembered that I had tucked a plastic shopping bag into my travel bag. In the end, the mind-over-matter approach failed. I felt the matter in question reemerging from my fiery gastral core. Knowing full well that others can become ill at the sound of someone else retching, I tried to be as quiet as I could while I literally bagged my lunch. In the end, I felt as if I were the lucky one as endorphins rushed in and the fatigue from the nausea granted me a legit pass to lie down for several hours. Meanwhile, my colleagues went to work teaching a four-hour boot camp in a zombie-like mental haze. Eventually, their need for food overwhelmed them. They roused me from my sleep, and I ordered a bland meal of chicken and rice and went back to sleep. I *almost* felt guilty.

After dinner, the team reviewed the afternoon's activities. By this time, I was eating and felt restored after several hours sleep. We decided we were so focused on our mission to be there, as well as having a desire to accommodate our overseas host's request, that we had failed to take into account our own physical limitations; specifically, the need for restoration after three flights and hopping six time zones. In short, we were so zeroed in our mission that we forgot our own needs and suffered the consequences. We decided that we weren't going to do that again! This was the start to my new Nigerian experience. Fortunately, it got progressively better.

Many pioneers have taken journeys, some lasting months and even years, to reach their destinations. They've endured more than just a twenty-four-hour journey of flights and van rides. Theirs was a more hazardous voyage. Others, while knowing the perils and potholes that awaited them, have attempted the same expedition even after several failed attempts. Fixated on accomplishing their goal, they have literally pressed forward again and again to the ends of the earth. As tireless as they may seem, the human body must recover through rest and diversion.

If the body doesn't get the recovery it needs, it may call activity to a halt and demand rest through some form of mounting physical ailment, emotional breakdown, or mental lockup. The body has its way of saying "I've had enough," even when the mind wants to press on. Pioneers, who are more prone to hyper-focus on their quest, need to recognize the warning signs of fatigue and take action to prevent a full blowout. In some cases, that first wake-up call is one from which one never wakes up, as is the case with some stroke and heart attack victims.

In his book *The Overload Syndrome: Learning to Live within your Limits*, medical doctor Richard Swenson highlights two types of people who are likely to suffer overload. First, he describes HPPs or Highly Productive People. These individuals are visionaries, driven by their own incredible work ethic. In Swenson's words, "Much of our national success can be attributed to their efforts. They do much of the work, make most of the decisions, develop most of the new products and create most of the wealth that the rest of us have grown to depend on." Some of these people could be considered pioneers. We owe them a great deal, but we also can learn from them. On the downside, they are often unaware of the warning signals their own bodies are giving them. They set up standards for themselves that are sky high and expect other people to meet them too. These unhealthy mindsets, if unheeded, are destabilizing. Swenson warns that human performance is only "one criteria by which acceptance is handed out, but it should not be the only criteria, or even the main criteria. We must always be careful to value…things like love, compassion, service, and justice."[1]

Swenson then turns his attention to HSPs, or Highly Sensitive People. Unlike the HPPs who can be overwhelmed by the toll their schedules and output put upon them, HSPs can be overcome by overload through sensory stimulus. They have a heightened sense of justice, are highly impacted by toxic environments, hurtful verbiage, and, as Swenson states, they "can feel the pain in the room."[2] While our culture has become very sensitized and feelings-oriented, HSPs are extremely so, not because they have learned it (though this may play into their sensitivity), but because it is part of their personality structure. The world to them clamors at a volume that they have trouble turning down on their own. They are often creative, prefer solitude, and may even isolate themselves socially because they are just worn out by overstimulation. However, their gift to the world is their sensitivity to others and to things that should change, yet they often offer their gift at great cost to themselves. Many pioneers throughout time have been HPPs and HSPs, and some, I venture, have been both.

Pioneering also demands considerable rest in various forms to add energy and infuse supercharged creativity and productivity to the pioneering process. For example, innovators on task to create or improve a medical solution or refine an invention have used rest to amp-up creativity, used play to problem solve, or kept journals to mark progress as a form of self-encouragement. Whatever form restoration may take for the individual pioneer, it is a vital component of the journey, and without it, accomplishment of the mission may not be realized.

The Beauty of Sleep

The need for physical restoration is well known and established through ample research. And yet, many people live in sleep-deprived cultures. Pioneering types may feel an urgency to get things done, keeping them wakeful. Ideas and methods may course through the mind like wild horses when the head hits the pillow, keeping their owner awake. There's a pressing desire to advance just a bit more, and if that additional thing on the task list can be done, pioneers reason they will sleep better, as they are that much further down the road.

Though many of us need a solid seven to nine hours of quality sleep each night (I fall on the side of needing more), individual needs do vary. Sleep keeps us functional as the body presses its restorative powers into service to cope with what the owner has experienced during the daytime. At various stages of the sleep cycle, we disengage from everyday surroundings, breathing slows, and muscles relax. Allowing the body its daily respite aids in boosting the immune system's response, improves the ability to learn, enhances memory recall, and helps maintain emotional balance. In addition, a simple online search instantly brings up other benefits, including cancer prevention, promotion of heart health, and even weight loss. Yet so many of us suffer during waking hours because we have pushed the envelope too far and not allowed ourselves enough sleep, trading the immediate benefits for the long term.

A plethora of cascading problems haunt us when we fail to slumber, including many that negatively impact mental health. Depression may develop, or if it's already a pre-existing condition, it may worsen. Anxiety may heighten, and symptoms of associated disorders, such as obsessive-compulsive disorder (OCD) and post-traumatic stress disorder (PTSD), may worsen. Those who already have difficulty with attention ailments may find that they struggle more. Improved sleep has shown to mitigate the severity of these issues or stave off their onset. Maybe one of the reasons the proverbial pioneering mad scientist was so cracked was because he was up all night.

Humor aside, there are times when extreme conditions imposed upon pioneers have made a solid night's sleep impossible. Perhaps the mission or the pioneers' lives are endangered. During the *Endurance* crew's six-man rescue journey from Elephant Island to South Georgia, six men, including leader Ernest Shackleton, sailed for their own lives and for those they left behind on the island. They knew they would be navigating one of the roughest patches of sea on the earth, but to fail was to bring a hard end to their story, and they knew it. During a time when there was no advanced communication, the only way others would know that they were not lost at sea and that the remainder of the crew needed rescue was to show up in a civilized place. They knew that they were not likely to be found in so remote an area. They had to sail for it.

It wasn't long into the journey before the extreme conditions began to take their toll. In Shackleton's own words, "real rest, we had none. The perpetual motion of the boat made repose impossible; we were cold, sore and anxious." Yet some sort of rest had to be imposed on the men in order to sail the *James Caird* from Elephant Island to South Georgia Island. Shackleton set up a work-rest schedule. He created a four-hour shift where three of the men worked and three rested as they could. The working team handled the sail, the tiller ropes, and bailed the seawater out. Those who were trying to recover shivered in sopping wet reindeer skin sleeping bags that had begun to slough off hair so badly that Shackleton described it as getting into everything, even their drinking water. At the end of the two-and-one-half-week ordeal, the sailing team was so exhausted that Shackleton said, "Our thirst was a torment and we could scarcely touch our food; the cold seemed to strike right through our weakened bodies." With a diminishing supply of good water, food, and sleep to comfort them, they were occasionally cheered by singing and growing signs of land in the forms of kelp and birds. As they reached the shores of South Georgia Island, Shackleton recognized, "Our united strength was not enough to get the *James Caird* clear of the water…. We attempted to pull the empty boat up on the beach, and discovered by this effort how weak we had become…. Time after time we pulled together, but without avail. I saw that it would be necessary to have food and rest before we beached the boat."[3]

Have you ever felt that you used all your strength up, and have gotten to the point where you pulled time after time without avail? Reflection may reveal that perhaps some basic human needs are lacking after you have spent mounds of effort "rowing" toward your pioneering end point.

Give Me Space!

One of the most extreme conditions in recent history that pioneering individuals have to navigate is the ability to function in space. The human body was not made to live and move and have its being in zero gravity, but thanks to scientific advancements, it can. When astronauts make the transition from native earth to a very low gravity environment, say aboard the international space station (ISS), there is a time when they can become very disoriented, making the motion sickness on my journey into Nigeria look like a walk in the park. Think back to the doctor's advice to me to locate the farthest point on the horizon that I could see and fixate on it to help my brain (and by extension, my stomach) reorient. Those directives would be impossible for an astronaut. After all, in space, where is the horizon anyway? Add to that the lack of gravity, and you have real disorientation. Remember that last meal you had? Imagine if it was just floating in your stomach. That's right—your food is floating as the rest of you is floating. About half of all astronauts suffer from space adaptation syndrome (SAS) for several days until the body acclimates to the new environment. Undoubtedly, I'd be one of them if I took to space.

This sort of disorientation also impacts the ability to obtain rest through sleep. Studies have examined how sleep patterns change once people enter space. This type of research is ongoing and is considered "a new medical research frontier."[4] Since sleep is an important component of peak performance and copious resources are being invested in the health and training of the astronauts as well as the experiments they are to perform, it is in everyone's best interest to ensure that they are sleeping well. Some of the challenges they face include uncomfortable temperatures, a sleeping bag that doesn't quite provide the comfort that gravity and a bed might, an inability for the body to detect its own position, and more noise in their surroundings.

Another challenge with sleeping in space is a disruption of the body's own circadian rhythm or its internal clock that helps regulate sleep cycles. One of the cues that the body receives as a signal to get out of bed is an increasing amount of light. Likewise, diminishing light signals the ending of the day and is a prompt for the body to prepare for rest. Astronauts do not experience day and night as we ground dwellers do. On terra firma, we are apportioned one sunrise and one sunset per twenty-four-hour day. However, people working on the ISS are orbiting the earth at an incredible speed. "The International Space Station travels at a brisk 17,100 miles per hour. That means it orbits Earth every 90 minutes—so it sees a sunrise every 90 minutes. Thus, every day, the residents of the ISS witness 16 sunrises and 16 sunsets."[5] This brings new meaning to the saying "Time flies when you're having fun." The fact is that time passes for the astronauts just as it does for us, but the light cues aren't the same, which makes sleep all the more challenging. Sudden changes in schedule or a need to attend to station operations have also had an interruptive impact on astronaut sleep. All of these factors can play into a variety of wear and tear in the orbiting astronaut body and psyche, and mistakes can become all the more likely.

Fortunately, research on orbiting sleep conditions continues to offer improvements for the benefit of the astro-pioneers who are serving aboard the ISS. Improvements have been made to the sleeping arrangements, including the cabin temperature, creating small spaces for private sleeping, and dampening noise levels. The sleeping bags in which they retire have been made more comfortable, and because of the lack of gravity, they are strategically fastened to the wall.

Sleeping pills are the friends of many earth dwellers, so it stands to reason that this type of medication also helps the astronauts when needed. Likewise, caffeine is also an ally that is used when needed to stay awake and alert. Of course, coffee is a favorite stimulant, and studying the behavior of fluids in space helped solve the conundrum of getting a warm cup of coffee to the astronauts in microgravity.

Initially, astronauts got their coffee—the yummy freeze-dried version—by sucking it from a sealed plastic bag. Sensory pleasures, such as inhaling the bracing smell of fresh brewed coffee in the morning, were nonexistent as the sealed, warm bag kept the fragrance away from the nose. Furthermore, hot coffee, as well as other liquids, behave differently in space. Liquids have a sticky quality when in a cup, due to surface tension in space, along with other factors. With a traditional cup, you might not be able to reach your warm beverage unless you have a very long tongue or try to pour it out. Now, your globular, steaming coffee is floating freely near you until you catch it and swallow it like a fish glomming on to a fishhook. Talk about getting burned!

Astronaut Don Pettit had an even more compelling reason to try to find an answer to the coffee conundrum. In an online video, he described that drinking coffee out of a bag "makes you feel like you're a big insect sucking juices from another insect."[6] Lovely. Caffeinated necessity being the mother of aromatic invention, Don went to work (or perhaps play?) when he remembered some of the lessons he had learned from chemistry. He notes, "When you're in space, you can't run down to the store to buy parts. You have to be able to improvise with what you have on your mission. And so I looked around and found a piece of plastic. I cut it up and used tape." The end result was a small, transparent container that looked like a teardrop or Wonder Woman's almost invisible airplane wing. It worked. When Don put his coffee in his newly designed Zero G coffee cup, the liquid crept up the side to the lip, but without spilling. Don was able to sip and smell his brew.

The 2008 original Zero G coffee cup received the first patent for a product invented in space. The original version has received some upgrades, and it is now made on earth. If you want one, you can get one, provided you want to pony up about five hundred dollars. Because few have been made, they are rare finds. But they certainly have an appeal for individuals who love a blend of art and science, as well as space innovation.

As much fun as astronaut Pettit has had telling and retelling the story of his coffee cup creation, he makes a solid appeal to other pioneers and creators:

> Frontiering requires making skills. Frontiers are all around us, and my frontier happens to be space. My urge to make [things] is so that there's something at the end of the day that wasn't there at the beginning of the day. It is an incredible sense of accomplishment when you have made something. It could be simple.

> It could be complex. But the fact that you made
> something and it fulfills a unique function, there's no
> better feeling than that.[7]

In addition to sleeping-stimulant interventions for the astronauts, work schedules were re-assessed to allow for enough time to disengage from the jobs assigned, and this included recreation. Light therapy, psychological support, along with crew training and selection have also been recommended. The more that we are able to learn about how the human body can function well in orbit around the earth, the more we will be able to learn from the experiments astronauts conduct in microgravity. Who knows what we may discover in the coming years that may be of help to all of us who live below in the firm gravitational pull of our earth?

"All Work and No Play..."

Rest for the human body goes beyond just a good night's sleep. It also includes diversion when one is awake—in other words, play. Play can be simply defined as "physical or mental leisure activity that is undertaken purely for enjoyment or amusement and has no other objective."[8] However, play can fall on a spectrum. Certainly, play can be blended with work, hence the saying, "If you love what you do, you'll never work a day in your life."

I have only to look a few feet away from my computer screen to see a living demonstration of this concept at work in my husband Jack. Jack is a rare broadcast engineer who is as comfortable with computers as he is with transmitters, radio consoles, microphones, and the like. One day may find him changing the light bulb in a studio on-air sign, standing in a satellite dish changing out an LNB,[9] or out on a boggy site trying to figure out why one of his transmitters (I call them his "hot girlfriends") is overheating. Some of his "girls" are higher maintenance than others, and when they call his cell phone with alarms in the middle of the night, he has to get out of bed to figure out how to make them happy again. That's the nature of the radio business; as the saying goes, "the show must go on." For every second of dead air, revenue is lost, and it's Jack's job to keep the equipment up to snuff.

The quirky part of Jack's lifestyle is that when he is off the clock and all the girls are happily singing on their various legal frequencies, the last thing I would expect him to engage with is a computer, or anything else with a plug, motor, or wires. One would think he would need "space" from these sorts of things, yet I have witnessed him drawn back to computer guts like vultures drawn to roadkill. As I was getting to know him, I asked about some of his favorite pastimes, and he replied, "tinkering, puttering." I have observed him long enough now in our marriage to see that his self-described tinkering and puttering have positive outcomes, not only in our own household, but also for the growing string of senior adults who have discovered that Jack is happy to address their technological issues. We hardly ever have to call a repairman. Jack *is* the repairman. For him, the lines between play and work are blurred, and a person cannot tell by watching him which end of the spectrum is operating at any given time. It confounded me early in our marriage as Jack would not disengage from what outwardly looked to me like work. I would say, "All work and no play make Jack a dull boy...and I mean you!" But as time has rolled on and I've learned more about Jack, I've learned not to nag.

Jack's penchant to play problem-solve has not only saved the Epperson household budget from taking some heavy hits when the sump pump or some other form of equipment fails, but his practice in blending play and work have had benefits beyond a job well done at work or at home. Ever so rarely, get-'er-done Jack will recount his day and reveal that he was faced with a problem that he didn't know how to solve. This is not the kind of talk you might overhear at a Society of Broadcast Engineers' (SBE) meeting. There is nothing more fearful for an engineer of Jack's ilk to admit, "I don't know how to fix this," or worse, "I don't know what resources I have to help solve this," which includes help from other people.

A few times throughout our eighteen-year marriage, Jack has told me of exceptional circumstances, when after doing what he knew to do failed to work, he would enter into a cycle of thinking, attempting a fix, and assessing the results, only to end up with a subsequent fail. He has described that fearful point when he was confounded but kept at his thinking-trying-assessing cycle. Eventually, he has shared how a clarity formed in his mind, allowing a solution to manifest. It was a "eureka moment." And the application of the solution finally yielded a humming transmitter. No one was there to slap him on the back and say, "Great job!" He couldn't hear any expressions of relief or thanks from listeners who were able to hear their favorite programming again. It was just him and his girl, the transmitter. Yet, a grand sense of fulfillment and victory flooded over him. He experienced the human soul cry "Yesssss!" that many achievers live for. He just had to share it with me when he got home.

Pioneering people press hard toward the type of experience that I described in Jack. It's the equivalent of a supreme soul fist-pump, if the soul had a fist to pump. It's the thrill of successfully arriving where no one else has been, or discovering a solution that no one else has derived. For me, this is a fascinating example of how play, work, creativity, and new discovery intersect.

There is evidence to support this. Play has long been thought of as an activity that children do in order to develop their mind and body before they get to the serious work of being adults. While this is true, play—even for adults—is serious business. Though there is a "history of research exploring playfulness in children, empirical attention on playfulness in adults is in its early stages," say researchers Cale Magnuson and Lynn Barnett. In their 2013 study called "The Playful Advantage: How Playfulness Enhances Coping with Stress," Magnuson and Barnett found that people who were more playful perceived less stress in their lives and used coping styles that helped them adapt better than others who were less playful. The subjects of their study were university students, the more playful of whom appeared to "believe they have the inner resources necessary to overcome their stressors and are typically successful in their utilization of coping strategies. The results clearly indicated that [they] had a propensity to attack stressors directly and that they more infrequently utilized less adaptive coping styles."[10] In their conclusion,

Magnuson and Barnett offer that the quality of being playful may take on a very important role throughout our lives, most notably in helping a person remain resilient, even when going through highly stressful situations.

As science begins to uncover how important play is to our health, it makes sense that individuals tasked with scientific research on the ISS must have time to reflect and even have fun in space in order to maximize their resilience along with their creative and analytical ability. Months of isolation and work in orbit can cause stress, which requires healthy ways to burn it off. Offering a playful margin enhances mental effectiveness while engaging with the pioneering experiments conducted in space. Like Jack, the infusion of creativity that play provides is not limited to time spent in play. It spills over into work. One never knows when a Eureka! moment may erupt, but creating the mental climate in which it might happen is working wisdom.

One of the relaxing pastimes for astronauts includes gazing out of space station windows. Those of us on earth have benefited from the many videos and pictures the astronauts have taken of the earth from their perspective. Based on the photos I've seen, witnessing an aurora borealis (northern lights) and aurora australis (southern lights) from space must be magnificent. My guess is that these video and photo likenesses don't do the actual image seen by the human eye any justice. Do an internet search. They're just beautiful!

As astronauts work full-time, they get weekends off. They may spend this free time talking to family members, watching movies, playing and listening to music, joking with fellow crewmates, and withdrawing to meditate and pray. Spending time with other people (including God, for people of faith) and engaging with the arts provides both positive stimulation and socialization. Exercise also plays a positive role in burning off stress both here and in space. There are some fairly sophisticated gadgets aboard the ISS to provide resistance and aerobic training in a microgravity environment. Part of astronaut workload may include experiments playing with games, especially to see how ordinary or scientific toys behave in microgravity. And while playing with your food may have been verboten at the dinner table, astronauts have amused themselves and made scientific advances while playing with their food.

Space PBJ

In an online instructional video on how to make a peanut butter and jelly sandwich in space, NASA astronaut Shane Kimbrough says, "Every time we eat, it's kind of fun. Everything will float around if we don't manage it…. If I let it go, it will kind of float there for a little while and then eventually the air conditioning system in here will take it away somewhere else, so I don't want to lose it, so I'm just going to stick it [with Velcro] on the table."[11] Peanut butter and jelly on a flour tortilla shell is great, but after a while, human beings begin to crave the sorts of fresh foods they can get on earth, like fruits and vegetables. It's just a fact of life that humans want more out of food than just nutrition. They want eating to be a fun, pleasurable experience.

To be sure, astronauts may get an apple or an orange every few months when supplies arrive from Earth, but what if there was no ability to return to Earth? That's a rough scenario to think about, but that's what pioneering is: it's pushing the boundaries of the possible. Some of us might have to live on Mars someday, and that's where learning to garden in space comes in. Even if we didn't have to live on Mars, knowing that it's possible is intriguing and opens up another world of possibilities.

How Does Your Garden Grow?

This is where the idea of experimenting with space gardening comes in. Thought has been given to how plants might thrive in microgravity. Shane Topham, an engineer with the Space Dynamics Laboratory at Utah State University in Logan, explains, "Growing food to supplement and minimize the food that must be carried to space will be increasingly important on long-duration missions…. We also are learning about the psychological benefits of growing plants in space, something that will become more important as crews travel farther from Earth."[12] Did he say, "psychological benefits of plants in space?" Yes! In January 2016, when the northern hemisphere was experiencing winter, the first zinnia bloomed in outer space, nurtured by astronaut Scott Kelly. He had several of them in a growth chamber that had previously been used to successfully grow red romaine lettuce. The zinnias had a tough go of it, overcoming too much water, not enough water, and then a mold problem. After the mold was addressed, the zinnias showed their bright, orange faces. Kelly was delighted, and he tweeted his success and a photo of the flower with an elated world. So there you have it, a psychological benefit of growing plants in space. Plants brighten our homes and beautify our earth landscapes, so why should it be any different in the confines of the ISS that several individuals call home throughout the year?

Even though zinnias are flowers and we don't usually eat them (although you could since zinnias are edible), the positive growth results ushered in the opportunity to try tomatoes, a more complicated plant to grow. So far there has been success with leafy greens, and experiments are designed to push the boundaries with different types of plants to learn how they react to microgravity, and, of course, how they taste to the astronauts who get to care for them and harvest them. Caring for live plants also adds to the variety of work in which astronauts are involved.

According to a report created for NASA that outlines some of the effects of long space habitation, one of the losses people may experience is engagement in work that they personally find fulfilling. Another such activity is "information foraging" which refers to how people seek out different sources to learn, stimulating parts of the brain that learn and engage with what an individual finds to be meaningful work. Pair this with other needed segments of activity, such as restoration and relaxation (restorative touch, interaction with nature either real or virtual, creativity, and habitat design) along with active release (exercise, celebration, and play, to name a few), and you see how plants bring together a number of renewing activities that serve to refresh astronauts who are far away from home. I guess there are scientific reasons why I find pulling weeds out of my midwestern flower gardens not only stress relieving but also rewarding.

Full disclosure: while writing this segment, I had to be careful not to allow myself to become too distracted by watching astronaut video postings from space. It was easy to press play and watch one video after another about how to wash your hair in space or how to brush your teeth in microgravity, all skills that I'm unlikely to use. Many of these videos brought a smile to my face. I learned a lot, and sorely wished I had one of the cool and convenient "space barf bags" on my bumpy ride in Nigeria. In truth, people on earth have benefited from many of the inventions created for space, such as scratch resistant glasses, memory foam, certain kinds of athletic sneakers, foil blankets, Dust Busters (cordless, handheld vacuum cleaners), and more. Who knows what else will be created in space that will benefit humanity?

Man's Best Friends

In the not-so-distant past, movement around the globe was limited to only the adventurous few. Those who had healthy personal bank accounts had the greatest access to global travel, though they may not have had the penchant for it. Those employed by the military (whether by choice or not) also had a shot at experiencing life beyond their native borders. Still others engaged in fundraising to explore or advance their lives beyond their native territory.

Animals were often included as part of early pioneer supply lists. Their inclusion was multipurpose. Many were included as food for the sojourners, and others were used as working partners. Some animals provided both. Early sailors, perhaps the Egyptians, brought cats aboard, realizing they were valuable in keeping the ship free of rodents that most certainly would have found their way into the sailors' valuable stores. Some saw felines as a lucky charm on the turbulent seas. Sometimes, sailors would adopt an animal as a ship's mascot. The practice continues today, though animals do not typically travel with ships anymore. Take the US Navy's mascot, Bill the goat.

It would be impractical to sustain a goat on a lengthy submarine mission. Before long, both the goat and the people would get on each other's nerves.

Still other animal companions found their way on board as a sort of souvenir from the land visited, or as gifts. British soldiers brought back many such animals, including monkeys, kangaroos, exotic birds, and polar bears. The menagerie grew, and soon a sort of zoo was established on Whale Island in Portsmouth, England. The little known "sailor's zoo," as it was called, nurtured sailors' "strong affection, curiosity and abiding respect for the natural world, especially for the animals and birds they met on their travels and maritime superstition engendered a feeling of obligation and reverence towards the non-human world."[13]

Perhaps the simplest explanation for their presence was to provide human counterparts with entertainment and comfort. While the dogs on board Shackleton's ship *Endurance* were intended to fulfill a practical mission of pulling supplies on sleds, they also provided the stranded men with comfort during the long Antarctic nights. Sadly, the time came when Shackleton had decided that the limited food supplies could no longer sustain both the men and the dogs, and he made the decision to have the dogs shot and eaten.

> Among the men, reactions ranged from simple resignation to outraged shock. Stormy debates on the value of the dogs against the food they consumed broke out in each tent that night. But the fundamental, underlying factor in these discussions was that, for many men, the dogs were more than so many pounds of pulling power on the trail; there was a deep emotional attachment involved. It was the basic human need to love something, the desire to express tenderness in this barren place. Though the dogs were vicious, surly beasts with one another, their devotion and loyalty toward the men was above question. And the men responded with an affection greatly surpassing anything they would have felt under ordinary circumstances.[14]

As harsh as it may sound, the men were also grateful for the "dog steaks" served after the difficult deed, as they offered a variance in the monotony of seal diet. The dogs sustained them, first with their affection, and then nutritionally, giving their all to support the men.

Pioneering pooches have also been sent on space missions, along with monkeys, chimpanzees, and mice. Fruit flies were the first animals in space in 1947, reaching the lower thermosphere, at an altitude of sixty-eight miles. Upon arrival back on earth, they were found alive. The Soviets sent the first rabbit into space in 1959 along with two canine companions, and Félicette, the French cat, reached an altitude of one hundred miles in 1963.

Laika was a stray dog found in Moscow—a mixed breed. The American media called her "Muttnik." Thought to have withstood extreme conditions as a stray, she was chosen to ride aboard Sputnik 2 in 1957, and she had the distinction of being the first animal to orbit the earth. Sadly, she died in space within hours from overheating. A 2008 monument that honors her and her contribution to space travel was unveiled in Moscow. Several Sputniks later, Sputnik 5 to be precise, Belka and Strelka were the first dogs to return alive from orbit in August 1960. Within a year after that (April 1961), the Soviets finally sent a human being into space. Yuri Gagarin went up in the capsule Vostok 1. He orbited the earth once for about 108 minutes, and upon completion became the first man to orbit the earth.

Without animal participation in several countries' space programs, putting human beings in space likely would have been delayed, as well as our collective knowledge of space and the inventions that have come as a result. Though the animals were unwittingly pressed into service (some might use stronger language), and some lost their lives, they are owed the sincere tributes given them. Today, animals are still in space, joining astronauts in research to understand the impact of microgravity on living creatures.

In April 2019, a research paper was published that described the behavior of mice on board the space station. It's the first study of its kind. These furry creatures lived in a special NASA rodent habitat. Throughout their stay, they remained healthy and active. The researchers observed typical "mousey" behavior, such as self-cleaning and eating. What did change was the way the mice learned to move in microgravity. Over time, they adjusted their movements, even using their ability to float. They began to anchor themselves with their rear legs or tails. Of the two groups of mice (one set was thirty-two weeks old and the other sixteen weeks old at launch), the younger group adopted a circling or "race-tracking" activity around their habitat that interested scientists. Overall, this was the first experiment with mice in a NASA rodent habitat on the ISS. While the role of the mice was not to serve as companions to the astronauts, their presence offered a look at how humans might endure longer spaceflights to Mars or elsewhere. And who knows? The space station may yet adopt a mascot like Bill the goat or a comfort animal for longer missions. It would certainly be in keeping with the pioneering tradition.

Reflection

Several pioneers throughout history have made use of journals. Through them, we've seen the drawings of John James Audubon, the musings of Mark Twain, and the calculations of Marie Curie and Albert Einstein. These personal journals have taken us beyond their own body of finished work and offered insights into their cognitive process. Beyond capturing details related to the pioneering work, journals also serve other purposes.

For many people, writing may seem like a chore, but an article from the University of Rochester claims that if journaling is approached with the proper mindset, its use can serve as a personal release, a time to de-stress and relax. For those who struggle with stress, depression, and anxiety (and don't we all at one stage or another?), journaling can serve as a means to process emotions and cope with daily stressors. As the written word is applied to the page, the mind is given space to make sense out of chaos, which is valuable, not only when feeling overwhelmed but also when the mind is trying to problem solve.

For example, the pages of Leonardo DaVinci's journal are a beautiful mélange of drawings and comments about his inventions, scientific observations, and architectural ideas. DaVinci was curious and delved into a spectrum of topics. Like the rest of us, pioneer Leonardo DaVinci had a life, so amidst his profound ponderings, he jotted down reminders as part of his daily to-do list.

Marie Curie also kept notes about her work, but due to the nature of her quest, her journals are housed in lead-lined boxes as they are still radioactive. Those who are willing to put on the proper protective clothing and sign a waiver to look at Curie's journals will see her calculations and gain insight into her process (if you can read French and understand her area of expertise). She was pioneering in the area of radiation, and what she didn't know did eventually kill her; she died of a condition caused by radiation poisoning.

Lewis and Clark's venture west was documented by the people in their party, as requested by U.S. President Thomas Jefferson. The president told them to observe "the animals of the country generally, and especially those not known in the U.S. the remains and accounts of any which may [be] rare or extinct."[15] As they traveled, they not only recounted the day's happenings and the weather, but also the land they were traversing along with their botanical and animal observations. They also kept accounts of the native people they met along the way. There were even comments about their health and challenges. Upon their return journey, their documentation kept a growing United States population fascinated with their pioneering trek. Through modern technology and financial investment, Lewis and Clarke's journals are digitized and available for anyone to see online, and reproductions can be purchased. However, they are considered so important to our nation's history that an original cannot be touched, unless you are an archivist wearing gloves. Pages are turned with a small metal spatula.

Shackleton distributed journals to his crew, and all of the members kept diaries. At the time, the world had been bit with the exotic pioneering bug, and Shackleton knew that there was value, even fiscal value, to the experiences they would chronicle. "As was the custom, Shackleton...mortgaged the expedition, in a sense, by selling in advance the rights to whatever commercial properties the expedition might produce. He promised to write a book later about the trip. He sold the rights to the motion pictures and still photographs that would be taken, and he agreed to give a long lecture series on his return."[16] Little did he or his team know that, not only would they fail in their attempt to cross the Antarctic Continent, but they would also be enduring its harsh climate (including its limited menu) far longer than they dreamed or desired. History has cherished the account that many of the men have left in piecing together just how incredible their journey was. They have left us their thoughts, feelings, and records of their actions under the harshest of conditions.

Journaling can be a special part of the pioneering journey. The process of documenting in words and pictures (drawn, photographed, or videoed) can keep the pioneer grounded as to why he or she is undertaking a trying journey. When the stressed pioneer asks, "Why am I doing this to myself," rereading one's own journal can be the closest consoler within reach. After all, one's own inspirational words written in the past and reread in a difficult time can firmly anchor and realign the soul by reminding a person why all the strain and effort will be worthwhile when the mission is accomplished. Soul alignment provides a deep sense of purpose and peace needed to keep the hard work of moving the pioneering vision forward.

Points for Your Compass

→ Considerable rest is needed when pioneering, in order to regain energy along the way to infuse the individual with supercharged creativity and productivity for the pioneering process. Healthy eating and exercise are also requisites.

→ Even pioneers must have recess time—time for play. Socializing with others over a meal in light conversation or playing games can give the brain a needed break from the work of the pioneering process.

→ Spending time in nature, such as stargazing, caring for gardens, and interacting with animals, provides refreshment and brings delight.

→ Reflection in the form of recording personal thoughts in writing and drawing observations can provide perspective, helping to spark potential breakthroughs by looking at problems in different ways.

The Conflict
"Managing skirmishes in the backseat"

THE EIGHT MEN WHO RETURNED HOME TO ENGLAND IN THE SHIP *Discovery* had a lot of explaining to do. First and foremost, where were the ship's captain and the rest of the crew? Then, there were other nagging questions: Why was there blood soaked into the sea-worn wood decking? What about the secretly stashed letter that was found? And there were questions about that letter: its content recounted a mounting tension among crew members. Apparently, a critical mass among them had come to loggerheads with their leader. They were greatly disturbed that the tenacious captain had decided to resume his search to find a northwest passage, after having been trapped in the wilderness during the harsh winter months. The beleaguered seafarers had had enough of it. They wanted to return to England with or without their hero captain. Taken as a whole, the pieces of the puzzle looked pretty damning for the living members of the *Discovery*. This was at a time when the penalty for mutiny was death. However, the survivors had their own story to tell, with none living to contest them.

It was 1611, and the missing captain was the famed explorer Henry Hudson. Hudson was no lightweight. Having made several daring journeys to the northwest, he was acutely aware that his supporters relied on him to find the quickest trade route to Asia. As always, time was money, and the nation that was able to crack this mystery stood to prosper handsomely, as would the explorer. Now on his fourth voyage, he had heretofore failed to find his way to Asia, but each time he returned to Europe, he added more discoveries to western knowledge. The public was intrigued, and investors were hungry. Previously, Hudson had sailed under a Dutch flag, but on his fourth journey, the English were determined to keep their own. England's leaders told him that he was never to sail for another country again.

Several months after setting sail from English shores, Hudson and his team had made their way across the Atlantic, stopping at Iceland and Greenland respectively. They then made their way through what is now known as the Hudson Strait. The ship sailed into the bay looking for a way west. Yet, without the modern benefit of satellite imagery, they had little idea they were heading into a cul-de-sac offset from another cul-de-sac, otherwise known as Saint James Bay. There they were stuck. It was too late to go back. The ship became trapped in the ice. They chose to ground it and wait out the winter, which proved to be a tough one. With little knowledge of the area and diminishing supplies, the men suffered, further deepening their burning anger toward the one who had gotten them into this mess in the first place: Henry Hudson.

With the passage of time, the sun shifted, and the ice melted. The men felt relief with the lengthening daylight on their faces and the spring song of the birds in their ears. Surely, their misery was coming to an end. There remained one obstacle: they failed to take into account the tenacity to which Hudson held to his mission.

When the ship was able to sail again by June 1611 and the expedition leader announced his renewed intent to sail west to find a trading passage instead of eastward toward their home, it was more than some could bear. Whispers and plans of mutiny spread through the crew. Sides were chosen. Then action was taken. The mutineers gathered up Hudson, his adolescent son, and those loyal to him and set them adrift on a lifeboat. The ship set sail eastward, leaving the little crew in the southern waters of the Saint James Bay area. One can imagine the horror that overcame the abandoned crew as they realized the permanence of their situation with the mother ship moving further and further away. The horror of a slow death by starvation or death by exposure in an unknown place was worse than taking a well-placed bullet.

Did Hudson and the loyal crew attempt to row after the ship, calling out for mercy?

Or did they stoically accept their fate?

We don't know. This was the last that any white man saw or heard from the Hudson party again.

The eight survivors, necks on the line, shed no such insight on the situation. They offered up their own version of events to the English authorities when questioned about Hudson's fate. They admitted that they had set the smaller team on a lifeboat before making their way back home. Other clues (such as the bloodstains on the deck) have caused conjecture that perhaps Hudson and his loyal party met a more violent end. At any rate, without any more evidence, the real fate of the abandoned party is a mystery buried deep in the murky past.

Pioneers like Henry Hudson have always had to navigate, not only their own mission, but also the many conflicts with and among team members that may ignite along the way. Whether a parent driving unruly children to band practice, a business leader on the verge of closing the deal of a lifetime, or a scientist on the brink of a breakthrough, no leader likes conflicts among team members in the back seat. Depending on the sort of exploration attempted, these troublesome situations may take a variety of forms, such as waning financial resources, harsh weather in a hostile environment, defection to another effort, unmet deadlines, or a lack of anticipated results. Layering these challenges can add to the stress factor among the team, sending morale, tempers, and even hope swirling down a black spiral.

The "driver" may be plied with endless questions: "Are we there yet?" "Can we pull over?" "Will you get me something else to eat?" Some challenges might even come from the front passenger seat, which may prove even more aggravating. "I think we're lost again; do you know where you're going?" "Didn't you foresee this?"

Then there are the accusations: "I can't believe you forgot to bring the _____ (fill in the blank)," "You want us to do what?" or "I don't remember signing up for this."

Finally, there are the last resorts—ultimatums designed as a final effort to get the pioneer to change course: "Stop the car!" "When hell freezes over, I will," "You're out of your mind!" and one of my favorites, "You first."

Stress is high, the mission is at stake, and resources wane while squabbling continues. A pioneer on the brink of a new frontier may taste the outcomes of achieving the success that he or she has longed for, while the team behind can only taste the bitter reflux of their own empty stomachs. Explorers of Henry Hudson's ill-fated team faced a breakdown as conditions became increasingly extreme. Layer tough conditions one upon another and a recipe for a crisis is brewing. Sheer desperation for survival from worn team members can cause even the most loyal among the exploring party to question a boss's sanity, and there may be an attempt to grab the car keys and drive for safer places.

During these bleak spells, history has offered us many examples of how desperate times have led to desperate measures. Pioneering leaders who are not able to manage conflict have found their hopes dashed, the mission abandoned, or have personally suffered from team-inflicted wounds. It cost Hudson and his loyal few their lives. However, other pioneers have offered insight as to how to navigate the narrow path and keep the team engaged while navigating the choppy waters of conflict.

Change the Mission:
Shackleton vs. Hudson

Three hundred and three years later, fellow English countryman Ernest Shackleton and his team found themselves in nearly the same conundrum. Icebound in the southern hemisphere, Shackleton and the crew settled into their floating home away from home until they could stay no longer. From Hudson to Shackleton, three hundred years of exploration had been added to history, and Sir Ernest had done all in his knowledge to have enough goods stored to last for the foreseeable future of the expedition.

Explorers like Hudson and Shackleton knew that no matter how prepared they were, there might always be life-threatening contingencies around the corner. It was the nature of the work and part of the adrenaline rush that came with exploration.

There's something invigorating when going against the all-natural will to live. The spirit makes the hard choice in the name of the mission, whether it be discovery, human relief, or innovation, to go to the danger zone and live to tell about it.

There are some significant differences between Shackleton's story and Hudson's. Most notably, Shackleton lost his ship to the crushing ice, whereas Hudson was able to ground his ship, allowing his crew to retain hope for a return in the same vessel. Both crews waited out the winter in harsh environments, and it took its toll on the men in body and spirit. However, in Shackleton's mind, there was a major shift in objective, and that was to bring everyone home alive. Who knows how he might have recounted previous stories of his Antarctic endeavors that had fallen short of his expectations as his team was hunkered down on the ice? One thing was certain: Shackleton had set a precedence of valuing life over glory, and his men knew it. The boss would do what he could to get them home safely. There was trust, even though it was tested at times.

Hudson had no such change in thinking. Despite the gnawingly bitter winter his men had endured, his rugged determinism offered no room for a change. He would not turn back, and when the reality of his intentions sank into the consciousness of his team, a group of them took a huge gamble by initiating a course of action that, should they arrive safely back home, was punishable by death. In this way, Hudson also lost his ship, not by the pressure of a crushing ice pack, but as a result of failing to see his crew's mounting internal pressure and making a decision that would ultimately crush the spirit of his men.

Leave the Fighters Home

It is a fact of life that certain situations create conflict. Putting two male betta fish in one tank is a no-no. If you are thinking about keeping chickens, there had better be enough hens to keep the roosters placated. Places of nuisance are labeled as such because they are trouble. One online commentator defined places of nuisance very simply as "places your momma told you to never go." Momma knew that avoiding the situation entirely is often the best course of action. A well-known proverb says it this way: "The best offense is a good defense."

During the trail-blazing process, forecasting potential conflicts through situational anticipation while taking steps to avoid them is a practical means of averting mitigating circumstances. For example, in preparation for his Iditarod run, the young musher Karl Clauson had to build a winning sled team. He not only had to find loyal, powerful dogs that would go the distance to carry him to Nome, Alaska, but they had to be of a temperament that would not be combative or prone to distraction. In considering potential dogs for his team, Clauson becomes emphatic in describing a deal-breaking trait: "One of the most vital things that you cannot have in any Iditarod dog ever is a fighter. No way. Fighters destroy a team."

But fighters are not always evident at first blush. My mother gave me some valuable dating advice: "Give him enough time, Jennifer, and he will show himself." This is good counsel for anyone considering a venture into an unknown situation with unknown characters. While Shackleton's method of choosing certain team members was unorthodox, those who composed the spine or primary support of his team were known to him and had weathered previous expeditions. They were tested. Time and experience had revealed character and temperament. If possible, it is wise to give anything or anyone a trial before the fixture becomes permanent—or irreparable.

Before adding any dog to his team, let alone adding them to his racing lineup, Clauson learned a proven process in order to assess their nature:

> Temperament is huge. It is critical. You cannot have fighters. How do you [discern] that? Believe it or not how we measured temperament in Alaska [is by watching] how dogs ran side by side with other dogs. How did they do? Did they give others space? Did they nip at them for no reason at all while they're going down the trail? Do they share a bowl of grub when it's put down in front of them, or do they dominate that grub? There's ways to determine that with dogs; there's ways to determine it with people. I bet you any amount of money, Shackleton would never have brought a fighter.[1]

Good words. But Shackleton did, inadvertently, bring some fighters. And true to my mother's wisdom, time revealed their nature. When these fighters showed their true stripes, it didn't take long for Shackleton to show them the ship's door. Fortunately for the rest of the team, these fighters' tenure was cut short even before the ship left its last port of call for the icy unknown. Only once subsequent to that event was The Boss publicly challenged: after he had made the decision to move the party forward, dragging their lifeboats with them over tough, icy ground. The men were weary, and it seemed like they were getting nowhere. That's when carpenter Harry McNish announced he would go no further, which evoked an equally intense response from Shackleton. "McNish's position was absurd... [his] one-man mutiny was simply an unreasoning, exhausted protest, called up by an aging and aching body that demanded rest. Even after Shackleton's talk, he remained obstinate."[2] Afterward, The Boss remained alert, continually sniffing the crisp, southern air for any other signs of mutiny. He had a keen sense of cultural barometric pressure, along with a winsome ability to head off challenges to his leadership through well-placed levity, or if needed, iron will. He also knew that naysayers and complainers have a way of infecting a mission like a virus. If only Hudson had developed such a skill. If only he had understood that his team had interests too, and attempted to reconcile theirs with his own. His story might have ended differently.

A Better Way

Sled dogs, betta fish, poultry, and yes, people become entangled in power struggles. When larger groups of people are involved, greater conflicts may ensue, sometimes with devastating consequences. Any history class devotes a share of its time to wars that bookend and pockmark the rises and falls of civilizations. Time periods like the French Revolution or the Vietnam War are often named for the conflicts that define them, because the cultural change the conflicts brought on was so pervasive in reach. While not as bloody, organizational failures can also be cataclysmic. Take, for example, the fallout from a number of companies whose lapses in leadership (in some cases deliberate) produced misleading financial reporting that cost their stakeholders billions of dollars. "In the early part of the twenty-first century, it came to light that the leaders of numerous companies had failed their investors, employees, vendors, and even entire communities that were dependent on them."[3]

As these events unfolded, as well as those that kicked off the subprime mortgage crisis of 2007 and the subsequent global recession, Ken Schuetz thought long and hard about the organizational enablers (as well as the people who created them) that led to the cascading financial failures. Ken is a little different from the rest of us. He knows a lot about organizational machinations, with academic specialization and real-life experience on how boards operate. He has spent untold thousands of hours teaching business in university classrooms and leading as a university executive. He has also benevolently given much of his time serving on school and church boards as well as other nonprofits. He knows how various organizations work, so why didn't they? While some people would have nothing but a cursory interest in such financial roadkill, Ken was highly curious as the results of the autopsies came to light. From his vantage point, if organizations were bodies, many were dropping unnecessarily with a ripple effect that engulfed investors who had trustingly invested their assets in the organization's leadership care.

As someone who has served on boards, Ken intuitively tapped his understanding of how organizations are run as he began work that would eventually set him on a pioneering course. Like an investigator of a failed airline flight, Ken tapped into his experience as he examined the wreckage: Where did the failure(s) occur? Was it due to faulty equipment in the form of operations, or was it human error? More importantly, was there a "black box" somewhere that might provide some "recordings" or insight as to why the economic plane took the devastating flight path that it did? He recalls reflecting on the internal structural integrity of how organizations were run, and it brought him right to the cockpit: the boardroom and C-suites. "I think that the events that caused me to think about starting to do work [in this area]…were catastrophic in the sense of that executives and boards in organizations were seeing each other as combatants rather than as allies in some way. Because of that, everyone was losing."[4] Indeed, conflict is a well-known corrosive that can internally eat away at organizational integrity no matter how solid the vessel may look on the exterior. This is where we need to pull out our own magnifying glasses to see the fine cracks that Ken is about to show us.

To understand how such failures happened, some foundational understanding of how organizations are led is in order. Legally, two kinds of corporations are required to be governed by boards: nonprofits and publicly held for-profits. This is largely due to the role these organizations play in managing other people's money. Careful attention needs to be ensured that there is a good return on stakeholders' financial investments along with a division of power among the board members in order to avoid corruption.

Among these board-governed organizations are *nonprofits*, which are largely mission driven. For the nonprofit donor, there is an expectation that some meaningful value is being created as a result of the donation, such as the creation of more affordable housing for struggling community members, fairer treatment of animals, or providing food and occupational training for the underemployed. Society greatly benefits from the nonprofits and the work of their boards, employees, and volunteers to create a better life for others.

Also included among organizations required to have boards are civic organizations, municipalities, schools, and all the branches that these authorities create. Stakeholders in this case are taxpayers who also expect a return on their investment in the forms of solid and reliable community infrastructure. Taxpayers also have an expectation of effective and efficient use of their enforced tax contributions, and if unhappy at the quality of governance are able to display their displeasure the next time a visit to the voting booth is available.

The second major type of organization required to have a board are publicly held for-profits. These manage investors' money in exchange for some type of hoped-for financial return. It was in this realm that the catastrophes of the early 2000s were incubated and hatched.

Ken Schuetz knew that there were unhealthy power struggles occurring in these types of organizations and, in his words, "ways of thinking that...needed to be addressed."[5] Some of these ways of thinking included making conflict "go away" in a very unhealthy way, such as allowing the CEO of the organization to also play the role of chairman of the board. In this way, both roles were played by the same person and conflict would supposedly evaporate. With this structure, however, accountability through checks and balances would also disappear. In order to understand the nature of the ugly critter that was allowed to grow in many boardrooms, we need to take another leap back in time.

Several decades ago, a lone voice was beginning to be heard in the area of what today is referred to as policy governance. Dr. John Carver began to develop a model that would be an innovative way to "empower boards of directors to fulfill their obligation of accountability for the organizations they govern," with the purpose of enabling "the board to focus on the larger issues, to delegate with clarity, to control management's job without meddling, to rigorously evaluate the accomplishment of the organization; to truly lead its organization."[6] In the years since, the Carver model has helped many organizations better fulfill their missional work, laying the foundation for future efforts to meet the needs organizations face in a rapidly changing culture. As one who would become a student of policy governance and its related body of literature, and then who would go on to serve as an academic practitioner in the area himself, Schuetz observed:

> The name itself [policy governance] should help you understand what Carver thought the problem was and what the solution was. International policy governance really implies that the problem is the lack of policy and the solution is to implement policy. So, actually being in that space, I understood that in many ways Carver had picked up on at least some of the answers, like policy is probably an important thing. But like most things, in the world of innovation today, it was part of the solution, not all of the solution.[7]

A Pioneer with Only Part of the Solution

Pioneers rarely start out with a full map or a complete solution. Yet, it is here, facing a pictorial "end-of-the world-as-we-know-it" document, where the pioneer's most unique traits are most evident in contrast with those of a simple leader: Passion for the unknown drives her forward. Her own skin or reputation is put on the line. Internally, time is spent in deep thought gnawing on the object of the pioneer's passion, running various strategies to make the mission become a reality, while significant effort is spent in persuasive evangelism to get others to comprehend the mechanics and importance of the ideas, inventions, and places needing to be explored. In the end, all of the hard work may leave the pioneer with only part of the map. For her, it is never enough, but occasionally time, resources, or life run out, and she must leave the incomplete pieces of the puzzle for the next pioneer to take up and continue. While this may never bring full satisfaction to the pioneer and is a hard pill to swallow, it is how life works. In those cases, the best the pioneer can do is pass on the knowledge and the burning flame to others to continue for the good of humanity. Though perhaps unfulfilled, there is no shame in it for the pioneer, even though it may be in her nature to go to the grave pining, "If only there were more time…money…help…."

As Ken Schuetz was sketching out his part of the map, using the context from the one that John Carver and those that others in the field had given him, he began to realize with growing clarity that a fresh model for governance was needed. And this he created. Called Aligned Influence®, his paradigm goes beyond leading through policy. It "defines the roles of both executives and board members 'as they influence' the organization, [stressing] that the key to successful organizational operation is 'aligning' those influences appropriately. The…model defines the role of the board as directing, protecting and enabling the work of the organization, and the work of the executive director as leading, managing and accomplishing the work of the organization."[8] Carver's work on policy sets and boards supplied part of the solution to the organizational governance problem. But Schuetz saw that much more was needed. And now he has supplied it.

Saving Lives through Resource Allocation

Today, the phrase "landing the plane" is invoked when a conversationalist is rambling, and the listener is asking for a verbal cessation by "getting to the point." In the context of business meetings, it's usually a request to move to a wrap-up of concepts by way of a summary, which hopefully includes action steps and closure of the meeting.

Then there is the literal need to land planes. Like business meetings, flights are only intended to last so long as they transport people and goods from one point to another. There are limits in the distance and speed aircraft can travel. Though flying is one of the safest ways to go places, things can still go wrong, and at that point, the lives of hundreds of people are in the hands of a skilled few, typically those seated in the nose of the plane. Depending on the nature of the problem, what these crew members focus on, and how they choose to react during the crisis, could mean the difference between life and death.

Dr. John Lauber, a neuropsychologist who at the time was working with NASA, had been examining how people interact in the cockpit, noting that human error was a significant factor in several plane crashes. He, along with others like him, were building on the seminal work of Royal Air Force pilot David Beaty, who authored the controversial book *The Human Factor in Aircraft Accidents*. Today, it is understood that human error can lead to accidents, but when Beaty wrote his book, the world was different. He revealed that "pilots were human beings, not supermen. Some were meek and easily led. Others believed the publicity and considered themselves incapable of mistakes. Some were left-handed in a right-handed world. Cockpits were fashioned for contortionists. Pilots even suffered from tiredness like others."[9]

A decade after Beaty published his book, Lauber hypothesized that better training might help the flight deck crew to better manage their resources, leading to increases in life-saving outcomes during crisis situations. In a 1979 paper presented in a NASA/Industry workshop called "Resource Management on the Flight Deck," Lauber noted: "Generally, those pilots who mentioned training during…interviews expressed satisfaction with the training they received in the technical aspects of flying and in flying skills. The difficulty related more to issues such as how to be a more effective leader, and how to achieve more effective crew coordination and improved communication within the cockpit."[10]

So, how do people skills, otherwise known as "soft skills," help save lives? Soft skills are not about saying "please" and "thank you" in emergencies. Rather, the study that Lauber and his colleagues conducted revealed some frequent commonalities that all seemed to fall into the realm of resource management. They included "preoccupation with minor mechanical problems, inadequate leadership, failure to delegate tasks and assign responsibilities, failure to set priorities, inadequate monitoring, failure to utilize available data, failure to communicate intent and plans."[11] Note that none of these problems are specific to flying planes. They are common human errors that occur across many industries. After citing the details of a cargo jet crash, the National Transportation Safety Board (NTSB) summarized the reason for the tragedy as being due to a "dynamic situation…because the aircraft must be flown while the malfunction is resolved, it follows that *the captain must manage the flight crew* in a manner which will insure absolute safe operation of the aircraft during the interim…. It remains that the captain's first and foremost responsibility is to insure [sic] safe operation of the aircraft. To achieve this objective, he must relegate other activities accordingly."[12] In other words, there must be aligned leadership and open communication. Without it, the safety of air flight is jeopardized.

These were building blocks of what would come to be known as Crew Resource Management, or CRM, a moniker that Lauber created. The practices emphasize cognitive and interpersonal skills of leadership rather than actual skills needed to fly an aircraft. At its core lies the need to have development in enhancing situational awareness and solid competencies in performance, along with leadership, decision-making, communication, and teamwork skills. CRM also helps with flexibility, adaptability, becoming more self-aware, and boosting assertiveness, especially if a crew member is not the captain of the flight. Traditionally, the captain's actions and decisions were not to be questioned, but with CRM in place, others in the cockpit were empowered to bring up relevant information that a captain in a crisis might be overlooking.

Training in the classroom is fine, but can it work in the field during a life or death situation? In the case of United Airlines 232, it did. About an hour into the flight from Denver to Chicago, a large "boom" signaled a main engine explosion, shattering the hydraulic lines. Without any hydraulics, the DC-10 had no flight controls. It virtually assured a crash that would kill the 296 passengers and crew. The incident, however, occurred on July 19, 1989, and by then, United Airlines had initiated CRM practices—the first airline to implement a comprehensive training in the United States by 1981. As a result, Captain Al Haynes and his team were able to remain calm, giving them mental and emotional bandwidth to think through the problem, implement solutions, and correct efforts that didn't work.

Though one engine was gone, two remained—one on each wing. Haynes, First Officer William Records, and Second Officer Dudley Dvorak discovered that they could control the plane by adjusting its thrust with two remaining throttles. A fourth person joined them in the cockpit. United Airlines instructor Dennis Fitch was in the first-class section of the plane, and his specialty was in DC-10s. He assumed control of the throttles. As the crippled jet spiraled its way down to the earth, the Sioux City airport in Iowa prepared to receive the passengers. At United 232's approach, the right wing dipped and hit the runway, sending it into a cartwheel. Fuel spilled and an explosion blew the aircraft into four pieces. Though 111 people died, 185 lived, including the four men in the cockpit.

Captain Al Haynes was injured in the crash landing he oversaw, as were the other three men in the cockpit. He would recover and continue to fly for United Airlines until he was sixty years old, when company policy dictated a mandatory retirement. Afterward, he kept up a hefty speaking schedule, emphasizing the need for teamwork that came through CRM. Rather than accept the title of "hero," he focused his praise on the skills of his whole team, along with the teams of ready rescuers, medical practitioners, and citizens of Sioux City for their help in saving lives. "The NTSB later cited Haynes' practice of crew resource management—in short it's the art of leading while empowering team members to speak up and to leverage their experience—as one of the reasons why the tragedy wasn't worse."[13]

Back to the Board Room

Fortunately, organizational spirals are rarely as accelerated as an inflight crisis. While a pilot and team may have only minutes to deduce a solution, organizational pilots may have months and even years to make course corrections. As it relates to the role of the board in the organization, Ken Schuetz relates: "Someone has to see the big picture during crisis, while others must execute [and] all must communicate. However, communication is hardly effective if everybody has a different understanding of the goal and the role that one must play while achieving those goals. Teams work best when there is frequent, meaningful communication, along with task assignments that add to organizational flow. There is nowhere better to model this than at the top."

As to the role of boards, Schuetz has found that boards function most productively when they "direct, protect, and enable the work." The *directing* role "involves thinking about the future of the organization. And the unique role of the board in thinking about the future of the organization is to define what should be accomplished by this organization, who should be served by this organization, and the executive, whatever that person is called, determine what ideals they ought to maintain as they're doing that."

Under the Aligned Influence® model, the board's second role, which is one of *protection*, extends, in part, to the executive. In its governing policies, the board establishes day-to-day working boundaries in which the organization must function. According to Schuetz, in essence the board is saying to its executive, "Executive, you can do anything you want, just don't cross these boundaries."

Finally, Schuetz identified a third role for the board and that is to *enable* the work of the organization, which encompasses advocacy, a full understanding of the organization's mission, and recognizing its opportunities and challenges. Says Schuetz:

> I like to tell boards when I am training them on this is that you either metaphorically or literally wear your organization around on your lapel [like a lapel pin]. Every conversation you have at coffee, at work, at church, wherever, someone might ask, "Wait, what's that symbol on your pin? What do the wheat stalks mean?," or "What's the little roof with the little people under it?," and a board member can say, "Oh! That's the food shelter," or "That's Habitat for Humanity." That opens the conversation where, as a board member, they get to advocate by asking, "Do you know what we're doing?" or "Do you understand the challenges we have or the opportunities we have?"

Now, [that's when board members need to] shut up and listen for the talents and resources that this person might have and influence they have and how those talents and influences might help the organization accomplish this work.

In this way, simple advocacy discussions morph into needed resource development exchanges that enable the organization to move forward.

But there's more: Schuetz explains that the board's gift of executive enablement is "to be dedicated to these roles and not move over into the executive's roles. Rather than enabling, it disables the organization when they move into the executive's [domain]."[14]

Stay in Your Lane!

Passing.

No passing.

Left turn only.

Right turn only.

It's amazing how painted lines on the roadway direct drivers, and how they are taken for granted until they are no longer visible. New pavement provides its challenges, especially in high traffic areas, creating stress and possible confusion until the road painters appear and restore order again. So it is with Aligned Influence® in directing the flow of the executive's work in tandem with the board's. Like on the roadways, an executive can see the other drivers out the windshield, but with his or her own roles to navigate, course collisions are reduced, and organizational traffic is kept flowing.

Under the Aligned Influence® model, Schuetz draws a contrast to the board's roles with that of the executive's. While the board is to *direct*, *protect*, and *enable* the organization, the executive is to *lead*, *manage*, and *accomplish* the work of the organization. These are more than just mere shades of the same terms. Like painted roadways, these six key terms provide meaningful difference in the execution of organizational roles. Schuetz provides a practical example, distinguishing the executive's role of leading with the board's role of directing. Both roles are future oriented but in different ways. The board lays out the overall goals that the organization must achieve. "In a similar way, the executive also must think about the future, but they think about the future by leading the organization. Its leadership is engaged in three-to-five-year planning on how they're going to strategically accomplish this work, supported by budgets." The board doesn't go into this level of detail in its directing work, which is just one of the ways that the board's directing role and the executive's leading role differ.

In the executive's managing role, necessary documentation is required as it is with the board. But once again, documentation at the executive level fulfills in greater detail the overall direction that the board has provided in its governing policies. The executive and his or her team develop overseeing policies and procedures that will help guide the day-to-day work of staff and volunteers in order to accomplish the organization's mission in a way that's safe and appropriate to its culture. Finally, executives are not worth their salt unless there is tangible accomplishment. Schuetz notes, "In the end, the work of the organization is accomplished by the executive side of the organization."[15]

Drive-Time Alignment

Taken as a whole, the Aligned Influence® model that Ken Schuetz has pioneered has offered both nonprofit and for-profit entities with boards a roadmap that maximizes organizational accomplishment through clearly defined and aligned role assignments. It also minimizes wreckage that comes as a result of crossing over that all-important double line. Many employees, departments, boards, and executives wish they could do more at work, if only _____ [you name it] would stay in their lane. It's a cry of frustration heard in many places of work today. As he discusses the benefits that his Aligned Influence® model offers, Schuetz grows animated at the benefits that are realized as people learn how to more effectively navigate wasteful power conflicts.

> Think about those two columns of three words side by side, with the board directing, protecting, and enabling, while the executive leads, manages, and accomplishes. We can look at them horizontally as ordered pairs of influence. The board enables and the executives accomplish; they have a dual role now. The board actually gets engaged in the work, but they get engaged in enabling the work.... They make that work visible so that other people understand how they might help that move forward. You also see that in the past we had this power struggle about who owns the future. Is it the board that talks about the future or is it the executive that talks about the future? And now we have an aligned way for both to talk about the future. The board thinks about the future of what's to be accomplished, and the executive thinks about the future of how it's going to be accomplished. We don't have to fight about that anymore. We have aligned ways of sharing that work.[16]

Putting the Pioneering Pedal to the Metal

No doubt about it, conflict can be a killer, not only to the pioneer but also to his or her team and the ultimate accomplishment of the mission. Wherever there are people, there will be conflict. Sometimes, the best way forward for the pioneer is to identify the source of conflict and confront it or remove it if necessary. Other times, conflict can be avoided in the process of pioneering by changing the thrust of the mission, if necessary, or by not combining two combustible elements together in the first place.

Since many pioneering efforts require the use of teams, resource allocation, especially through the assignment of roles, has proven effective, as Ken Schuetz is discovering through the practice of his Aligned Influence® model. Resource allocation requires training and practice. For example, board members must understand their roles and where they may best invest their efforts. For the board member who wonders why in the world she is sitting on a board, resource allocation such as that offered through Aligned Influence® provides relief and motivation. Likewise, the executive is set free to practice his craft, having a full understanding of the parameters that the board has assigned to him. In a similar way, when an airline crew boards an aircraft, they know full well that any relevant information they might contribute to a solution will be heard should a crisis in the skies arise.

For those up and coming pioneers who will need to navigate conflict, Ken Schuetz offers the following advice: maintain a posture of learning through humility.

> I say this to my students, when you get done with your four-year education here, you'll have your education, but your training will start on the first day of your job. So, I would say be ready, be humble, be listening for everything that somebody says to you. Take it as feedback. Do your best to understand that you may not have all the answers. Maybe a critique that somebody has of what you are doing may actually help, so encourage those critiques, don't be afraid of them, lean into them. Try to understand if that critique has something that will actually help you to be better at what you are doing rather than seeing it as someone who is working against you.[17]

That's precisely what a successful pioneer who created a win-win model like Aligned Influence® would say: see every conflict as an opportunity to learn and grow.

Points for Your Compass

→ Ethical pioneers value the lives of their team members over mission accomplishment. They are not afraid to change the thrust of the mission to preserve life, knowing that they may live to pioneer again.

➔ One way to navigate conflicts is for the pioneer to "leave the fighters at home." In other words, the pioneering leader mitigates the likelihood of unnecessary internal struggles by leaving the combative off the team.

➔ Pioneers rarely have a complete plan when they begin their mission. Rather, they are more likely to build on the knowledge of other pioneers to advance into new territory.

➔ Wise pioneers encourage their team members to speak up and add their expertise, especially in critical situations where time and loss of life are factors in the outcome.

➔ The clear assignment of roles and alignment in mission helps team members concentrate on their individual roles and tasks, mitigating squabbling and power grabbing. In other words, a clear definition of assignments keeps team members moving forward in their own lane.

➔ If you want to be a future pioneer, maintain a posture of humility and be open to learning from those who are more experienced. This includes a willingness to ask questions and receive respectful, constructive criticism.

The Slippery Path
"I've fallen and I can't get up"

IN HIS PLAY *AS YOU LIKE IT*, WILLIAM SHAKESPEARE DIRECTS HIS character Rosalind to ask, "Why then, can one desire too much of a good thing?" Centuries later, actress Mae West comically offered the response, "Too much of a good thing can be wonderful," while writer Mark Twain turned the phrase to praise his favorite beverage, "Too much of anything is bad, but too much of good whiskey is barely enough."

While witticisms provide a temporary escape, reality has a way of overtaking the one trying to outrun or out-pun it. Too much of anything, even if good in moderation, may inflict its own sort of nasty consequences. Take spinach, for example. Some souls find the bitter taste of cooked spinach acceptable, and its mouth feel, albeit slimy, amenable. By consuming spinach, they reap the benefits of a green leafy vegetable full of nutrients (like vitamins A and C) as well as disease defending antioxidants. Eat too much spinach and look out! You open yourself up to kidney stones, abdominal pain, vomiting, tremors, convulsions, low blood pressure, and a weakened pulse. If you like spinach, don't despair, you'd have to eat about seven pounds of it per day to be at risk.[1] If you're not a fan, you've just received several more reasons to avoid it.

Beyond the practical advice offered by the refined proverb "Too much of a good thing is a bad thing," a deeper examination of what we say, do, or consume creates insight into our own behavioral patterns, effectively raising self-awareness. Astute individuals know that strengths are also likely fountainheads of personal weaknesses. If intentionality is applied to self-analysis, and enough light is shed and the proper lens is applied to the facets of personal strength, we might perceive something very different about ourselves than if we had not undertaken the exercise and left our foibles to go undetected and unevaluated. For example, self-confidence applied to work is a good thing when it comes to performing music, preparing a meal, or caring for the sick. However, too much confidence in self has the potential to turn a more sinister corner, morphing into ugly cockiness, arrogance, and overly self-reliant thoughts and actions. These are behavioral characteristics that are unattractive social repellants and may even result in injurious behavior to self and others.

No matter how discerning we think we might be when it comes to self-assessment, even the most introspective among us can't always see the fissures in our armor. This is especially true when visually diminished by the light of success that brilliantly dances off the metallic garb we've crafted for ourselves (Tony Stark/Ironman, anyone?). There's a blinding effect, a false feeling of impermeability. It's at these times when trusted friends and advisors may be lifesavers. An ancient proverb wisely offers, "The wounds of a friend are faithful, but the kisses of an enemy are deceitful."[2] By the time an enemy feigning friendship is close enough to offer kisses, he is also in proximity to put a knife in the gut. Moral of the story: Even when we don't think we need deliverance, we do, and most often, we need rescuing from ourselves. This is when the gift of others is most needed. That ugly thing you don't want to hear about yourself? You probably need to hear it, and more than once. Then you need to do something about it.

Passionate, risk tolerant, stoked-to-get-in-the-game pioneering types are at greater peril just by their nature. It's easy to bypass personal character assessment for those "let's get cracking" jobs on the to-do list. And yet, by creating space for personal self-reflection and allowing some wounding to personal pride in order to embrace humility, the pioneer and those along for the journey might be spared from actual physical pain, financial loss, mission abandonment, and even death.

If you consider yourself a pioneering type, see if some of these sticky quagmires ring true of you:

- Are you likely to risk too much?
- Does your inquisitive nature take you to harmful places from which there is no potential return (curiosity has killed more than the cat)?
- Do you fail to desist, even when your actions are injurious to yourself and those around you?
- Have you found yourself willing to compromise your own principles in order to achieve new outcomes or experience new things?
- Are you so persuasive that even you have begun to believe your own press against loved ones' better judgment?

Maybe none of these apply to you, but you're on a pioneer's team along for the journey. With him or her at the helm, you may find yourself in a sticky situation you never expected, given that the whole point of the endeavor is to do something that's never before been done. Your role is one that must provide balance, feedback, advice, and even warning if necessary. Every balloon must have ballast and every boat must have an anchor. Without these vital means of control, a vessel and all on board may be lost, and the purpose of the journey left unfilled. The following pioneering experiences are vivid examples of what might happen when innovators are left to themselves.

Risk and Regret

Life experience plays a significant role in a pioneer's success. With experience comes the ability to properly apply knowledge in areas relevant to pioneering achievements. This is why it is a big deal when younger people innovate and break age barriers with previously unrealized accomplishments.

Now a father himself, Karl Clauson, the youngest musher to finish the Iditarod in his time, is able to appreciate the sacrifice his parents made to help him complete the race and realize his adolescent dream. He trained and refined his dog team. He sought advice from seasoned mushers, yet naysayers pelted the young man with taunts that he would scratch the race or would die trying. Karl knew he actually could die if he made errors or exercised poor judgment. How does an eighteen-year-old prepare him or herself to mount a venture that may not only go down as an epic fail but could lead to death? He remembers: "The test in front of me was brutal without a doubt. Fear would creep in at times during the months of training leading up to the start. But here I was, [at the start of the race], staring down the trail that would lead me into danger like I'd never really imagined."[3]

Pioneers are not fortune-tellers; it is impossible to imagine all future contingencies. No matter how hard one has trained or how precisely one has prepared, risk of harm is always a percentage of the pioneering prognosis, depending on the type of venture attempted. No guts, no glory, as the saying goes, but guts and glory hardly matter to a dead pioneer. As Karl reflected on his particular challenge: "You know, you hear horror stories, but I don't think you can prepare for that. [You might] find some better man or woman than me, but I couldn't prepare for it. As a matter of fact, I don't think you can. The prospect of death is an interesting thing.... [You] try to gear your mind for the trial, [but] I don't [fully] think you can." Though he had hoped to avoid it and thought he couldn't prepare for it, Karl's worst nightmare played out as he was alone on sea ice. Thinking he was a dead man, he brought back soul-stretching lessons from which all pioneers may benefit.

Partway through his quest to reach Nome during the Iditarod, Clauson had reached the village of Shaktoolik and was headed for Koyuk. The wind blows incessantly on these coastal villages that are on the Norton Sound. Reaching Koyuk would necessitate crossing the icy bay as one competed with the wind. But before Clauson left, an Iditarod checker who was also a native of the area questioned him. Clauson remembers the exchange: "He asked, 'Are you going to go?' and I said, 'I'm going to go,' and he urged me, 'Karl, don't go. It's going to blow hard tonight. Don't go out on the ice.' But I went. I'm eighteen years old, and I thought I knew better than this guy, even though he was born and raised there. So, I headed out. I was naïve."[4]

As the checker anticipated, the wind picked up into gales, and Karl found himself in blinding conditions. The blasting snow left him unable to see beyond the front bumper of his sled. With the going so incredibly difficult, he resorted to futile attempts to kick and push the sled with his own feet. After some time and effort, a disheartened Karl realized the sled wasn't moving. He was stuck in a blizzard on sea ice. If he was to survive, he had to wait it out, but he had to be smart about it.

> I got down on my hands and knees, and crawled up to my team, one dog at a time—carefully, because if you crawl away from a tow line into a white out, you'll crawl to your death because you have no bearing. None. You have no way of seeing anything. So I crawl up to my team, saw where they were, [and] one by one got them into a pile, carefully holding on to the gang lines of their harnesses so I wouldn't lose my way. I crawled back to my sled, got up into it, and put up a windbreak with a snow shoe and some Gore-Tex, and crawled into my sleeping bags.

With his dogs safely in a pile to maintain heat and a makeshift shelter in place for himself, unwanted images began to press onto the gallery of Karl's mind:

> I was going to be on the front page of the *Anchorage Daily News*: "Karl Clauson dies on Norton Sound." It

was [completely] flat on the sea ice. There was nothing to hide behind, not even a pebble. I found out later that the wind was gusting to ninety-two miles per hour, with wind chill factors between seventy to one hundred below zero. So was I a dead man? I thought I was, because I couldn't move and I knew that the wind could last for a week to ten days, so I thought, *Yeah, I'm a dead man.*

When pioneers have dug deep in the face of adversity, they return to the well of the soul and pull from untapped depths from which more comfortable souls may never draw. He did things that many desperate men and women have done in moments like these: He prayed and made deals with God. "Often when we're running from God, and I was, he's still extending mercy to us. It's amazing. So, he let me live through that one." While Karl was taking a beating from the Alaskan weather, he feared for his life, but he did not panic. The thing that made the difference? Clauson responded:

> You begin to dig into a deeper part of yourself than you ever have before…. It was a few hours later that I thought I heard the wind subsiding and I stood up my full six feet—glad I wasn't five feet tall because I could just see over this horrible ground storm. I could see way, way off in the distance just a glimmer of light that I thought was Koyuk, and I got my team strung out and we headed off to Koyuk and we made it, by the grace of God. That situation was nip and tuck, a do-or-die situation. If I hadn't gotten off that ice in that window of time, I'd have probably perished out there.[5]

Relief in Retrospect or Driven to Death

One hundred thirty years before Karl's near-death encounter with Mother Nature, down in the much smaller, milder Nutmeg State, Hartford dentist Horace Wells was finally a free man. After the first successful use of nitrous oxide as an anesthesia gave him the gift of a painless wisdom tooth extraction, Wells was not only physically liberated, but the murky fog that comingled pain and dental work was finally lifting, and with it, Wells's spirits. Wells had been a fellow sufferer alongside his own dental patients, even to the point of occasionally placing his own practice on hiatus, because he had difficulty tolerating the pain others bore as he worked to solve their dental dilemmas.

After his own wisdom tooth extraction on December 11, 1844, Wells was energized. Eager to put the new discovery to work as the practitioner and not the patient, traveling showman "Colton taught Wells how to administer the gas, [and Wells] performed a dozen painless procedures over the next few weeks. Always intense, Wells became more excited with each successful procedure."[6]

Wells decided it was time to take the next step in revealing his discovery, but where would he go? Hartford had no hospital at the time, but it was situated between the two high-profile cities of Boston and New York. It is possible that the familiarity of Boston beckoned to him. He had studied dentistry in Boston and had some known associates there. Going with what you know is always a good place to start, but sometimes contingencies that are not known or planned for are what end up biting you.

Wells left for Boston in January 1845, and his initial efforts to bring attention to his claim proved to be frustrating. While there, he made contact with former apprentice and fellow dentist William Thomas Green Morton. The two had established a practice in Boston in 1843 while Wells continued to mentor Morton, but it was dissolved in October the following year. Just several months later, Wells was back in Boston, claiming he had found a way to offer pain-free extractions. It was too much for Morton, who was dismissive. Stoked by his former protégé's disbelief, an animated "Wells exclaimed, 'I have done it and can do it again.' Wells intended to place an advertisement in a Boston newspaper for volunteers for a demonstration of nitrous oxide."[7] Subsequently, Morton told friends that Wells had only one person show interest and that no operation was attempted.

Failing to be dissuaded, Wells dug in, taking rooms in Boston. He was determined to promote the use of nitrous oxide and ostensibly, himself as the innovator. He met with various dentists but gained little traction. According to Wells, Morton and physician Charles T. Jackson of Harvard (who would subsequently recommend the use of ether to Morton) refused to believe him. Others, such as Dr. Abel Ball and partner Dr. Fitch, put Wells off even though he offered them a trial. They rebuffed him with the excuse that they were too busy. Even a January 20, 1845 announcement in the newspaper the *Boston Bee* gained little attention. It read, "A dentist in Hartford, (Conn.) has adopted the use of nitrous oxide gas, in teeth pulling. It is said that after taking the gas the patient *feels no pain*."[8] Apparently, it sounded too good to be true, and many readers reasoned that was all it amounted to and turned the page.

Wells was facing a barrier that many pioneers face: disbelief. But indifference of others to such a monumental discovery initially added fuel to his fire. Fires are helpful if they can be contained and used appropriately: unwanted material can be destroyed, heat brings relief to a cold body, and even time spent watching the flames lick up into the air can relax a tense soul. But if igniting sparks fly outside the hearth, the whole house is endangered, potentially subject to a total loss of possessions, shelter, and even life. While on a mission to raise awareness to the relief nitrous oxide could provide, Horace Wells was suffering with the knowledge that each day, people underwent extraction procedures that caused unnecessary pain, and the fire in his soul raged higher and burned hotter.

The following day, January 21, 1845, an advertisement in the *Daily Evening Transcript* began with the eye-catching, capitalized, bold print: "**NOTICE EXTRAORDINARY.**" In it, Wells solicited volunteers to undergo extractions to demonstrate that "nearly or quite all of the pain which is caused by the operation may be avoided." Wells warned in his advertisement that he would be forced to abandon the project as his time in the area was limited. A more desperate announcement appeared the following day in the same paper. In it, Wells tweaked his colleagues by publicly asking, "Cannot our Dentists take enough interest in this matter to furnish patients for the occasion?"⁹ Wells's expenses, including the costs of the ads, were mounting, and he had not one bite for his demonstration. The apathy was eating him up.

Finally, Wells got the break he was looking for. While the exact date is unknown, Wells, with Morton and medical students present, did perform a public tooth extraction with nitrous oxide. After a lecture given by Dr. John Collins Warren at the Massachusetts Medical College, Wells and the group gathered in a different hall. What happened then would not only change the course of Wells's career but also his life.

The High Price of Pioneering

Like Horace Wells, Sophia Gregoria Hayden was a young, rising star. Born in Chile in 1868 to Elezena Fernandez and Bostonian dentist George Hayden, she was sent to the United States to live with her father's parents and attend school. She became fascinated with architecture, and though her family had moved away from the Boston area, was accepted at Massachusetts Institute of Technology and returned to the area. In 1890, she became the first female to graduate from MIT's four-year architecture program, and she did it with honors.

Her training in the École des Beaux-Arts style at MIT prepared her well for her next adventure post-graduation. While teaching mechanical drawing, Hayden became aware of a contest that was especially for female architects. The opportunity was associated with the upcoming World's Fair to be held in Chicago in 1893. Bertha Honoré Palmer, an influential and powerful businesswoman and member of Chicago's high society, was determined that the exposition would feature a grand building exhibiting works from women around the world. As the leader of the fair's board of lady managers, Palmer was determined that a woman would design the Women's Building, and she got her way. Back east in Boston, Hayden got to work to compete for the design that would win Palmer's vision. She used her thesis project, "Renaissance Museum of Fine Arts," as an inspiration for her contest entry. She sent away her drawings and waited.

Palmer and her board of lady managers had taken a bit of a gamble in their insistence that the Women's Building actually be designed by a woman. After all, how many capable female architects were there in the early 1890s? Not many, they surmised, but the choice had been made, and a renowned male architect had already been dismissed as a possible designer. Though the prospects seemed unlikely, entries began to make their way in for consideration. "You can well imagine our surprise and delight," Palmer wrote, "as drawing after drawing was opened and spread before us, until we had 13 plans, almost all of which were good, and five or six excellent."[10]

In the end, twenty-one-year-old Hayden emerged the winner. For her efforts, she received $1,000, which was three to ten times less than the compensation her male counterparts were collecting for fair buildings of a similar stature. Of course, Palmer was thrilled. Celebrated city planner and chief architect of the expo, Daniel Burnham, commended Hayden and saw in her a flourishing future career. In his opinion, the young architect would readily find employment in Chicagoland. "'She could soon be at the head of a lucrative business,' Burnham optimistically forecast."[11] However, it was not to be. Sophia Hayden's dream come true would soon turn into a nightmare.

The Beginning and the End

As the winner of the design contest, Hayden was brought to Chicago to supervise the construction of her building. Almost as soon as she entered her domain to oversee the creation of her masterpiece, far too many cooks swept into her kitchen to spoil her soup. Construction personnel wanted to make multiple changes to her design, which she rejected. Most detrimental, though, was Palmer herself, who butted heads with Hayden about the number of exhibits that were being allowed into the building. After all, Hayden was an artist as well as a skilled architect, and she balked when she learned of all the visual clutter the exhibits would create. Hayden was striving for a clean, simple interior that was in harmony with her design. Palmer had different ideas, and when push came to shove, Palmer was the weightier of the two women, given her status as the President of the Board of Lady Managers. Hayden was fired and another designer of Palmer's choice was given the job.

The construction combat had an eroding effect. Sophia Hayden found herself in her first professional position, set in an unfamiliar context. She was navigating continual criticism and challenges to her design. Hayden's internal framework was taken down to the studs. As a fellow architect, she logically turned to William Burnham for assistance in the matter. Apparently, the stressed, young architect boiled over and melted down in her meeting with him. Instead of receiving the artistic assurance she sought, Hayden was humiliated and agreed to withdraw to recuperate.

The events served to bolster patriarchal opinion at the time: architecture is not a woman's field. Though supportive of Hayden initially, Burnham's attitude toward her and female architects in general soured. He "express[ed] reservations about a woman's ability to leave the comfort of a drafting studio for the muck and mire of a construction site, where an architect's dreams are converted to brick-and-mortar reality."[12] A writer for the *American Architect and Building News* in 1892 also showed initial support for Hayden's design resolve, reporting, "It is said that Miss Hayden had an especially aggravating experience with her superiors, 'the Lady Managers,' in their desire to incorporate into her building all sorts of bits of design of work, whether they harmonized with it…or not, simply because they had been the work of women. Many of these designs though good in themselves were totally unfit to be incorporated into Miss Hayden's composition."[13]

As understanding as the writer appears to be, he deftly turns the corner by assigning her difficulties to weakness he associates with her gender: "It may be that Miss Hayden's experience has been unusual, but the planning and construction of any building with the accompanying dealing with clients is always liable to be 'especially trying'.…

If this building of which the women seem to be so proud...is to mark the physical ruin of its architect, it will be a much more telling argument against the women entering this especial profession than anything else could be." If this were not enough, he cites "brain fever" as a possible cause for her illness, and finishes off with a personal jab that, as women go, she in particular "may have been especially weak and nervous."[14]

Sophia Hayden's first building would be her last. While she appeared at the dedication of the Women's Building, she withdrew and did not return to the exposition. Her building was the first to be constructed, standing long enough to accommodate visitors during the World's Fair, but it was demolished at the fair's conclusion, as were the other buildings that had been erected just for the event. Hayden designed one more piece in 1894 that was never constructed, and this was the end of her architectural ventures. She married artist and interior designer William Blackstone Bennett and spent the rest of her life in Massachusetts as an artist herself. She died in 1953 in a nursing home. The world would have no tangible architectural heirloom left by MIT's first female architectural graduate.

How might the trajectory of history have changed if Sophia Hayden Bennett had received support from Daniel Burnham instead of more shame? What if Sophia Hayden had an advocate in Bertha Honoré Palmer and not an adversary, despite some of their disagreements? What if Sophia Hayden's pioneering experience had not been so traumatic? Perhaps she would not have abandoned architecture, and the world would have benefitted from her achievements. At any rate, we'll never know.

Any pioneer might find himself or herself in a similar situation in which an advocate or supporter is needed. If you're a trailblazing type, don't go it alone. Seek out support. If you have a young innovator like Sophia Hayden Bennett in your life, do your best to provide the healthiest soil to support the growth of that tender, healthy plant. The world may bless you when it's time to share the fruit of your cultivation.

The "Gas Wars": Protégé to Partner to Rival

After removing the bag containing the nitrous oxide from the mouth and nose of his patient, Dr. Horace Wells got to work on the tooth extraction. This time he was not operating within the quiet of his rooms in Hartford but was in a public hall in Boston with on-looking Harvard medical students and former partner Dr. W. T. G. Morton among them. It was a public trial as he set out to prove that he could perform a painless extraction. He had conducted several successful operations in Connecticut. But this was Boston, and its population had never seen such a thing. To the Boston elite, the prospect of pain-free dentistry seemed as nonsensible as Wells's patients had become as a result of inhaling nitrous oxide.

Once the gas took effect, Wells began the procedure. At some point, the patient cried out in pain, and the spectators' skepticism appeared warranted. Some called it a humbug affair. The patient told Wells later that he didn't experience as much pain as one usually would during such an operation, but it was too late. The public experiment was deemed a failure. Wells blamed himself for having not given the patient enough nitrous oxide. Wells's former colleague, Morton, was harsh about it: "Dr. Wells administered the gas, and extracted a tooth, but the patient screamed from pain, and the spectators laughed and hissed."[15] Wells was humiliated. He returned for Hartford early the next day.

Wells then began to unravel. In 1847 he wrote, "The excitement of this adventure immediately brought on an illness, from which I did not recover for many months; being thus obliged to relinquish, entirely, my professional business."[16] He advertised his Hartford home for rent on February 5th after returning from Boston, and he closed his dental practice shortly after. He reopened it in September of the same year only to close it again. He is also said to have ventured into other fields, such as sales of his invention of a "shower-bath."

In addition to physical and mental suffering, Wells was facing another hard knock. His former partner, Morton, was on his own quest to provide painless dentistry. It seems that Morton realized the altruistic, financial, and celebrated advantages of being the first to demonstrate the use of anesthesia. Wells had publicly failed. Morton had been party to his shaming. This left Morton with a window of opportunity to succeed where Wells had failed. He took it.

While at Harvard, Morton had been working with his teacher, Charles T. Jackson, on painless dental surgery with the use of chemical agents. Jackson recommended using ether. On October 16, 1846, Morton successfully performed the first public demonstration of a painless surgery at Massachusetts General Hospital in an operating theater now called the Ether Dome. The event made medical history and was a profound benefit to humanity. It publicly and permanently demonstrated that pain-free surgery was possible. It also set off a torturous controversy that imploded the lives of those involved, most immediately Horace Wells.

While aware of ether's numbing effects, Wells had steered clear of using the substance because he believed that nitrous oxide was the safer of the two gases. Some say that Wells had actually introduced Morton to ether.[17] When Morton made his pioneering claim to have been the first to employ anesthesia, both Wells and Jackson stepped up to challenge him. Wells published an article in December 1846 in the *Hartford Courant*, claiming discovery of dental anesthesia. He also wrote to Morton directly the same month stating as much, but he also indicated that he wouldn't take any action against him. "Wells…sought to strengthen his claims by publishing *History of the Discovery of the Application of Nitrous Oxide, Ether, and Other Vapors, to Surgical Operations* (1847). Morton and Jackson entered into protracted legal battles in their attempts to prove their claims."[18] The contentions got ugly, extensive, and convoluted.

An abstract from an article in the *American Association of Nurse Anesthetists* journal summarizes the "Gas Wars" well:

> The discovery of anesthesia occurred during a narrow time span in the mid-19th century, but *there is no agreement about who deserves credit for this important American contribution to medicine.*… We suggest that credit for the discovery of anesthesia be divided among 4 individuals who played specific roles. Crawford W. Long first used ether as an anesthetic during

surgery, Horace Wells introduced nitrous oxide for pain relief during dental surgery, and William T. G. Morton gave the first public demonstration of ether anesthesia and spread the word about its efficacy. Charles T. Jackson suggested the use of ether as an anesthetic agent to Morton…. Had these individuals not known one another, the discovery of anesthesia would have [perhaps] proceeded in approximately the same timeframe, but Wells, Morton, and Jackson would have enjoyed more productive careers as well as longer, more peaceful lives.[19]

Productive careers as well as longer, more peaceful lives: What's not to love about that? These pioneering journeys did not need to be as painful as these doctors made them. Ironically, in trying to claim priority in the discovery of techniques that vastly diminished pain and promoted health in others, their actions diminished the quality in their own lives. "In 1873 Jackson was admitted to an asylum for the mentally ill, where he spent the remainder of his life."[20] Morton continued to try to prove he was the originator of anesthesia and his patent for Letheon (merely ether with a tinge of orange oil to kill the smell) tanked. His legacy suffered as he "became increasingly bitter as his legal battles failed. He died…at the age of 48, deeply in debt."[21] On Morton's tombstone, the east side states, "W. T. G. Morton, Inventor and Revealer of Anesthetic Inhalation, Born August 9, 1819, Died July 15, 1868." As a passerby walks counterclockwise, the monument reads:

> Before whom, In all time, Surgery was Agony [north side]
> By whom, pain in surgery was averted [west side]
> Since whom, science has control over pain. [south side]

I beg to differ. While I understand the spirit of these words, humanity still suffers physically, mentally, and spiritually even in light of the advances of science. This is why new pioneers are needed to extend the work of doctors like Wells, Morton, Jackson, and Long. Trailblazers such as Ferrans and Powers are still necessary to contend with the intersections of ethics and medicine. Modern boundary challengers like Clauson, Wilk, and Felix must break barriers in order to create new spaces for healing and forge new paths to community-oriented cities.

As for Horace Wells, he was far from his home support network, alone in New York City. Coping with the humiliation of recent failures while grappling to find another form of income must have overwhelmed him. He turned to some new friends, ether and chloroform, for relief. While under the influence, Wells threw acid at two prostitutes. While no one was harmed, one cannot simply throw caustic chemicals at others. The police were called, and Wells was hauled off to the Tombs prison, known for its own forms of exploitation, scandals, and squalid conditions. When the fog of the anesthesia cleared his mind, he took his condition hard. He thought himself irredeemable, and for the first time in his life he was determined to use his medical knowledge to inflict harm—to himself. He cleverly obtained some chloroform, and after inhaling it for the last time, he cut his own femoral artery. Horace Wells was dead, three days after his thirty-third birthday.

In 2005, after struggling with an erupting wisdom tooth for years, my dentist referred me to an oral surgeon. Physiologically, my mouth was proclaimed too small for the entrance of any more teeth, and frankly, I was tired of swallowing my own blood and dealing with the gum irritation caused by the recalcitrant tooth. Most people have wisdom teeth extracted in their late teens, but I was thirty-eight, having never had surgery or anesthesia of any kind. I was nervous, calmed only by the reward of a chocolate shake and long nap I would have at the close of the surgery.

Dr. Moretti was to perform the job. Not only was he an oral surgeon, but he also taught dental students at the local state college. Having performed many extractions, he had nowhere near the trepidation I had over the outpatient procedure. Sensing I was curious as well as nervous, he diverted my attention away from the imminent extraction to a distraction in the form of some interesting information. "Now, what I am about to give you is nitrous oxide. It's the first anesthesia known to man. It was discovered by Horace Wells in 1844. I'm going to put this mask over your mouth and nose, and I want you to inhale slowly." It was the last thing I remembered before I fell deeply asleep. I don't remember the surgery at all, but I will never forget Horace Wells.

Points for Your Compass

➔ When an error in judgment is made, the pioneer will often have to dig deep within her being to keep a cool head and make mission-saving or even life-saving decisions.

➔ The process of pioneering can exact a high price from the pioneer, which may include stress, burnout, physical exhaustion, and the misunderstanding of others, to name a few.

➔ Pioneers should seek out support from others to guard against succumbing to internal and/or external stressors.

➔ Pioneers must work hard to keep their ethical compass fixed on what is true and just. They must temper desires for glory, wealth, and fame. Fixation on any one of these prideful objectives can cause personal misery that ripples out to friends and family.

LEG THREE

The Arrival

Create Constellations
"Aligning the luminaries"

THOMAS CAMPBELL WAS RIDING HIGH. FROM THE FRONT PERCH OF his wagon, he hazily gazed over the backs of the mules far down the lane ahead of him. The animals dutifully pulled the weight of their driver and his well-stocked cart along the country road. On this mild November day in Alabama, the sun cast its light through the gently waving leaves of the trees overhead, creating a shifting, speckled carpet rolling out on the dirt road that lay before him. Behind him, the sandy dust kicked up by the animals and their four-wheeled burden appeared to sparkle in the light rays that escaped the shaded tree canopy. Campbell allowed his mind to wander as he slowly rocked back and forth in his seat.

It wasn't unlike Campbell to give himself over to wakeful dreaming. As he reflected back over the past few years of his life, he could hardly believe how kindly Providence had treated him. Born to a traveling Methodist preacher who also farmed land that he did not own, Campbell had worked alongside his father, learning not only how to successfully coax crops out of the soil, but also how to best cultivate fruit from a life well lived. His father was fastidious about a soul telling the truth and earning an honest living. The work and the life associated with farming were hard yet rewarding to his dad. But working the soil and being hired out to others by his father was not enough for young Tom, as he was more often called. He had ambition to get an education, but his father found no value in it. Even Tom's stepmother, a former schoolteacher herself, interceded on his behalf, but to no avail. Eventually, it occurred to him that if he were to better himself, he would have to take matters into his own hands.

Determined to leave farming behind, he undertook a hard, solo journey on foot, inadequately clothed for the chill of the winter. Inspired by stories his brother had shared as a college student, he doggedly made his way to the Tuskegee Institute (now University) in Alabama. As Tom journeyed back in his mind that November day, he amused himself by recalling his first meeting with the registrar. The registrar got right down to business when Campbell entered his office, asking him what trade he would like to take up. He took a big breath before he responded—may the good Lord help him. Anything but farming!

"Sir, I'd like to be a wheelwright, or a blacksmith, or a carpenter."

"What about farming? Wouldn't you like to study farming?"

"Thank you, sir, but no. I've had quite enough time farming, and if it's all the same, I'm not eager to learn anymore about it."

"Hmm. I see." The registrar paused for reflection, then continued enthusiastically. "Well, what about agriculture?"

Campbell's face brightened.

"Agriculture? Why, sir, I think that would suit me just fine!"

Campbell couldn't help but break out in a smile at the recollection of his younger, naïve self, and how the wise registrar had snookered him back into farming. Again, he reasoned it was Providence at work in his life, directing him back toward the work for which he was made. A healthy dose of pride filled his chest, and he exhaled.

A Harvest of Pioneers

Just a few short years after his first meeting with the registrar and many hours of hard work later, Thomas Morgan Campbell graduated in 1906 from the Tuskegee Institute. He was esteemed by the great Booker T. Washington and a student of the famed scientist George Washington Carver. Both of these men believed in their young protégé, advocating for Campbell to the United States Department of Agriculture (USDA). The results of their efforts paid off, and he became the nation's first African American extension agent. And now, here he was on his first assignment in rural Macon County with his moveable school of agriculture, representing the school he loved to the people he loved. He was an emissary to pass on the knowledge he had learned to the struggling rural black farmer, with the hopes of improving their farming methods and thus their yields. Campbell brought with him firsthand experience of a black farmer's life, along with the knowledge Tuskegee had equipped him: the latest advances in farming science and best land management practices. He was also armed with the "Farmers' College on wheels," a buggy designed by Carver, who had stocked it with all kinds of demonstration items, including seeds, farm equipment such as plows, fertilizers, a milk tester, charts, diagrams, as well as other needful farming implements.

Campbell didn't know it at the time, but he would go on to make history while making the rounds on country roads in Macon County, Alabama. He was pioneering an innovative yet practical educational method. He not only educated black and white share-cropping families in farming practices that were advanced for the day, but he brought learning to students who could not practically leave their fields for the classroom. Campbell rode in a wagon imagined by George Washington Carver who tapped the generosity of New York Philanthropist Morris K. Jesup, for whom the wagon was named. Carver's Jesup wagon concepts, along with Campbell's educative demonstrations among the tenant farming communities, were so successful that they were eventually adopted by the USDA's outreach program. Campbell became a shining light, a luminary of hope shining for others, for he was not only showing these families a path to better farming, but he was giving them a way to create a better life for themselves.

In two years' time, Campbell's light brightened as he was appointed by the USDA to be the district agent for Alabama and nearby states. He was seeing a huge unmet need among people he was in a position to help, and he took pioneering steps to meet that great need, such as creating agricultural fairs and conferences for farmers. He was also carving a path for other black leaders. By 1913, thirty-two African Americans had been appointed as extension agents, and together they had "enrolled 3,500 farmers in demonstration work. At the heart of the work were youth clubs among [black] boys and girls," and these clubs were one of the spokes in the wheel that would eventually become the 4-H Clubs. "Although he retired in 1953, [Thomas Campbell] remained active in 4-H until the time of his death in 1956. He paved the way for the many [African American] extension agents who followed."[1]

It's Getting Better All the Time

"To make the best better" is the 4-H club's motto. For thousands of young people across the United States and internationally, 4-H has helped them to become better versions of themselves. I speak from experience as a 4-H alumna. While I settled on public speaking as a concentration, the program gave me many opportunities to try various disciplines, such as stripping furniture finish, growing strawberries, creating a hand-braided rug, and building a wooden marionette. It also offered me some life experiences I might not have had otherwise, like showing my handcrafts publicly in a fair exhibit, properly setting a table, and gaining feedback for my speaking ability, which laid the foundation for my radio career (sadly, neither speech nor theater classes were offered in the public schools I attended).

Now, what long-term benefit did I receive from building a wooden pink flamingo marionette? Honestly, I'd have to look around to see if I even still have it stored away in my basement somewhere. It's not like I use it every day or it helps me earn an income. However,

I still remember the lessons the construction of that silly-looking thing taught me: how to properly trace a pattern onto wood, how to cut the wood pieces using a band saw and drill press properly, not to mention how to experiment with assembling and balancing it to make it work properly, along with painting it so that it would look attractive. As a child, I also enjoyed playing with it. But the flamingo and other similar 4-H projects gave me something that can never be undone: the confidence to try something new. This trait, I believe, wanes as we age unless we nurture it, and by extension, cultivate it in others through encouragement. Furthermore, receiving informed instruction while trying something new is a very basic way to practice risk. I also believe that lessons learned in one field often manifest when needed in other areas. There are times when applications are interdisciplinary, and pioneering personalities are often called on to draw from a variety of subjects and skills at a time of need.

About two years ago, I realized that I needed a way to productively deal with stress. At the end of the day, I found I still had anxious energy to spare, but my mental capacity had diminished. Playing games on my phone was fun and portable but not productive. I began to ask myself, *What might be fun and portable yet produce something tangible to show for the time I spent with it?* Because I liked to work with my hands, I decided on knitting, but how would I learn? My paternal grandmother was a knitter, but by the time I became old enough to learn, rheumatoid arthritis had twisted her fingers. So I turned to the internet and began the awkward process of knitting and purling from kind strangers who posted tutorials online. While I was crafting my first uneven scarf, I received encouragement from a knitting neighbor who helped me to dream of what I wanted to accomplish one day. For fodder, she loaned me some books, and I imagined making my first Fair Isle-styled sweater. It kept me going. When I was tired of scarves, I tried making colorful socks and flashed them around the office to the oohs and ahs of coworkers. Then I attempted my first pullover sweater. I found people to encourage me, and when I got stuck, I laughed at my own mistakes and found a sympathetic soul to help me. I still haven't made that Fair Isle sweater yet, but I've made a cardigan. Give me some time. I'll get it done.

There's no doubt about it, trying something new is daunting. Just picture how Thomas Campbell must have felt the first time he approached a country community on his Jesup wagon to share his knowledge and demonstrations. He had to lean on what he already knew, draw energy from others' belief in him, and focus on what he hoped to achieve. In other words, he had developed a concrete idea of what success would look like as he sought to help others create a better future for themselves. Just imagine how many pioneering efforts might never have happened if an individual had not bothered to try something new because he or she lacked the confidence to experiment. Our lives would be much different now, and not for the better.

Other Luminaries in the Sky

At the same time Thomas Campbell was drawing community crowds and inspiring their youth, other bright lights appeared to meet similar needs. In the early part of the twentieth century, rural communities were feeling the hard loss of their youth to the pull of industrialization and urbanization, despite the fact that advancements were yielding economic agricultural prosperity. "In less than one hundred years, American farmers had penetrated a wilderness from the Atlantic to the Pacific and mastered the vagaries of climate and soil to create one of the world's most productive enterprises. An international marketing system carried American farm products by rail, wagon and ship throughout the world, while sophisticated technology and rapidly advancing scientific discoveries poised American agriculture on new thresholds." Even so, the cities still held a shiny allure for youth (as they still do for many today), and rural communities at the turn of the twentieth century were concerned, desiring to "instill in their children the same sense of purpose that had conditioned their own lives." A worthy, counter-philosophy began to take shape: "Farming and rural living were not just for those who failed to find a place in a growing urban environment, but were cherished and nurtured as a way of life."[2]

"Learning by doing" is 4-H's slogan, a reflection of its very practical "Now, you try it" educational method. Theory and application are woven together in a way that satisfies both the learner and the doer—traits that are typically found together in a curious young person. In short, clubs like 4-H fill in the educational and experiential gaps that many schools created as they emphasized reading, writing, and arithmetic.

It is in this context that the origins of 4-H are found. Because many communities across the nation faced similar challenges, concerned parents, mentors, and educators sought to ignite rural young people's interest with disciplines that were part of the environment around them. For example, in Ohio, A. B. Graham kicked off early efforts to organize young people into clubs. As an educator, he became aware of efforts to instruct urban students in technical training that would prepare them for the new industrial context in which the United States was entering. He reasoned that rural, relevant subject matter should be taught to country-dwelling children. In 1902, he began to gather young people for training on Saturdays while their parents were shopping in town. He gave them projects to do, such as soil testing and selecting the corn kernels from their parents' plots, in order to create an experimental garden that would demonstrate which varieties yielded the best corn. One of the virtues of A. B. Graham's methods was his belief in teaching all children similar educational content. "He may have been ahead of his time regarding equality. The first clubs included white, black and Hispanic children, and he did not limit club members to traditional topics. He taught girls gardening and boys cooking."[3] Many scholars attribute Graham's early efforts to be the origins of 4-H.

Others who are considered 4-H founders include Jessie Field Shambaugh, who was a school superintendent in Page County, Iowa. She grouped young people into corn clubs, since corn was a crop on which many farmers depended in the area. She and Oscar H. Benson, who was the superintendent of Wright County schools, began using the first 4-H clover as a symbol, though it consisted initially of only three H's on three leaves standing for head, heart, and hands. Shambaugh's clubs also used the motto that would be adopted by all of 4-H: "Learning by doing, to make the best, better."[4] Others who are named as founders all contributed to what would eventually become 4-H Clubs: Ella Agnew from Virginia, Dr. Liberty Hyde Bailey of New York, South Carolina's Marie Cromer, T. A. Erickson of Minnesota, Dr. Seaman A. Knapp who worked with the USDA in the early twentieth century, Iowa's Cap E. Miller, William B. Otwell from Illinois, and, of course, Thomas Campbell who educated so many in Alabama. Because several individuals had similar concerns for their rural youth and turned to practical educational methods that suited their needs, 4-H historians acknowledge that "no one individual or place can be credited as the founder of 4-H, or the place where 4-H began. 4-H type programs began in a number of places at about the same time and were shaped by the environment and conditions of each area."[5]

The Power of Alignment

As each club founder's light appeared, they eventually aligned, creating a constellation that would become 4-H Clubs for boys and girls. "The passage of the Smith-Lever Act in 1914 created the Cooperative Extension System at USDA and nationalized 4-H. By 1924, 4-H clubs were formed and the clover emblem was adopted."[6] 4-H would explode during the twentieth century, offering numerous projects and opportunities that would expand the horizons of the nation's youth, one of whom is me. The fascinating history of how 4-H clubs were birthed provides an example of how powerful uniting the pioneering work of several individuals can be when the mission and vision are similar.

In today's highly competitive and litigious environment, there is a temptation to believe that such associations are a thing of the past, a relic of a kinder, gentler age. A pervasive hostility in culture has made many individuals, groups, communities, and organizations cynical, siloed, and self-protective. Perhaps this is out of fear or out of a desire to win in what is perceived as a win-lose society. For some, their perspective lies somewhere along this spectrum. But one thing is certain: The need for collaboration (coalescing minds) remains great as stakes remain high—lives are still lost to substance abuse, a cure is still needed for cancer, treasured animals are still in danger of extinction, better ways are still needed for disposing of our refuse, educational opportunities still remain elusive for many worldwide, homelessness is still an ongoing problem, and on and on the list goes. Fill in the blank with your irritant. Whether it be large or small, technological or relational, research-laden or adventure-driven, there are plenty of issues—including yours—for which pioneers are needed. And there may be other pioneering spirits around you with the same passion you have. What might be accomplished together?

William Bratton and Zachary Tumin, authors of *Collaborate or Perish!*, do not shy away from exposing the chafing difficulties that working together may create: "Even when groups or organizations share a vision, collaboration takes a conviction that it's better working together than going it alone." Conviction, especially in the mission and vision of the work, is the glue that continues to draw parties back together even when the going gets difficult; and when the work is pioneering, it *will* get tough. However, Bratton and Tumin are quick to point out the transformational properties of collaboration:

> [It] takes people, platforms, incentives—hard work at first, but once you've started, [it gets] easier and easier. In the end, it's all worthwhile. Done right, collaboration unleashes assets, your own as well as others'. It allows companies to reuse, recombine and transform resources; to cut costs, improve performance, and deal with every opportunity and challenge that comes along. In a world where everyone is connected, collaboration is the difference maker, the force multiplier, the game changer.[7]

What Shape Is the Earth Really In?

There was a time in human history when even the very best minds believed that the world was flat. Then along came Aristotle who around 350 BCE reasoned that the earth was round. He offered several logical arguments based on experience. One of these rationales is the shape of earth's umbra that is cast during an eclipse; it's round. Aristotle wrote:

> The evidence of the senses further corroborates [the spherical shape of the earth]. How else would eclipses of the moon show segments shaped as we see them? As it is, the shapes which the moon itself each month shows are of every kind straight, gibbous, and concave—but in eclipses the outline is always curved: and, since it is the interposition of the earth that makes the eclipse, the form of this line will be caused by the form of the earth's surface, which is therefore spherical.[8]

Aristotle also pointed out that the night sky seems to change depending on the viewer's position, and he used this universal observation to support his concept that the world is round:

> Again, our observations of the stars make it evident, not only that the earth is circular, but also that it is a circle of no great size. For quite a small change of position to south or north causes a manifest alteration of the horizon. There is much change, I mean, in the stars which are overhead, and the stars seen are different, as one moves northward or southward. Indeed, there are some stars seen in Egypt and in the neighborhood of Cyprus which are not seen in the northerly regions; and stars, which in the north are never beyond the range of observation, in those regions rise and set. All of which goes to show not only that the earth is circular in shape, but also that it is a sphere of no great size: for otherwise the effect of so slight a change of place would not be quickly apparent.[9]

As a pioneer, Aristotle used persuasive logic to combat flat-earth theory.

Aristotle's earth may be "of no great size," but exactly how big (or small) was it? As the old supermarket tabloid, the *National Enquirer,* described human curiosity, "Enquiring minds want to know." Pioneering minds take it this one step further: They *need* to know. So more than a hundred years later (240 BCE), another Greek mind engineered a way to determine how to measure the circumference of the earth. Born in ancient Cyrene (now called Shahhat in eastern Libya), educated in Athens, and ultimately based in Alexandria as the chief of the famous library in the region, Eratosthenes' curiosity was piqued by a strange story passed along by travelers who had been further south along the Nile River. The tale was told that no shadow could be seen at the bottom of a well in Syene (modern-day Aswan, Egypt) at noontime on the day of the summer solstice. The bottom of the well was fully illuminated, pointing to the fact that the sun was directly above it. From a modern perspective, Aswan is on the Tropic of Cancer, so it makes sense that the tilt of the earth would allow direct sunshine overhead on that one day of the year.

Eratosthenes got out his gnomon (a vertical rod) and waited for the same moment in Alexandria. At noon on the summer solstice, he placed his rod in the sand, and unlike the well-wishers in Syene, he got a shadow. He measured it and found it to be 7.2 degrees, which works out to one-fiftieth of a circle. But in order to get his answer as to how large the circumference of the world might be, he needed one more figure: the distance between Alexandria and Syene. So he did what most busy, well-resourced chief librarians would do: he hired some bematists (professional pacers) to walk the distance and count their steps. The distance he was given was 5,000 stadia, putting a final calculation of the earth's circumference at about 250,000 stadia. Translated into modern-speak, each stadium was estimated at about 500 to 600 feet, putting his circumference calculation between 24,000 to 29,000 miles.

With the technology available to us today, we know that the earth's equatorial circumference is "24,901 miles (40,075 km). However, from pole-to-pole—the meridional circumference—Earth is only 24,860 miles (40,008 km) around. This shape, caused by the flattening at the poles due to its constant rotation, is called an oblate spheroid."[10] Eratosthenes' rough measurement turned out to be right in the ballpark.

Historically, the human perspective of the earth's shape has gone from a flat, two-dimensional disc, to a sphere, to an oblate spheroid. With increased knowledge, we've changed the nomenclature that describes the shape of the earth, and with each new moniker, we have a more precise understanding of the shape and size of our planetary home.

The Mother of All Measurements

Gladys Mae West was born in 1930 in a rural area south of Richmond, Virginia. Her African American family members were farmers, and she often joined them in their tasks. She recalls, "I told myself that I did not like being out in the sun, working from sunrise to sunset and all that, so I made good grades in all of my subjects." Despite her hard work in school, West was born in a time when opportunities for young black females were less than stellar. She went to a segregated school and learned from books that were not new but were discards from white schools. This had an impact on young Gladys and her peers. It was unfair and unacceptable, to be sure. However, looking back with a true pioneering spirit, she commented: "But all of that, helped to make us, I think, work harder because you were behind the eight ball to start with, you know, so you had to work harder. But I always was motivated by doing something new, and completing something, having a goal, because usually, I had a mind of my own. I tend to think for myself."[11]

West engaged her mind, and fueled by her internal drive, she emerged as the valedictorian of her high school, earning a scholarship at Virginia State University (VSU). Because of her good grades, she was told that she could pursue any subject she wanted but was urged to study mathematics because of its difficulty. She was up for the challenge, enrolling in a major that very few women had entered. "You felt a little bit different," West recalled. "You didn't quite fit in as you did in home economics…. You're always competing and trying to survive because you're in a different group of people." Upon graduation, West taught math and science for two years, then returned to VSU, graduating with her master's in math in 1955.

West continued to forge her own uncharted path after graduate school. Instead of returning to teaching, she was brought on at the Naval Proving Ground (now the Naval Surface Warfare Center) in Dahlgren, Virginia. At the time, she was only one of four African Americans who worked there and only the second black woman ever hired. Her persistence, talent, and work ethic yielded crop after successful crop. Her job as a mathematician working in the U.S. Naval Weapons Lab allowed her to complete "a path-breaking, award-winning astronomical study that proved, during the early 1960s, the regularity of Pluto's motion relative to Neptune." Later in the mid-1970s into the 1980s, she worked on creating an extremely accurate model of the Earth, using complicated algorithms. These calculations would take into account the varying forces, such as tides and gravitational pull, that change the shape of the earth. "She programmed an IBM 7030 'Stretch' computer to deliver increasingly refined calculations for an extremely accurate geodetic Earth model, optimized for what ultimately became the Global Positioning System (GPS)."[12]

Retirement for West came in 1998, but this pioneer would not remain still. She traveled with her husband and embarked on PhD studies, but then something tragic happened: She suffered a stroke. Though it left her suffering with challenges to her vision, hearing, balance, and mobility, she pushed through her impediments by reminding herself that she had a doctorate to complete. And finish it, she did.

Though she worked for years without recognition, West's accomplishments were finally spotlighted and celebrated by the military. She was inducted into its Air Force Space and Missile Pioneers Hall of Fame at a ceremony held in her honor in December 2018 at the Pentagon.

As a mathematician, she did many of her calculations without the use of electronic systems, but when electronic computers came along, she didn't let the new technology stop her. She didn't complain, "We've never done it this way." Rather, she learned how to use and leverage it to accomplish even greater work that led to the development of the GPS technology, without which we could say we might be lost.

West also adds humility to her pioneering traits. When asked if she saw herself as a trailblazer for other women, she indicated: "I think I did help.... We have made a lot of progress since when I came in, because now at least you can talk about things and be open a little more. Before you sort of whispered and looked at each other, or something, but now the world is opening up a little bit and making it easier for women. But they still gotta fight."[13] Thanks to Dr. Gladys Mae West and her pioneering spirit, women, African Americans—all of us really—find our way around much better than we used to.

Aligning Pioneers

Unlike collective societies, there is a tendency for people in individualistic cultures to work like a lone wolf. Fiery, innovative personalities may also default to private pioneering. After all, if the innovative effort succeeds, there are more rewards and glory to be had for the "I" than if shared with the "we." Sometimes, however, it takes "us" to get it done. In reality, discovery is always a group effort as history hands us the available, collective human knowledge from the time of our birth. For example, when I was a young girl, I was hospitalized with pneumonia. Had I been born at another time, the infection might have meant my demise. As it was, the technology and knowledge available in the early 1970s were enough to save my life, that, along with a stern nurse who warned me not to try and escape the frequent shots in my posterior by climbing over the bars of my hospital bed.

Ken Schuetz, creator of the Aligned Influence® model, acknowledges that he, too, has built upon the work of others just as scientists did before him in their areas of expertise:

> Interestingly enough, Einstein has become a really important focal point for me in understanding why I'm doing what I am doing. I [watched] a biography on public television and that encouraged me to pick up one of his biographies. In the biography, I noticed

that he was constantly referring to Newton. That made me think, 'I wonder what Newton says?' so I found a biography of Newton. [I found] that Newton was constantly referring to Galileo in his biography. It hit me that [even] today, people acknowledge that Einstein's work really was [fueled] by Newton's and Galileo's, but nobody confuses Einstein's work with Galileo's work…. In other words, in my own work, there was a need for the next John Carver's voice.[14]

Through this experience, Schuetz grappled with his concern that his work might not be "original *enough*," and came to grips with the fact that innovative solutions to current problems are built on concepts that were created by earlier pioneers. Once these concepts were new and innovative too, but as times change, needs change. Solutions and models naturally become outmoded or must be amended, making room for the work of new pioneers. Schuetz took inspiration from what he learned about Einstein. Pioneers build on the work of other pioneers, much like skyscrapers are erected upon a strong foundation and progressively rising scaffolding. In fact, this is how all great work develops. And one stage of discovery need not be confused with another: all are important to advance the pioneering work. This can be a freeing concept for the pioneer. Carol Ferrans expressed it more bluntly and her statement bears repeating: "There's lots of room at the [pioneering] table and it's not just that one person ever wins. And if anyone ever says, 'It's just me. I did it. It's my work,' they're lying! They're forgetting that nobody, nobody succeeds alone. Nobody. Nobody accomplished anything of importance alone. Nobody."[15]

Schuetz proceeded in a bold way: he looked for experts in the field to critique his emerging model. Rather than defend "his baby" along the way, he sought out informed, tough thinkers to beat it up to make it better. He explains his process:

When I worked in higher education administration, the faculty who had been on those boards with me said, 'You know what you're going to do, so go do it like we would do it.' [I understood] that meant,

'Don't go try to apply what we already know. Go use what we already know to build new knowledge.' Like all academics, I did the literature review to understand what [had been done]. I wrote about what I was observing, putting that in front of other people who knew something about [the subject] in the academic genre, and got to critique what I am doing. We all know that the voice of the faculty is a negative voice as we critique each other's work. So, I got them to start punching holes in what I was writing [and] I started seeing some patterns emerge. That pattern was: what we have been doing the last forty years using Carver's work was applying a very important tool, but not really solving the problem. The problem was not the lack of policies. The problem was a lack of some framework, some structure, that allowed the person playing the executive role in the organization and the persons in the board role of the organization to understand how their work was unique in its own way and aligned with the work of the other. And that's where aligned influence came from.[16]

Aligning the Luminaries

No matter where you are on the planet, looking into the night sky is always an education. Beyond being awed by the multitude of stars and humbled by the vast expanse of the universe beyond us, it helps to also learn about what you're looking at. Star charts are readily available online as well as apps that allow the user on a clear night to point the smart phone right at a celestial object in the night sky for quick identification. Star charts in particular offer us what appears to be a timeless perspective on the heavens, as the constellations are mapped out between the stars that have been our celestial canvas for centuries. Some believe that humans have been fascinated with the sky since ancient times, and that early cave art depicts some of the elements of the night sky. Today, the International Astronomical Union recognizes eighty-eight constellations and attributes over half of those as given to us by the ancient Greeks, one of whom was Ptolemy. If we search the sky for constellations, we find a veritable menagerie of animals, interesting objects, and people from Greek and Roman mythology. Finding them in the celestial palette is like playing the original game of *Where's Waldo?*. And it leads to hours of fun and education.

Technically, the definition of a constellation is simply a marking of line patterns between the stars that represent the shapes that inform the name of the figure. As astronomy has advanced, so has the mapping of the constellations. Interestingly, "the International Astronomical Union (IAU) defines a constellation by its boundary (indicated by sky coordinates) and not by its pattern, and the same constellation may have several variants in its representation."[17] Looking at the Great Bear (Ursa Major) in particular, there are a number of stars that comprise the constellation, seven of which make up the Big Dipper (also known as the Plough). These stars vary in color, luminosity, and size. In short, these stars are diverse, they maintain their own uniqueness, and yet they make up the larger picture of what we know as the Great Bear. Two of the stars have pointed travelers to Polaris—the North Star that has provided a reliable navigational point for centuries.

Likewise, pioneers across time (building on previous work) and various regions (like the 4-H founders) may coalesce to advance human knowledge for the greater good. In contributing to a cause larger than their own, none of them need alter personal traits or diminish the nature of their own contributions, as Ken Schuetz has found. In fact, unique, personal characteristics brought to the pioneering work enhance the depth, breadth, and effectiveness of the collective pioneering effort. Gladys West's background directly contributed to her drive and perspective, enabling her to dig into advanced mathematical thinking that ultimately advanced global positioning. And while many individuals in the past and present have devoted their energies to refining human understanding of the world's size and shape, no one would confuse West's work with other pioneers in global measurement. Whatever unique pieces the individual brings to the pioneering puzzle at hand, these help complete the larger picture that leads to further successful discovery and advancement. "Together, we are better" is not just a feel-good meme; it's an undeniable truth.

Points for Your Compass

→ A pioneer's beginnings may seem small and insignificant but should not be underestimated. For example, Thomas Campbell came from a sharecropping family in the country, but his work as an educator in the Cooperative Extension program turned out to be groundbreaking.

→ Sometimes a pioneering idea may emerge from several different people who struggle to overcome similar challenges in various places at the same time in history. Uniting ideas and efforts may prove to create a powerful movement that has the potential to enhance many lives, such as what happened in the creation and development of 4-H clubs.

→ Diversity allows for variation in thought and perspective and offers individuals an opportunity to learn from others who are different. Respectful dialogue is the road on which meaningful thought may flow and solutions to societal challenges are found and implemented.

→ There are plenty of issues, large and small—including yours—for which pioneers are needed. And there may be other pioneering spirits around you with the same passion you have. What might be accomplished together?

→ Pioneers never accomplish their work on their own. There are always other people behind the pioneer who help him achieve his goal and who deserve his gratitude.

Ensuring a Future
"Choose what happens next"

It was a late winter snowy day, and southern New England had already had its share of snow. To make matters worse, the precipitation was assailing the area in what is known as a "wintry mix," a kind of soupy concoction consisting of snow and freezing rain. Its weightiness causes great tree limbs to bow in humble obeisance to Mother Nature or snap in absolute submission. Worse still, the temperature that day was forecast to plummet, encasing the already yielding limbs in ice. More weight would be added to the trees, powerlines, and fragile rooftops. With a New England snowstorm often came wind, whipping the loose white stuff around the corners of centuries old wooden buildings, howling as if it were taunting the groaning old structures and the hunkering dwellers inside.

My mother and I dawdled that morning, prolonging breakfast while the storm continued. Occasionally, Mom would get up and poke at the flaming embers in the kitchen woodstove until she was satisfied with their position, and then feed the hungry fire another log. That morning, the backdoor of our mid-eighteenth-century farmhouse opened, startling my mother and me. It was followed by synchronous, raucous, throat clearing and stomping feet, announcing the entry of my mother's brother. I had long abandoned the formality of calling him Uncle Arnold, since he was known to family members as just "Bub." Bub lived in a freestyle house he had built himself on a small hill overlooking the old family property, and it wasn't uncommon for him to amble down to the "main house" from time to time, convenience store coffee in hand. This morning, however, there was something on his mind. Mom and I looked up from our reading at the kitchen table as my uncle announced the purpose of his visit.

"I dunno, Betty," he grumbled. "I don't know how much that mill can take."

"I know it, Bub," was my mother's stock answer, inherited by female family members for anything that required empathy. To be sure, she felt my uncle's concern but was at a loss for any solutions.

My uncle paused and then gruffly responded to his own thoughts: "All it takes is a day like this and that mill would go right over into the Moshassuck. I wish they'd do something about it."

My uncle was right. I could hear the earnestness in his voice, and I could feel my own muscles tightening in response. The mill in question was the Moffett Mill, an early nineteenth-century survivor believed to be the first machine shop in Rhode Island. The Moshassuck was the nearby river that had originally driven the mill's water system, and the "they" in question were the owners of the mill. By that time, the property had passed out of the hands of our family.

Built around 1812 by George Olney, the mill came into the possession of Arnold Moffett Jr. Eventually, it continued to run under the proprietorship of his son, Edmund Burke Moffett, until early into the twentieth century. It was subsequently closed by his son, Edmund Everett Moffett, my great grandfather. At the time, it was outpaced by the sprawling industrial mills that had sprung up around the rivers of southern New England.

As the saying goes, "If you can't beat 'em, join 'em." So after he received his degree from Brown University in 1909, Everett Moffett moved his family away from his family of origin and the small mill in Lincoln, Rhode Island and traveled southward to work on the electric turbines in the Arkwright Mill along the Pawtuxet River in Kent County. When he left, my great grandfather and his siblings did little to change the mill. The doors were shut, and most of its contents were left as they were. Knowing my family, I can't help but think that when he closed the doors signaling the end of the operation, he may have done so with a stoic wish that any emotions wrapped around the building and the livelihood it had provided the family and others in the community would be locked inside as well.

As the decades slid by, the silent, wooden soldier weathered many winters—some mild, some wild. The mill's great drive shafts, leather drive belts, wheels, and pulley system remained still, no longer driven by the iron turbine that responded to the Moshassuck River below. Once state-of-the-art wood and metal lathes, along with a table saw and drill press, collected dust as the world passed them by. Externally, generations of new machinery were developed, bought, and sold in a growing market to which the mill no longer contributed. As a result, the old mill evolved into a unique survivor. Likened to a time capsule, industrial historians who dared to venture out onto the creaky mill's floorboards nearly a century later were treated to a living example of what early American manufacturing looked like. It had a great story to tell. But would anyone have the chance to hear it? The mill was in danger of being lost as it continued to lean dangerously over the Moshassuck River.

Most of the time, my family tried to put any thoughts about the mill out of mind. It held a tender place in our hearts, but it seemed that there was very little that we could do about it. After all, who were we? We were just the progeny of machine shop owners who ran a business in a structure that now looked like a dilapidated relic. Furthermore, we lived further south, still dwelling in the area to which our great grandfather had brought us. It spared us the ache of seeing the neglected mill every day.

Winters passed, and the mill was still standing. Spring would come, and family members who cared about the nondescript two-story building would heave a sigh of relief, only to reenter the emotional cycle when the snowy weather returned. It seemed only a matter of time before the mill would be lost forever if there was no intervention. We wondered if anyone beyond ourselves even noticed or cared.

But there *was* someone else who noticed. A resident of Lincoln, Rhode Island her whole life, Kathy Chase Hartley drove by the Moffett Mill frequently, as well as other buildings in the immediate area that held former significance. These structures populated an area along what has become known today as the Great Road corridor. Daily, she and other motorists who traveled along this former artery between Providence, Rhode Island; Hartford, Connecticut; and Worcester, Massachusetts were treated to the sight of degenerating buildings, some of which had so obviously been grand buildings during their heyday. Now they were just eyesores. Peeling paint, greying wood, rotting casements—it all became part of the scenery. One piece of property was especially worrisome for Kathy. She recalls:

> I could see [the decline of] my grandparents' house (the Chase Farmhouse), with it being empty for so long. It was so sad that the house seemed to be screaming out to take care of it.... I think that I started to really appreciate the fact that these buildings had so much history to them, and they were closed up. The town [of Lincoln, RI] owned them, and with an empty building, it does not take long to start to deteriorate. And one by one, that's what all these buildings were starting to look like—sad relics by the side of the road, and it just...it tugged at my heart.[1]

One of the anchors among these buildings along the Great Road corridor was what locals called the Hearthside House. The imposing two-and-one-half-story mansion was a glory in its time. Stephen Hopkins Smith built it in 1812 while only in his twenties; he "used a great deal of imagination and care in the building of the house. He chose unusual materials, finished with exceptional design details. The walls are built of Smithfield [fieldstone], a smooth, easily-cut stone with soft shades of gray, quarried from the area and trimmed with granite.... While simplicity is the keynote of the design, Hearthside is quite unique, with a sense of charm, dignity and stateliness."[2]

Hearthside is also referred to as the "house that love built."[3] It has romance woven throughout the stones of its foundation. Stephen Hopkins Smith was originally a country boy from a rural Lincoln, Rhode Island farm. He had an opportunity for a change of scenery and pace and took it, venturing to the "big city" of Providence for his education. He also eventually scored an apprenticeship. While there, he became smitten with a city girl and sought to win her. But what was he to do? He did not come from a family of means, and he soon discovered that she was looking to wed a wealthy gentleman who was able to build her a grand house. Feeling fortunate, he bought a lottery ticket and "through either sheer luck or divine intervention, he won $40,000."[4] That's about $900,000 by today's standards. Surely, Smith was on a successful streak, so he quietly began building the grand home that was to become Hearthside House. It took him four years, but when the job was done, he brought his love to the site. But she rejected his mansion. It was too far out in the country for her. With her decision, she rejected the man who had built the beautiful house for her.

The mansion featured a grand entrance that continues to awe guests. Visitors approach a main entrance with four pilasters supporting a portico. As they draw closer, they come to a six-paneled front door topped by an elliptical fanlight. When the door opens to the foyer, guests are treated to an elegant "flying" staircase. The stairs wind around a Tuscan column, so those who ascend it go upward in a counterclockwise direction. One of the home's later owners gave it the moniker Hearthside because it has ten rooms that feature a fireplace. Outside, the attractive multi-shaded gray stone walls rise, ending in s-shaped curves trimmed with beaded cornice. Hearthside's front portico is also thoughtfully adorned with a dormer facing front, which repeats the theme of the curved walls and cornice.

As to the spurned man, he never married. It appears that he poured all of his love into the home he built early in his life. However, Stephen Hopkins Smith would continue to make good use of his education. He built and ran the Butterfly Mill, the remains of which sit across the street from Hearthside. Textile printing was accomplished there. Smith also eventually became the commissioner for the Blackstone Canal project that would help drive commerce by connecting the cities of Providence and Worcester, Massachusetts. He was personally involved with buying the land, and he participated in the layout of the canal's reservoirs and gates. He had a special interest in beauty created through landscaping, collecting exotic trees and giving them a permanent home on his land. He eventually went on to become the first president of the Rhode Island Horticultural Society.

Many more families would enjoy life in the home that Smith constructed until one of its last owners passed away in 1996. The remaining family sold the home to the town of Lincoln in order to preserve it, but it appeared that the town was at a loss as to what to do about it, other than to decorate it for Christmas and open it to the public at that time of year. Hartley recalls:

> [In Lincoln, RI], we don't have a mayor; we have a town administrator. The person [at that time] had been in office for twenty-eight years. It was under his leadership that these buildings were purchased by the town, yet he had no vision for what to do with them.... So, I kept asking him what his plan was; what he was going to do with them. He kept saying, "There's nothing we can do because they're not handicapped accessible." So, I thought, that's no answer.[5]

After the yearly Christmas showing, Hearthside would be locked back up again and stand empty, waiting for another Christmas to come to life. Hartley would continue to drive by the building as she went about her daily business. It got under her skin. To this longtime Lincoln resident, it became nothing short of an irritant. "It was so beautiful at Christmastime; it just had so much potential. I could not understand how the town owned something like that and would not do something more with it. It lended itself to bringing the public in and enjoying it."[6] Whether Hartley was entirely conscious of it or not, a strategy was forming in her mind. She was imagining a brighter future for Hearthside where she and others could enjoy the magnificent house during other seasons of the year. But if its rightful owners, the Town of Lincoln, would do nothing about it, then neither could she. She was at an impasse.

Seasons come and seasons go, as do election cycles and politicians. After nearly three decades, the Lincoln's town administrator was voted out of office. At the next Christmas gathering at Hearthside, shortly before he was to take office, the new administrator made an appearance. Kathy saw her chance to make an impression, not for her own sake, but for Hearthside's sake. Decked in all its glory, Kathy saw that Hearthside was already working its way into the new administrator's heart. She remembers well the gift that this Hearthside gathering gave her that Christmas:

> [The administrator's] mouth was hanging open at the beauty that he was seeing as he was going through [Hearthside House]. He said, "This is incredible!"
>
> And I asked, "What is your plan for the building when you take office?"
>
> And he said, "I have no idea. I really haven't given it any thought." So, he turned to me and asked, "What would you do with it?"
>
> So I said, "Oh! Well, I would open it four times a year, at least every season. There are some wonderful things you could do with it, not just at Christmastime."
>
> He asked, "Like what?"
>
> I responded, "Well you could do a fall festival here, spring tea, or garden party in the summer."
>
> So he called a few days later and asked, "You know what you were talking about? Why don't you come to my office in about a week with a plan?"
>
> Quickly, I sat down and sketched out some ideas. I went in to see him the following week and [presented my plan]. He said, "I love it. Go for it." So, he kind of gave me free rein to do whatever I wanted with the building to breathe some life into it and raise some money.[7]

A deteriorating house, a town with a rich history that failed to preserve it, and a single resident who treasured that history. These were the ingredients that brought Kathy Hartley to a crossroads. She could be the one who steps up to take the administrator's challenge or not. If she did nothing, she would continue to live with the irritating decline of the landscape she loved and had learned to treasure from her childhood. When plans began to form in her own mind, she was imagining a new future for Hearthside—one that led it down a path away from what seemed like foregone destruction if no one intervened. By the time she met with the administrator, her creative powers of persuasion had convinced him, with the backing of his office, to get involved. At that point, how could she say no to a brighter future for Hearthside, one in which she would be the catalyst for change? The path that Hartley was creating not only meant good news for Hearthside House, but whether she knew it or not, it was taking her to the brink of creating something altogether new. She was on the pioneering path.

Risk—for a Higher Mission

Don Larson was always a little crazy. In fact, friends from his youth might tell you that he's a *lot* crazy. Not content with the usual adolescent activity, he would indulge in recreation that pushed the limits, like cliff diving. Young women wary of Larson's persuasive ability and penchant for risk warned him, "Stay away from my boyfriend because you're going to get him hurt."[8] Larson was also drawn to things that seemed out of the ordinary and deviated from routine. In his own words, he wanted to "be unique and succeed." Fouled up situations would attract his attention. In his estimation, "the broker it was, the better" because he liked solving problems that required a measure of risk.

It's not surprising, then, that when Larson fell into a career, it would be as a "fixer." Originally an industrial engineer with RCA, he was hired at The Hershey Company and quickly rose through the ranks, excelling at continuous improvement. Soon he gained the reputation of being Hershey's turnaround guy. He recalls: "The senior level people would say, 'Just give it to Don. Don't tell him what to do, just send him off. He'll have fun, and a year from now, he'll be bored so we'll have to find something else hopelessly broken.' So, I had a new job every year." But there was another element to Larson's desire to be a change agent: he intensely wanted to fix things, because others would benefit from his work. "What I do is right wrongs, stop injustice, [correct] anything that's being done that's inappropriate. That's why I like to be a turnaround guy. They would send me to different places at Hershey where things were a wreck."[9]

Along with organizational improvement, another one of Larson's hallmarks was his ability to enlist the help of other people to get a job done, whether they reported to him or not. Other employees naturally wanted to be part of what he was doing, and before he knew it, he had an unofficial team working with him. They were people who, like Larson, wanted to be part of something larger than themselves and succeed while doing it. He had a way of persuading workers to get on board and pull together for a cause. He recalls the way in which he invited people to work with him: "It was not, 'Hey, I want you to do this. I want you to change.' [My requests] were not confrontational. It [was more like], 'Let's do something better together,' you know?" There were others who noticed Larson's ability to convince fellow workers to help him: Hershey's C-level executives who were actually the supervisors of the colleagues Larson was attracting. At one point, they pointed out, "'Don, you have people working for you that are not supposed to be working for you. I've got to tell my people, 'You don't work for him. You're not even getting paid to work for him.' You have so many people who want to be part of what you're doing that they do it even though they're not assigned to do it.'"[10]

At Hershey, Larson continued to tackle the tough situations assigned by the company's executives. As an adult, he resonated with each messed-up challenge given him, like the adrenaline-filled rush he got from the risky cliff-dives he took as a younger man. Even though Larson may not have liked every assignment sent his way, a comment coming from a C-Level executive like "Just give it to Don" contained a veiled personal challenge to engage and conquer the problem. And Don Larson would not let Hershey down. To succeed, he continually had to practice skills of problem-solving and continuous improvement, while tapping into some of his risk-taking temperament to implement novel solutions. Yet, he didn't do this work alone. He was able to complete numerous turnarounds with the help of others who voluntarily worked for him. His whimsical, persuasive style drew others to join his team. Larson muses: "It's not me, personally. They want to be part of something that's helping the world to be a better place. And that, I think, is the higher mission."[11]

Larson may not have known it then, but he was just warming up for his "big game." It was only a matter of time before he would face the biggest risk of his life—a pioneering adventure that was waiting just for him.

Taking on the Mantle...and the Lintels

With a mandate from the new town administrator, Kathy Hartley stood on the verge of entering new territory on a personal quest to help an unknowing public fall in love with a house that many in the area didn't even know existed. The State of Rhode Island and Providence Plantations may hold the record for the longest official state name in the union, but it also holds the record for smallest land area. So how hard could it be to get the word out about Hearthside to the locals?

For Hartley, it was much more than a mere marketing project. Formerly the Director of Leadership Rhode Island, a transformational program that offers groups of diverse people shared learning experiences and opportunities to identify and solve challenges facing the state, she had ample experience bringing people together. As a leader herself, she knew that she had a lot of work to do on the product of Hearthside before she could go public with any marketing for it. Frankly, the old home needed some gussying up before it would meet debutante standards. Furthermore, Hartley also knew that the public needed a compelling reason to actually come to the house. Though some old house aficionados might carve time out of their schedule to take in some unique, early nineteenth-century construction, Hartley's vision extended far beyond this. She wanted everybody to fall in love with Hearthside. Was that too much to ask?

Hartley began by getting a pulse for who else might be interested in preserving Hearthside House. She decided to start with one organizational meeting. She drafted a newspaper article with an appeal to anyone who might have a heart for Hearthside in particular, or who was interested in historic preservation in general, or who had a penchant for event planning. She cast her net wide, attempting to appeal to others who would want to join her in an organizational meeting. She then put the article into print. The response to the plea was surprising:

> [The meeting] was in March [following the Hearthside Christmas event], and forty people showed up. They couldn't all fit in the room. We had to borrow folding chairs from the local church for the meeting. We had no lights in the house, so it had to be early because there were no lights to turn on, but it was incredible to see the energy in the room. Everyone wanted to help. No matter what I offered up, the hands were flying up: "I'll take care of this," and "I'll do that." Six weeks later we opened. We planned a tea just because the house seemed elegant, and we said, "Let's do a Victorian tea." Nobody was doing teas at the time, so it was a very unique thing to offer.[12]

While the newly formed group loved the romantic idea of an elegant Victorian tea, as its leader, Hartley had to face the reality that she didn't have enough teacups in her cupboard for such an event. Nor did she have enough spoons or cubes of sugar or anything else. Where would she get all that she needed? Furthermore, how would this new team create an atmosphere in which one would want to sip tea? Laughingly, Hartley recalls the scope of the challenge:

> We had no curtains, we had no tables to seat people, we had no teapots or teacups or anything else, so we borrowed everything from [a local] church. When the day of the Victorian tea arrived, I'm telling you, there

were people out the door! We had three seatings and
sold sixty seats at each seating. So, we started without a
dime, and I think we made $80 after paying expenses,
and that was our first $80. It was incredible.[13]

Hartley also went to work creating a governing board for the
forming organization. With so much to be done to bring the house
back into its glory, she knew that it would only be a matter of
time before she entered into the realm of fundraising. After all, she
couldn't continue to borrow supplies from the nearby church, and
other places, into the unforeseeable future. Hearthside House needed
to have its own tables and chairs to welcome people. It also needed
a serious facelift if it were to be seen by the public more frequently.
One of the early members of the board was a lawyer who advised
Kathy "that if we were going to raise any money, then we had to be
a 501c3. So, she went right to work on getting that—writing some
bylaws and incorporation papers. I think it was by November of that
year that we were deemed a nonprofit."[14]

Missed Turns

"I am never going back to Africa," a beleaguered Don Larson vowed.
Having already served as Hershey's director of strategic sourcing and
its director of global sourcing, he was pressured into taking the position of director of cocoa operations. In fact, Larson was clear that
he didn't want the job, but cocoa is an essential ingredient to chocolate, and since chocolate is Hershey's bread and butter, so to speak,
the company found itself in a tight spot. The new position was a
highly taxing job that involved the strategic purchase of hundreds
of millions of dollars of cocoa on the futures market. Hershey had
tried several people in the role, and the stress had been crushing.
They were running out of options and personnel possibilities for the
position. Larson wanted none of it, as he believed the job would be
dreadfully boring. In the end, he relented and took the position, and
it was as a result of this decision that he found himself in Ghana,
Africa to assess the crops. This west African country is known for its

high-quality cocoa beans, yearly producing about one-quarter of the world's supply.[15]

Through a turn of events, Larson found himself on one of the rides of his life while in the Ghanaian countryside. In the dark of night, his drivers took a wrong turn and became lost. An astute observer of body language, Larson noted that they were in a full panic, and learned that some witch doctors had made it known that they wanted to process the food processor himself for their own potions. Larson protested, "Come on! That's ridiculous!" Whether such a potion was real or imagined, the drivers were responsible for their human cargo and took the threat very seriously, while Larson, sick in the back of the vehicle, was bounced around in darkness. When he returned to the United States, Larson quit Hershey and swore off any future visits to the African continent. But as the saying goes, "Never say 'never.'"

A Great Vision for a Great Road

With the restoration of Hearthside underway, Kathy Hartley could not corral the thoughts that would break free from the home fires of Hearthside and, with a full gallop, race to other buildings on Great Road in need of human tending. Of course, there was her grandparents' property, the Chase Farm. It continued to call out to her, but there were other voices as well, including the Moffett Mill, as it continued to lean toward the river just down the street. Gradually, what was to become the Great Road Campus took shape as Hartley and her Friends of Hearthside worked tirelessly to host events and raise awareness of the area's historic importance, while raising funds for the care of the buildings.

As Hartley reflects back on the years of determined hard work that carved out a new organization for the preservation of Great Road's past, she points to the importance of vision and its role in fueling pioneering perseverance. For Hartley, vision is a skill that a would-be pioneer can cultivate, especially when it is motivated by the desire to introduce change. It was a skill that she refined in her previous position as the Director of Leadership Rhode Island and brought to bear in her emerging role as the Friends of Hearthside founder, president, and CEO. She recalls:

> I never really understood the power of vision until I saw it and used it when I was running [Leadership Rhode Island]. [It] was first creating a vision, and then bringing other people around that vision to help it become a reality. I saw it happen over and over and over again. I just had to use [visioning] in the Hearthside project because it was so overwhelming to think about: What is the next thing to do? What should we do with this thing or that thing? It was so enormous that...I had to get the people around me that brought different skill sets that I didn't have, for example, the lawyer to put the 501c3, and people in event planning. I also brought in food service experts in particular, because we knew in putting anything out there to the public that they would come if food was involved. If you just throw history in there, they're not going to come, but get them there with food, then history comes second![16]

As Hartley demonstrates, the process of creating a vision, gathering people with varying skill sets around that vision, and coupling that with a solid understanding of human nature can metamorphize a community irritant into a community asset. If you offer food and fun, the public will come!

Another important lesson this seasoned pioneer offers is that leadership, like visioning, can also be cultivated. Though difficult to believe when you meet her, Hartley claims that she was always shy:

> When I was very young, I was so timid. I went through 4-H clubs, and all through school, and I wouldn't even raise my hand to ask a question in class. However, I was fortunate that when I got older, people noticed something in me. They would tell me that I was a leader and that I was able to do these things. At first, I didn't believe them. I thought, *Me? No, I could never*

do that. But they stuck with me and mentored me, boosting my confidence. Finally, I would say, "Okay, I'll go for it."

When I took the job at Leadership Rhode Island, I was kind of pushed into it. I didn't think that I would ever do something like that, but there were others who believed in me, saying, "Yes, you can do this." So, I accepted the job, and I thought to myself, *I'll never be able to succeed at this, but I'll do it for three months and give it a try.* I was there for [eighteen] years, and I ended up getting the first national award for excellence as a program director for a leadership program.[17]

Hartley's example illustrates a well-supported fact: leaders can be cultivated. Leadership is not a trait that only certain individuals are conferred with at birth; it can be learned and refined through practice. In their book *Learning Leadership*, well-respected researchers James Kouzes and Barry Posner offered: "'Our research shows that a universal set of leadership practices is associated with exemplary leadership, and these practices are within the capacity of everyone to follow.' In other words, leadership is a skill that can be honed and developed."[18] What is important is that individuals who aspire to be leaders, whether they are initially shy like Hartley or bold like Larson, invest in learning best practices in leadership, and then begin to exercise those practices within their own context. Refinement then follows, until a successful personal leadership style is found. Mentoring also plays a valuable role, and the emerging leader must be humble enough to accept correction as well as affirmation. Then the real work comes as the leader actively engages in continual observation, problem-solving, and ongoing improvement. This is the price of advancement coupled with the reality of "slogging," as Dr. Carol Ferrans has described it (see chapter 6). Hartley agrees: "I think that everyone has a leader inside of them, and it just depends on their circumstances whether it gets tapped and utilized. Ultimately, I think everybody's got it in them to do it. For myself? My own mother has said to me, 'I can't believe you're doing what you do. I could never do that. I would never have the courage to do it.' I said, 'Oh, sure you could.'"[19]

This is more good news for those who, at present, don't consider themselves leaders, let alone desire to take an even greater leap into the realm of pioneer. Leading and pioneering can be learned and can be accomplished—if, that is, one has the will backed by perseverance to make it work. However, there is a hefty price to pay, and in some cases, not everyone is willing to pay it.

Back to Africa

When Don Larson quit Hershey, he joined a team to build the largest, most ultra-efficient cocoa factory in the world near the ports of Philadelphia. Backed by foreign investors, the venture showed great success potential. But to Larson's dismay and contrary to his own input, he watched a cascade of poor decision-making and shady moves, verging on the illegal. In his own words: "It was the toughest part of my life, and I have never experienced such unethical behavior. I had to uncover a bunch of stuff. It was just a nightmare."

Larson became disillusioned. Even when it appeared that the nightmare was about to end, he was deeply disturbed: "At first I was upset. I was like, 'I just killed myself for two years doing herculean things that no one sees, not appreciated for it.'" Larson's pushback didn't go untested: "This guy [at the factory] would berate me, and I would just go out, find a corner somewhere, get in a fetal position, and think, *Man, how much of this can I take?*"[20] What Larson didn't know is that even the constant barrage of criticism he received for doing the right thing, albeit the uphill, hard, high road, was toughening him up for a pioneering adventure that would take him from the herculean to the even weightier realm of Atlas.

When Larson finally left the factory, he was in search of his next chapter in life. Campbell's Soup came courting, and Larson reluctantly began to explore whether this was to be the plot to his next chapter. He took a full day of interviews with the company. He recalls:

At the end of the day, the top HR guy comes in and says, "I don't know what you did, but they want me to create a senior VP position that's sort of a center of excellence, where all you do is help make Campbell Soup a better place."

I'm like, "That sounds pretty good!"

They said, "It's going to take three to five months to form the position, go through all the interviewing. But," they said, "there will be no one that'll top you to qualify. Can you take three to five months off?"

I said, "Absolutely. I've always wanted to have some time off."[21]

And that's just what Larson did. Previously, as Hershey's turnaround guy, he had been rewarded greatly for his years of effort and success. He had experienced the best life had to offer. By his own accounting, at midlife, Larson had lived a very prosperous life: "I've had a great job. I have the most wonderful wife, beautiful kids. I had everything. I was a hot air balloon pilot for twenty some years. I flew airplanes and tried to land it on a highway for the fun of it. I had a nice, fast, high-performance Porsche convertible. I had street bikes, dirt bikes, every toy you could think of." But all of it left him unfulfilled. During that three to five months away from work, he decided that he was designed for something more, a mission that would have a greater impact than he had ever experienced, and not one that would simply benefit him, his immediate family, or the bottom line of a corporation, but would resonate beyond his immediate world.

Larson entered into a time of personal searching and deep reflection. He looked for answers to the "What's next?" question in every encounter in his life while he continued to go about his daily routine. One day during that hiatus, in a way that he least expected it, a new vision in the form of words came to him: "Build food factories in third world nations to bring lasting economic transformation, and name it Sunshine." For Don, it was a profound, life-changing experience. It had such a deep impact on him that he describes it as "almost audible." He wrestled with it, determining in his own words, "That certainly wasn't me because I'm never going back into the food industry, and I'm never going back to Africa, but I gotta record it in my journal."

Larson was serious. He didn't want to go back into the food industry. In fact, he had enrolled in seminary, thinking he might pastor a church, and if he did, this prosperous turnaround guy was going to give it his all: "I was in that mindset of, I'm going to be poor for the rest of my life, and I'm going to give everything. I'm going to save plastic baggies and tin foil and things like that. I'm going to give everything to the poor, widowed, and the orphan."[22] While Larson had no yearning to remain rich for his own sake, what he would develop would offer others much more than the plastic baggies and tin foil he thought he might end up collecting.

A Quadruple Bottom Line

Larson's process was messy, but it had a method. He remained open to whatever might be in his future. He searched for it in everyday events and wanted to be ready for it. After he received the new vision for Sunshine food factories, he began to act on it. He started to develop a philosophy of operation that has come to be called the Sunshine Approach business model. While many organizations strive for a triple bottom line—profit (financial), people (social), and planet (environmental)—Larson took his model a step further to create a quadruple bottom line, adding "transformation" as another measure of success. Not only did he want to support materially poor workers in a community at a fair price, but he wanted to be a part of transforming the lives of the most vulnerable. In short, Larson dreamed of a day when he could not only support poor farmers but could also convert orphans into leaders! Currently, the social and transformational components of the Sunshine Business model reads:

> Our social bottom line focuses on supporting the materially poor farmers, orphans and vulnerable children. In addition to supporting our farmers by providing fair prices, 30% of our company's net proceeds will go back into supporting agricultural

development. Another 30% of the company's net proceeds will go toward caring for orphans and vulnerable children through direct donation to establish children's centers.

The transformational bottom line will be achieved by hiring adult orphans at the factory and equipping them to become tomorrow's business leaders through education and training. We will also be using our factories as teaching facilities in cooperation with local universities to teach food processing and international food quality requirements. The remaining 30% of the company's net distributions will go towards new food processing companies to grow the concept—thereby bringing economic relief to different regions involved in different types of farming.[23]

Larson completed his model and sent if off to an influencer he had met previously at a food conference, who he knew interacted frequently with presidents of African nations. He had no idea if his idea would strike a chord with her or anyone she knew, but apparently, the timely arrow he blindly sent forth hit a target, and she returned his communication. She had just had lunch with the chairman of the Tanzanian Chamber of Commerce, who was also the best friend of the President of Tanzania. He was bemoaning the fact that he needed help with the farming community, and the consultants who had been brought in weren't helping. He shared, "I don't trust anyone. I wish there was someone in the food industry who could give us great advice." And, of course, she now had just the guy for the president. Larson realized, "Oh my gosh, it looks like I'm going back to Africa and the food industry."[24]

Larson did visit Tanzania in Africa, but ultimately it wasn't where he would land. In 2011, two years after that trip, in an all-in pioneering style, he and his wife sold everything they owned and moved the family to Mozambique. Though his experience was in chocolate, he decided against it for his new company. "Chocolate I could do, but it took too much in the way of utilities and infrastructure. If any mistakes occur, you've got big mounds of melted chocolate. Whereas cashews are much more forgiving. I started off with cashews and built the brand. This is all about doing long-lasting economic transformation. So, the key words [here are]: sustainable, holistic, integrative, transformative."[25] And so began the Sunshine Nuts Company.

As Larson's pioneering story has unfolded, he has found that all of the effort he put into his previous roles have congealed, preparing him for this gargantuan pioneering effort that would give back to the area in which he would establish his business. He was creating a virtuous cycle that had the potential to not only change a region economically but to give hope to people in a country that had formerly been decimated by war. Larson has successfully built a world-class food factory and staffed it primarily with adult orphans. He and his family have developed relationships with orphanages and other community organizations throughout Mozambique where they support and develop projects, giving back 90 percent of their profits. In 2014, Sunshine Nuts landed on shelves in the United States.

The company's establishment and growth have not been easy. Mozambique is a country that has been torn apart by war, and it has struggled for decades to recover. "Mozambique used to be the largest cashew producer in the world until civil war and banking policies decimated their industry over thirty years ago. I think it's time to return Mozambique to its former glory."[26] Just because Larson wants to create a positive impact in the country and is determined to operate the Sunshine Nut Company ethically doesn't mean that everyone he's encountered has slapped him on the back and wished him success in his endeavors. In fact, at one time, he and his family were held at gunpoint while their cars were stolen. Larson estimates:

> It's probably the most difficult country of all countries to do business. We have endured such incredible hardship here: corruption, exploitation, bribe attempts, delays, and stealing. But we persevere, and we find a way through it. One of the things I've found is that there's always a solution. I [used to] negotiate with all these companies, but now I negotiate with government officials.... I am able to use my skill set, but to demonstrate a better way, an honest, ethical way. We have never once paid [a bribe], never done

anything wrong. When [government agencies] come in, our books are clean. I say, "I'm so glad that you're coming in here to evaluate us, because we want to be the best that we can be. So, if you find anything wrong, I'm going to be very appreciative."[27]

Perseverance is one of the main ingredients that makes Sunshine Nuts so successful, and many have marveled that the company has been able to stay in business. As a result, Larson has had the opportunity to speak at food shows all over the world, having been sponsored by the United Nations, the European Union, and the US government to share about his operation. U.S. Aid recently did an assessment on the viability of the company. Astonished that Larson and his team have been able to continue operations in such adverse circumstances, others are eager to learn the secret to Larson's survival where similar efforts have failed. He shares his secret sauce that few are willing to brew: Extreme generosity for the sake of the mission he is pioneering:

> Everyone thinks I'm crazy. At the end of the day, if I have a million dollars of profit I'm going to make, I don't have to make a penny of profit. Because I'm giving it all back anyway. If I encounter things that need to be changed and corrected, like exploitation, I can use that million dollars in the value chain of the business in order to do the right thing for the people and honor God. Does that make sense? People think you're crazy, but it allows me to gain trust with the government. It also allows me to go up against those who are exploiting, those who are trying to put me out of business.[28]

A House That Love Saved

Thanks to Kathy Hartley and her friends, Hearthside is not only the house that love built but also the house that love saved. From its earliest events that included the old-fashioned Christmas open houses and Victorians teas, Hearthside continues to frequently welcome guests into its warm embrace. Visitors are now able to enjoy other heritage-oriented events: for example, antique fairs, heritage crafts, Revolutionary War and Civil War reenactments, and classes on Victorian mourning customs. Hartley and her team no sooner finish adorning Hearthside and her sister buildings for one event that they then busy themselves dressing the buildings up for another.

There is a high cost to love. As the Bible says, "Love bears all things, believes all things, hopes all things, endures all things."[29] At the end of the day, Hartley admits that Lady Hearthside takes more than she gives, and if accounting could be put in a personal context, Hartley would admit that her own ledger is in "the red."

> [Hearthside has] taken a lot. Seven days a week, a lot of family time away, a lot of stress. I know that it affects my health because of the stress. I wish I could take more time off, but in a way, it feeds me…. On one hand Hearthside is a lot of work, on the other it's just something that I love doing so much that it is my hobby. It's finding that balance too, which is a little tough right now.[30]

Hartley echoes the honest thoughts and feelings of many who dare to pioneer. Life balance does not come easy to the pioneer, yet in order to continue the work, it is best accomplished in good health. Still, there are days when mission and vision fulfillment demands that little bit more, pressing into the fatigue that is begging the body to stop. What has kept Hartley going? Those characteristics that separate the pioneer from the leader: possibility driven, probing, peaumance, principled, persuasive, and, of course, hard-core persistence. Says Hartley:

> I think, again, keeping your eye on the future, knowing that it was so worthy a cause that there's no way that these buildings were going to be falling down under my watch. Something was going to work out—I was given a task here and I'm not about to give up on it. It will work. Some way. Sometimes it's not clear how, but it will happen.[31]

But was Hartley given a task, or did she take it on herself? For pioneers, it is hard to see the difference.

Though Don Larson's mission greatly differs from Hartley's, he also reflects how hardship and personal sacrifice are part and parcel of the pioneering endeavor. Though giving his all has personally put he and his family members in the red many times, he would never go back to the life he once lived:

> [My time at the cocoa factory was] nothing compared to now. I could multiply that times a hundred and that's what I go through here. It's tough. And you know, it has this progression of refining you.... At the end of the day none of that even comes close to being on this ride. I was designed for exactly what [I'm going] through. Before I was on this mission, I was doing everything to try to fulfill it with all these toys, all these things. I sold everything, and I don't miss it at all. I've got something much better: God is fulfilling how he designed me for the mission that he has me on.[32]

And for the pioneer, there is no higher resonance than fulfilling a destiny for which he or she was designed and bringing others along for the exciting ride.

Pioneering with the End in Sight

For Hartley and Larson, pioneering wouldn't be nearly as fun if they were doing it all in a vacuum. Both clearly speak of others: those who have caught the shared vision and those who benefit from it.

Even though a task may seem impossible, the pioneer will have a thirst to break the barrier so that others may come behind and share the experience. Larson points out: "I'd like to convey, someone needs to be the ice breaker, that breaks the ice that allows others to go through. What I've found is that people said this is impossible. And I like when people say it's impossible. I thrive on that. It's the same when people say, 'No one can break a four-minute mile.' Then someone did, then everyone did. And what I'm looking to do is be so successful here that it gives others the motivation and encouragement to persevere and to be successful as well."[33]

As Larson's children have matured, they have become active in the Sunshine Nut operation. One of Larson's sons remains in Mozambique and runs sales and operations, while the other lives in the United States caring for the company's finances and books. Larson's daughter is responsible for marketing and social media. With pride, Larson shares: "They've already aligned themselves that Cassie will be CEO, Brent will be CFO, and William will be COO. They are totally bought in. My wife is the philanthropic arm. She's heading up the foundation. She's the chief baby hugger." And there are plenty of babies in their orphanages who need a warm embrace.

As for those who come in contact with the Sunshine Nut Company, their future looks brighter as well. Larson's growing organization is bringing expanding hope to the people of Mozambique. Through their Sunshine Approach business model, "We're replacing hand-outs with hand-ups, we're replacing entitlement with earning and the pride of a paycheck, we're replacing despair with hope, adversity with opportunity, stagnation with transformation, worthlessness with dignity, failure with excellence. These are the things that I make part of the company."[34]

Just a singular example of the company's transformative effect is found in one of their own workers, Borges Domingos. When a child, he lost his father, plunging his family further into poverty. Without a working father, Borges could not return to school. His mother had to shoulder all of the responsibility for him, his younger brother, and sister. It appeared he would go the way of millions of disadvantaged African children living in despair—without an education, without resources, and without hope. Now working at Sunshine Nut company, he reflects on how his life has changed: "Sunshine [changed] a lot of things, not just in my life, but in my family's life. [It] is a different company, because what we do here is not just for us. Everything we do, we do it from our hearts to help the community."

More pioneers are needed to take bold risks like the Larson family. Perhaps some of them, like Borges, will be former disadvantaged children who emerge from the Sunshine Nut Company. They are learning that big risks with big rewards are possible. As others learn from Larson's transformative, pioneering model, they too may bring it to other nations that struggle to prosper.

For Hartley, preserving the past is not just about saving the Lincoln landscape and decorating buildings for others to enjoy. Mainly, it's part of pioneering a work in order to leave a legacy of place and people for those who come behind us, some of whom we may never know. Despite all of the sacrifices and long hours invested in Hearthside, she looks to the future as much as she has learned from Hearthside's past. She muses:

> I think when you get older, you start to see the end in sight. The older you get, you start to reflect on your life and ask, "What have I done?" I also had a child late in life. I started to think about the stories I needed to tell him…. Then, at the same time, I saw [the houses on Great Road] not being used. I wanted to learn the stories behind the buildings, save that history. It all started to become interesting to me, where in school, history was not interesting. It was about reading it in books. It wasn't real to me.[35]

Hartley and team have worked hard to make history real and Hearthside a living place to which people want to return. She is stretching herself now so that Hearthside's legacy will stretch beyond herself into the future. It may have begun with her, but she is hopeful that it will not end with her.

> I would like to see this continue on, the whole campus. I want it to be valued by the community. I want others to follow in my footsteps and carry it on. I'm fortunate in being able to get it going, but I'm only a steward in leading it for so long. I want others to be able to step in and take over and make sure that these buildings stand for the next one hundred years, two hundred years, and that they're active and part of

the community and not just old buildings sitting by the side of the road.

We learn from our past. If these buildings go, we lose those reminders of our past. If we're only living in the present moment…I can't even imagine. No. We've got to have the past. The past has got to be there for us because we learn the values of the past and what those who have come before us went through. Without that kind of appreciation, you're not grounded. You have no sense of self. It's the whole appreciation I think that makes you a better person inside by knowing what others went through before you.[36]

Kathy Hartley. Don Larson. Two very different pioneering personalities with two very different missions. One started out shy and timid, and the other bold and brash, but they both exhibit similar traits that have allowed them to create something new that they will leave for those behind them. They have truly embodied the phrase "Always leave a place better than when you found it," and they are taking steps to ensure that it will be so, by leaving their work in the capable hands of those who will continue it.

Letting It Go for the Sake of the Future

I met Hartley under hard circumstances. My uncle Bub passed away, taking with him the sole voice of the elder Moffetts in my branch of the family tree. With whom would I talk to now? Without my mother, I had turned to Bub for those long, family history discussions that no one else seemed to care about. Bub left behind generations of the family's treasures in nooks and crannies in his home on the little hill. He had gathered it all, placing it in the attic, garage, outbuildings, and beyond. Bub was so like his ilk: stoic in some measure, yet sentimental in others. He couldn't part with his family's things, yet he didn't know what to do with them either. He had no children to gift them to. I had already inherited my share of relics when my mother passed away, and now lived some distance away.

Knowing my uncle and his penchant for holding on to the family's history, I promised my aunt that I would help her when the day came, and eventually, it did.

After a few phone calls, I found that the friends of Hearthside had advanced their mission beyond their namesake property. I learned that they had become stewards of the restored Moffett Mill, and yes, they were thrilled to receive items that were once used there. With a great amount of joy, and no little sadness, my remaining family members would send the family history back to where it belonged. In the spirit of Don Larson, it was time to open our hands and give it back, after over a century in our possession. I couldn't help but think that Mom and Bub would heartily approve.

Points for Your Compass

→ Pioneers see the possibilities for a better future in what appears to be an insurmountable, irritating situation.

→ They persevere, sometimes for years if necessary, until they see and seize the opportunity to be a change agent, even if that involves courage to take the personal risk.

→ With their own efforts and resources, pioneers will enter the situation that needs transformation, persuading others with needed expertise to join them.

→ Principles guide pioneers as they work to create change, and they are careful not to violate personal core ethics. If necessary, pioneers run "iffy" practices past a trusted circle of advisors and thoughtfully measure their feedback before acting.

→ A pioneer's passion drives her forward until her dream becomes a reality. Often in the process, the dream will expand to include more new turf, positively impacting an increasing number of people.

Portrait of a Pioneer

S<small>AY THE WORD</small> *CANVAS* <small>AND THIS IMAGE LIKELY COMES TO MIND:</small> A piece of cloth backed or framed as a surface for a painting.[1] We may think of an unsullied, white square just waiting for some form of novel, painted expression to be applied to it. One artist's result may be wildly different from the next, with the final product bearing little resemblance to the canvas's original form. In reality, not all canvases are equal. An artist walking along a lakefront may come upon a small stone and see that a badger must be painted on it. Or, he might pick it up and decide that it is just the thing to include in a larger art piece. In this case, the rock is given new meaning as it is taken from its former context and placed into another. Alternatively, an artist in an urban context might find satisfaction working on scaffolding at great heights as she transforms the side of a building into a mural for onlookers to enjoy. In this case, her canvas is no longer cloth. Suffice it to say, canvases are as diverse as the human imagination, and the process may be as pristine or as messy as the individual artist's method.

Artists may care little for their appearance while creating, forming, and moving the medium into the image they envision. I had an art teacher in high school who once said to me, "I love it when artists aren't afraid to get dirty." Charcoal smears on cheeks, paint-saturated clothing, clay matter forced under fingernails, sawdust in hair—this shows the working artist's true joy. As one who enjoys working with pencils, pens, inks, and paint, I've experienced the personal oblivion that comes with crafting while "in flow." Others describe the experience as being "in the zone." You're so in love with the work that you are fashioning that your eyes are fixed on it, not on your appearance. You don't realize that you're dirty until your session is over, and you look in the mirror during cleanup. The artistic reward is a good laugh at the grimy face staring back at you, and, of course, a finished piece of art just as you imagined it. Others receive the fruit of the artist's joy when they experience it too.

It also bears mentioning that the word *joy* doesn't simplistically mean "happy." It's not merely a sparkly green and red wood cutout to be affixed to door wreaths once a year. Its meaning runs deeper. As such, one may have joy even in the agony and exhaustion of bringing something new into the world. Just ask any woman who claims her greatest joy is in being a mother. For those of us who have not had this experience, it can be very difficult to understand.

While in process, an artist may bring to bear every emotion that the drive to create draws upon, such as enthusiasm, determination, confidence, anxiety, frustration, optimism, surprise, and anger. Great physical energy to produce can be mixed with a critical eye toward the product and even toward the artist herself. In fact, it's not uncommon to have two opposing forces at work at the same time. One moment the artist may be dissatisfied, and the next, after an applied swoop of the palette knife, she may be extremely gratified. But she will only rest when her work is done. Even so, when the final brush stroke is applied and she declares the piece completed, she may look back and see ways in which the piece could have been improved. A true artist never arrives at an end that is beyond improvement, even though she may be considered a master. There is always something new to learn to apply to a canvas waiting to be transformed.

A Mosaic of Pioneers

Who, then, is an artist? Are artistic individuals defined by the medium in which they work, or by gender, age, ethnicity, or any other demographic label? No, artists are found in all these categories. Art is supra-demographic and has been conceived in different ways during various periods throughout human history. Across time and geography, artists are defined by what they all have in common: they render art using various types of canvas and a medium(s) of one form or another. While there may be subjective opinions and philosophical discussions about what "good art" is, all artists are driven to create, as writers are to write, architects are to design, and so forth.

And so it is that pioneers must pioneer. No one demographic trait defines them. They may be young or old, a citizen of one country or another (or hold a dual citizenship), from various economic backgrounds, or drawn from different faiths or no faith at all.

Consider again a young Haley Wilk. She is currently making an impact in her home state as she is driven to carve out a niche to assist those with mental health challenges through equine therapy. Her pioneering work is in progress, and she is moving toward her dream of one day owning her own facility where people can find healing through interaction with horses. It's hard work. A day might find her in muddy boots in the barn pitching in with all the dirty jobs that are required to care for horses. Another day might find her in an office designing a survey to add to the pool of knowledge in her field. As a pioneer, Haley's dreams are not merely confined to being a successful entrepreneur. And they are not to be confused with her ultimate mission, which is greater than providing help to a few. In typical pioneering style, she sees the impact of her efforts as surpassing the immediate relief that she provides her clientele, though the importance of this should not be diminished. Rather, in her own words, she hopes to be a part of providing natural healing with horses to entire segments of people. She sees what could be through her efforts: advancing understanding through research and applying that new knowledge to ever-improving practice.

And then there's Juni Felix, a trauma victim. Her battles for health and stability have been hard won. Anyone who has spent time with her knows that her smile is genuine and contagious. She is a joyful pioneer who, like Gladys West, is authentic about the obstacles that have been placed in her path. She embodies West's assessment that adversity can sometimes serve as a slingshot. If allowed, that slingshot may catapult a person toward exponential growth. It takes hard work, but sometimes those who may appear behind in life are able to advance when given an opportunity, undergirding their efforts with personal grit to achieve their own passion-driven goals. Like Gladys West, Juni Felix has "a mind of [her] own," applying herself to imagine compassionate communities where citizens not only help each other in person but may leverage technology in order to surface needs among them so that those who need specific forms of help may receive them quickly and efficiently.

Then there is Ken Schuetz. Ken nurtured an area of interest into an expertise that eventually became a full-blown passion. His fascination with leadership, specifically with board-governed organizations, came through participation and study. As a result of his many years serving on organizational boards, he began to see cracks in the best-practices system. Because of his placement in history, he was witness to a massive crumbling of the governance monolith that caused the subprime mortgage crisis. Picking through rubble is disturbing, especially when the collateral damage has a human face. In this instance, Schuetz wasn't looking for actual bodies, but he clearly saw the destructive impact on people's lives—a magnitude of pain and suffering imposed by personal financial loss.

As his exploration into the crisis continued and he received answers as how board-governed organizations failed, in true pioneer style, his thinking turned not only to constructing preventative measures by reinforcing an older system. He also went beyond a "never again" scenario into the unknown. He has imagined a future where boards and executives clearly know their roles and will not operate as adversaries but as collaborators. And now, after much work, he is actively presenting his ideas to the world.

Shades of Pioneering

At first glance, these innovators (Wilk, Felix, and Schuetz) appear to have little in common: they originate from and operate in different regions of the country, represent three different generations, vary demographically, and have very different stories of origin. In addition, they are all in different stages of their pioneering. Some are just setting out on the journey, some in the process of developing expertise, and others are revealing their ideas to the world and gaining practice with their implementation. And yet, if each of them was asked the right question, say, "What do you do?" the hearer would receive very similar responses, not in substance but in spirit.

Pioneering "the White Space"

During my undergraduate years, my mother also decided to advance her education beyond her high school diploma. While I was reading medieval French literature and banging out Prokofiev's Sonata in D on my flute, Mom was taking course work to inform and improve her day job in recreational therapy for the elderly. Unlike my well-designed programs in French literature and music, Mom entered into an amorphous scholastic journey that crossed the bounds between gerontology, education, and the arts, as a program for recreational therapy for the elderly had not yet been offered. One of her visual art courses was in drawing. Already accomplished in this area through her own efforts, Mom began to formally learn terms and techniques for concepts upon which she had already acted intuitively.

One of these areas that she discussed with me was the importance of white space, also known as negative space. In music composition, we might analogously refer to the strategic use of silence or rests to offset the sound that the composer intends. In an orchestra, some instruments rest while others play, creating unique combinations of sounds. Most interesting to me in Mom's schooling was learning to sketch white spaces, which is the ability to draw images, not by the mass that is typically used to define them, but by examining the shape of the space around the object, and putting charcoal to paper to recreate that image. Many times, a viewer can discern what the object is just by looking at a rendered image's negative space. For example, it is easy for the mind to pick out a plant or a chair, but sometimes more detail is needed in the picture to distinguish it if, for example, the object is actually a hat or Antoine de Saint-Exupéry's picture of an elephant that's been swallowed by a boa constrictor.[2] It's a fun exercise as it works on the brain's ability to see things differently, translate it to paper, and examine the result. Sometimes an artist will devote a study to implementing both practices: drawing half the object as it appears and the other half using its negative space as a reference. It is interesting to see the similarities and differences of the outcomes when using white space as a reference as opposed to drawing in a more traditional style.

White space can define an object or a problem or offer a solution in a different way, and this is what makes this awkward practice valuable. Likewise, it may also help to think of concepts in terms of what lies outside a definition in order to get a fuller picture of its meaning. A very simple way to try out this sort of thinking is to consult a thesaurus, which readily offers different shades of similar meaning through synonyms. However, at the bottom of the entry are antonyms—words that have an opposite meaning. Sometimes, these word "white spaces" offer insight into meaning that have been missed by the many synonyms offered.

Looking at conceptual white space is a good practice for anyone who wants to gain a fresh perspective on an idea. It may offer new insights, and it is with this benefit in mind that we may apply the "white space" concept to discover more about the inner substance of the pioneer.

POSSIBILITY-DRIVEN VERSUS CAUTIOUS

"Play it safe" is an idiom that's offered as an admonishment when someone we care about is going into a potentially dangerous situation. The expression communicates "don't take risks," instead, "take precautions." Many motorists might even recall an initial admonition to "drive defensively" when they were first taking to the road. I have often been amused when the automated voice programmed into my vehicle's GPS directional system advises me to "continue to follow the road." Does she think I will go off-roading in my passenger vehicle? The directive seems ridiculous in this context, but for the pioneer, a command like "continue to follow the road" flies in the face of his or her essence. It seems that a measured amount of certainty, security, or safety must be, in some ways, set aside if advances are to be made. The possibilities of a better understanding of a thing, a healthier future for a community, or an encounter with a creature heretofore unknown to humanity drives the pioneer to take risks.

This does not mean that risks cannot or should not be measured and mitigated, but the pioneer is always trading some form of safety for innovation. An example of this is James Cameron, who took the trip down to the deepest part of the Pacific Ocean's Mariana Trench on March 26, 2012. While the Challenger Deep was constructed and tested in order to preserve the life of the human pilot descending to the deepest parts of the ocean, there is still a fair amount of risk in boarding such a vessel and piloting it to a setting that is hostile to human life. No matter how much the design is refined and the mechanics are tested, things can still go wrong during exploration, as we've seen from a similarly named space shuttle.

Yes, pioneers must be willing to take risks. All kinds of risks. Rosa Parks took a risk when, in 1955 in Alabama, she refused to sit in a section of the bus designated for African Americans. Her action spurred the civil rights movement forward, inspiring similar protests throughout the country. When pioneers are successful, the results of their risk-taking are amazing. Humanity is still being introduced to some new sea creatures we never knew existed, and more people are being treated fairly as injustice is identified and rectified.

PROBING VERSUS DISINTEREST

I first learned the French expression *je m'en fiche* in my intermediate French class. Translated, it means "I don't care" or even "I don't give a rip." There are many phrases in English used to communicate unconcern, disinterest, and indifference. It's one thing to be strongly disinterested (and usually we begin or end these rants by saying, "for all I care"), but it's another to experience *ennui* that is a result of lethargy and listlessness of mind. For some of us, the business of modern living can be so tiresome that it whips any concern and curiosity right out of us. Thinking about something other than "the required" can feel exhausting, so we don't go there. But just for fun, let's "go there" for a bit.

Ever heard of a holothurian? How about a teuthidodrilus, otherwise known as a squidworm? These words are so new that my computer word processing program is telling me that I have misspelled them. The first two questions in this paragraph simply require a "yes" or a "no" response and may be left at that. If these questions were asked of a child, he or she would likely follow up with another question: "What's a holothurian?" Children are naturally inquisitive, and sometimes that quality remains with us through adulthood. Pioneers, at any age, remain curious.

In a debutant article, writer Ed Yong ostensibly introduces the squidworm to the world. He amusingly reflects on the importance of pioneering discoveries before he describes the creature: "Some scientific discoveries are exciting because they have the potential to save lives and revolutionize the way we live. Others are exciting because they fundamentally change the way we view ourselves and the world around us. And others are exciting because they involve a worm with tentacles on its head." Yong goes on to describe this aquatic animal found in "the depths of the western Celebes Sea off the eastern coast of Borneo:" "The squidworm looks like a fusion animal, half-squid and half-worm. In fact, it's all worm, a member of the group that includes familiar earthworms and leeches. It just happens to have ten long tentacles on its head."[3]

Obviously, a deep dive into the ocean isn't for everyone. The point is that curiosity can take many forms, especially if directed at an area of personal interest. Discovery becomes exciting if curiosity becomes the motivator for obtaining new knowledge. There is a certain delight that comes with discovery. There can even be sorrow, such as the day my world crumbled when I learned that a daddy longlegs was not a spider. Emotion signals care and personal involvement—something that all pioneers possess when they are pioneering.

PERSISTENT VERSUS YIELDING

An interesting antonym for the word *persistent* provided by thesaurus.com is "yielding." The verb *to yield* invokes a sense that some sort of challenge has been issued, and one of the challengers has failed to meet the test. If the test-taker is a person, there may be an image of throwing in the towel, as is done in the boxing ring when a contestant surrenders and admits defeat. A person may gesture by throwing her hands up or verbalize it by saying "I give up!" or "Uncle!" Subsequently, one walks away from the challenge or shows a resignation to defeat—at least for the time being.

Resignation is the bane of the pioneer's existence. It creates a sense of profound loss, especially if the challenge issued is one that is given to oneself. It seems that these personal tests are never more powerful than those that are developed within. They find their origins deep in the soul and by force of will become forged inextricably with a mission. For example, Henry Hudson was doggedly determined to find a northwest passage to Cathay (modern China) to the point of risking his life and the life of his crew to find it. The crew would have none of it, however, because they saw that Hudson's perseverance ignored the consideration of his own people. In stark contrast, modern pioneer Don Larson is also single-mindedly on a mission, prioritizing people by using his business to provide economic transformation to those in Mozambique. He and his family actively grow the business in order to "make a difference in the lives of the poor and orphaned" in this war-torn, debt-saddled country.[4] Pioneering perseverance can mean the difference between life and death as seen in the origins of the Iditarod, Jonas Salk's creation of a polio vaccine, and Carol Ferrans's continuing research to mitigate breast cancer, especially among underserved African American women in urban Chicago.

Whether you are a fellow pioneer or not, aren't we glad that some among us don't and won't give up?

PEAU-MANCE VERSUS PASSIVITY

It's easy to be a benchwarmer when there is no interest in the game. James Naismith, the father of basketball, knew this all too well when he was contending with a disinterested physical education class at the YMCA. These young men had chosen a course of study that would prepare them to be secretaries, not weightlifters or linebackers. Even so, they were required to participate in a physical exercise program as part of the Y's holistic approach to betterment. Naismith knew that he had to stir up some form of internal motivation in order to interest the non-interested enough to willingly participate. His prescription for passivity was basketball, which not only sparked interest but induced a drive that spread to many who wanted to get in the game, eventually making basketball a worldwide sport accessible to participants and spectators alike.

Most pioneers won't allow themselves to be left in reserve when there is exploring to be done. Rather, they willingly throw themselves into the thick of the pioneering game at whatever stage it is in. They cannot *not* participate, and this drive extends to their whole being. Thoughts, emotions, strength, personal resources, even relationships may all be sacrificed at the altar of advancement to the cause. Horace Wells was an extreme case of one who was consumed by his pioneering pursuit. In having his own skin in the game, he discovered nitrous oxide for which many are thankful. But he, along with others like him, was recklessly inhaling vapors without fully understanding the consequences. Driven by mixed desires for personal fame and other motivators that were certainly altruistic, Wells abandoned the ballasts of relational accountability and set off on a solitary journey that would lead to poor decision-making that would eventually lead to taking his own life at a young age.

Physical, emotional, and mental trials can be the result of pioneering with your own neck on the line. Possible outcomes such as depression, social marginalization, and physical trauma are no joke. It is important to count the cost, especially since success rarely comes with the first try. A pioneer who surrounds herself and listens to those who care for her is wise, and their advice and admonitions provide personal accountability that act as a ballast to her inflated, tugging, pioneering balloon.

Pioneers, there's no reason that your goals cannot be as high as the sky. Just remember, the laws of gravity are also at play. If something doesn't work, "going down in flames" is more than just a saying; it's borne out in reality. It's great if you can die doing what you love, but there's no reason that death needs to be premature.

PRINCIPLED VERSUS UNETHICAL

Pioneers are believers. They have conviction that a thing can be done. If doubts overshadow, why attempt a very difficult, costly, explorative effort in the first place? A lack of conviction leads to a lack of effort. In Henry Ford's words, "Whether you believe you can do a thing or not, you are right." This is not to imply that it is healthy to live in a fairytale of one's own making. For example, I might believe with all my being that I can fly. I might even see it in my dreams. But if I acted out on this conviction and leaped from a tall building without any aids, I would meet a swift end. The intensity of the conviction, however, *is* the sort that fueled the Wright Brothers to build an apparatus based on the laws of physics that would help a person to fly. As a result of their efforts, I can say with all seriousness that I can and do fly, as I hold an airline ticket in my hand and await my turn to board a jet. The substance of conviction, rooted in the reality of the world in which we live, is the difference. The pioneer must work with the limitations that reality imposes. There is a major distinction between a conviction based on real-world principles and one rooted in wishful thinking. And the difference is much more than semantics.

This brings us to another relevant meaning of the word *principled* as it relates to the pioneering process. It is beneficial to cite several antonyms: corrupt, dishonest, and unethical. Thesaurus.com even adds a word with theological overtones: sinful.[5] At the very least, taking action into the unknown without a well-developed, mature, ethical structure in the inner person is to risk pioneering without morals. On the other end of life's sour consequences, many people have asked, some from behind prison bars, "How did I get into this mess?" In the process of formulating his Aligned Influence® model, Ken Schuetz saw the damage close-up as he examined how the letter of the law, and not the spirit, was kept in applying the international policy governance system. When a critical number of board-governed organizations wandered from ethical intent, the harm they caused cascaded far beyond their organizational walls, and history has recorded the damage. Ken sought to rectify the gaps created by the international policy governance model and the faulty way in which some practiced it. He also sought to add meaning and harmony to the practice of executives and board members. In doing so, he became a pioneer.

Ethical pioneers know that just because a thing can be done doesn't mean it should be. An alert, fully aware pioneer will ask a series of questions and play out various scenarios, some of which may include: What are the likely outcomes of this effort if it should succeed? If there is a significant potential for harm, how will I live with the results? How can I combat negative results if they emerge? Is it my responsibility to combat such results?

In fairness, a pioneer cannot always foresee outcomes of his or her efforts, even if what she or he intended for good is used destructively. Should the pioneer be blamed if this is the case? A well-known example of this is Alfred Nobel's invention of dynamite. While there are plenty of beneficial uses for the explosive, it hardly takes much of an imagination to envision its destructive potential, and history has this on record many times over. Nobel had plenty of detractors, some calling him *le marchand de la mort*; translated from French it means "the merchant of death."[6] His aversion to leaving such a legacy motivated him to create the Nobel Peace Prize upon his death. Did Nobel succeed in altering society's opinion of his motives and his inventions? I guess it depends on who you ask. Outcomes and legacy should be taken very seriously. A healthy pioneer will want to put his or her head down on the pillow at night and sleep soundly with a clear conscience.

Then there are unhealthy pioneers. There is a reason that the word *sick* in English not only means lacking health but can also be used to describe those who have a propensity to seek their own gain despite a knowledge that their efforts will bring destruction to people and other living things. A healthy pioneer will scour his or her internal motives, and if, in balance, self-gain trumps overall beneficial outcomes to society, he or she will have the maturity to choose self-denial. Taking this one step further, a self-aware pioneer will also consult others while on mission to ensure that personal judgment is not becoming clouded during the pioneering process. A pioneer involved in exploration must have a functioning ethical compass, just as he or she must have a functioning geographical compass. Altruism and pioneering must go hand in hand. Motivational speaker and sales expert Zig Ziglar once said, "The most important tool you have in your entire arsenal is integrity." Speaking of sales...

PERSUASIVE VERSUS INEFFECTIVE

My father is a salesman as well as an avid reader. As a result, I grew up around books that had titles like *How to Win Big by Flipping Houses* and *A Fool-Proof Guide to No-Sweat Money-Making through Real Estate*. I also grew up hearing things like, "Sweet-haht, don't fall in love with the deal," "There's another Golden Rule: He who has the gold, rules," and other pithy sayings related to economics and power. My dad offered these maxims to his children to help them navigate the potholes of slick advertising. One of his favorite expressions was, and still is, "Nothing happens until someone sells something." While not universally true (the sun still continues to rise and set, doesn't it?), within a given framework, it describes the power of persuasion. When somebody sells something, it can initiate a cascade of events that, given the product that is bought and sold, may have virtuous outcomes throughout a community and beyond. Of course, the opposite is true as well.

Sometimes, the product is an idea. It's a concept of what could happen given enough time and resources. If placed within a pioneering context, it is a worthy idea that has not yet been attained. So the pioneer in whose mind the endeavor has incubated is pressed with the responsibility of convincingly sharing the vision with others. A prospective pioneer who appears incapable, weak, or unbelievable will have a steep climb in gaining the support of backers whose resources and other forms of support might be needed to bring the quest into reality.

Many pioneers have sprung from well-resourced families. However, there are many others who have not been born with a silver spoon in their mouth. Pioneers have come from backgrounds that have included economic difficulty, broken homes, and demographic disadvantage. This being the case, if pioneers lacked the ability to persuade others of their potential quest, where would they be? Who would they be? After all, Shackleton couldn't sail without a ship. An ability to persuade can make the difference between dreamers and doers.

In a modern context, acquiring resources has become more complex. While pioneers still meet face-to-face with prospective benefactors, there are other methods available. There is a skill to grant writing, constructing cases for support, and demonstrating a potential return on investment for stakeholders. Some of these steps have become requisites for obtaining available resources. There are individuals and organizations who specialize in helping pioneering people gain resources for their endeavors and efforts. If the prospective pioneer needs to build skills in persuasion, there are an abundance of websites, books, and blogs on the topic. Sales and marketing training opportunities also abound. Suffice it to say, however, that the pioneer himself must have some ability to honestly attract others to support and sign on to the mission.

Separating the Pioneers from the Leaders

While there is no one formula pioneers follow to achieve success, and there is no set background from which pioneering souls spring, they appear to possess similar traits that advance them into areas that beg to be explored, or demand social change, or require a remedy to mitigate human suffering. Previously, we may have thought these traits as integral to all leaders, but our understanding of leadership and its practice has grown. It now appears that those who pioneer have separated themselves from other leaders who guide groups using methods that have been tested and found true but are not necessarily novel.

Not all leaders display the courage to take risk. Rather, they lead through methods and means that avoid risk, while still advancing the mission and vision of the organization. This is not an option for a pioneer. Pioneering requires the courage to dig deep, to probe into realms that beckon to be explored. Pioneers are not afraid to take risks in order to find answers.

Typical leaders need not have their own skin in the game and may be known to quote a popular saying, "The sign of a good leader is the ability to delegate." While nobody can do everything, and delegation is an efficient way to complete tasks, the pioneer typically has her sleeves rolled up and is working right alongside other team members. And I'm not talking about micromanagement here. Simply managing others, no matter how closely, will not feed her. She must be all in. The task is her heart. It is this burning passion for her mission that makes her so persuasive and convinces others to become excited at potential outcomes. Leaders need not take such risks with their energy and emotions. To be sure, they may still provide direction, ensure alignment with the organizational mission, and add to the bottom line, but there is not necessarily a risk component in leading others toward a common goal.

Some may argue otherwise, adding that innovation, creativity, and passion are essential attributes of leadership. This type of discussion is welcome as we continue to more deeply understand concepts of leadership, pioneering, and the true essence of what makes a pioneering leader. In practice, I have observed many leaders at work. They have been honest and hardworking, having the respect of their reports, and that is commendable. However, there is something in the spirit of the pioneering leader that does not always manifest in many who lead these days, and that is a tangible conviction that new ways ought to be explored in order to apprehend the innovative. This is intrinsic to the spirit of someone who wants to advance an effort through new ways and means. And this person isn't afraid to take on current obstacles for the good of those who benefit from the organizational effort. That is a conquering spirit. That is the spirit of a pioneer. There is a yearning to risk something, albeit measured, and a willingness to speak up, even in a culture that is risk averse and genteel.

And so, we return to a definition of a pioneer: *a persistent, risk-taking individual who ventures into new territory in order to accomplish a goal and, in so doing, influences others to participate in realizing and expanding this goal.* This is the difference between a leader and one who is driven to pioneer.

The Art of Pioneering

There is, however, no reason to believe that a leader cannot leap into pioneering if desired. In fact, pioneers may start out as leaders. Like any expert practitioner in art or science, good leaders are not made overnight. They may spend ample time in study, receive valuable mentoring, and learn through observation. Like the 4-H motto, they learn through doing, applying what has been learned, and then making course corrections as needed.

There may come a time, however, when the leader discovers that the methods that he or she has learned and relied upon in practice no longer work. A desire, then a stronger drive develops to try something novel. Status quo practice becomes a throbbing irritant begging this leader to create and try some sort of a solution, much the way Henry Wells experienced his own nagging wisdom tooth. Given enough time, nagging can turn into agony. If the culture of the organization in which this leader practices is averse to any sort of change or risk, this leader now has a conflict. He can attempt to persuade those in power to try the new solution, or he can practice elsewhere or even set off on his own new course.

When Rhode Island artist Gilbert Stuart painted the picture of the first President of the United States, he made a deliberate decision to leave it unfinished. It seems that the President's wife, Martha, was so fond of the portrait that she wanted it. However, Stuart was satisfied with the likeness he created and knew that he wanted to use that particular piece as a reference for future commissions. As a means to keep the portrait, Stuart claimed that he could not part with it because it wasn't "finished." In fact, it was never finished. Crafty Stuart is said to have created and sold seventy more finished pieces from that particular sitting, which is now known as the Athenaeum. If you think about the number of people who reach into their pockets every day and draw out a United States paper dollar, the impact of this one rendering of US President George Washington is multiplied billions of times over, as it is the image that is seen on the American dollar bill. As of April 2018, it has been said that there are 11.7 billion dollar bills in circulation.[7] That is quite an impact! How could Gilbert Stuart have known that so many people would be seeing his work every day?

Just as we rarely give a thought to seeing Stuart's work as we make our daily transactions, so we may rarely think about the pioneers who have, through their courage, conviction, and conquering spirit, gifted us with our current way of life. Nobody likes to hear from the doctor that they need further testing or surgery, but we are comforted by hearing something like, "Oh, you won't even feel it. You'll wake up and it will be over." In our present context, especially in western culture, we have come to assume that something can be given to us to numb the pain, or that there are "people" who will fix things that go wrong in society. For many of us, especially younger generations, this has been our only experience. We cannot remember a time when this wasn't the case. However, the modern conveniences society enjoys were once brand new. Many of these inventions, inoculations, and ideas were hard won by pioneers who invested their time, talent, and, in some cases, their life blood to bring them into reality.

Still, even a cursory glance at the news demonstrates that, despite the advances that have been made, all is still not well. Inventions become outdated and need improvement. Disruptive technology might cause early obsolescence, making the useful life of some new inventions short as they are replaced by even newer technology. For example, mobile phones constantly add new features and capabilities. Who would have thought that in less than a decade and a half a person could hold a telephone, map, camera, alarm clock, address book, and radio (to name just a few) in the palm of one hand? Pathogens can morph and mutate into new subtypes or strains, which create more human suffering due to unprepared collective immunity. Pioneering scientists are still needed to decode these mysteries and create solutions to combat what may easily become a new pandemic. New ideas are needed to solve ecological challenges, educational dilemmas, and societal plagues, such as premature death due to violence and drug abuse.

Who will answer the call?

Many times, the pioneer arises to accept the challenge because he or she has been personally scarred by one of these bitter circumstances. The pioneer rises each day to the internal call of "never again" and is driven—often with the enlistment of other sympathetic souls—to shape a new reality where the harmful agent is rendered powerless and can no longer harm others. Are you one of these people? If so, the rest of us thank you.

Do you believe you could become one of these people?

Are you driven by the possibilities of what new frontiers hold?

Are you the owner of a probing, insatiably curious mind?

Will you pursue your new, envisioned reality with persistence and the passion of having your own skin in the game?

Are you the owner of a moral compass with a strong magnetic field pointing you northward? Or are you somewhere en route in this process?

Whether you are great or small, known or unknown, the rest of us implore you to continue your quest, because tomorrow will surely bring new tests and trails. Pioneers will always be needed. Will you be one of them?

ENDNOTES

Chapter 1

1   Linton Weeks, "Defeating Polio: The Disease That Paralyzed America," NPR, April 10, 2015, www.npr.org/sections/npr-history-dept/2015/04/10/398515228/defeating-the-disease-that-paralyzed-america.

2   Salk Institute for Biological Studies, "History of Salk," 2018, accessed September 26, 2018, https://www.salk.edu/about/history-of-salk/jonas-salk/.

3   The American Presidency Project, *Dwight D. Eisenhower*, "Citation Presented to Dr. Jonas E. Salk and Accompanying Remarks," accessed September 27, 2018, https://www.presidency.ucsb.edu/documents/citation-presented-dr-jonas-e-salk-and-accompanying-remarks.

4   *CBSnews.com*, "Relive! Apollo 11 with Walter Cronkite (Anchor of the First Moonwalk)," July 1969, YouTube, https://www.youtube.com/watch?v=5F6B1U77dgs.

5   *Merriam-Webster Unabridged* online, s.v. "pioneer," accessed September 19, 2018, http://unabridged.merriam-webster.com/unabridged/pioneer.

6   *Online Etymology Dictionary*, s.v. "pioneer," accessed January 10, 2019, https://www.etymonline.com/word/pioneer.

7   *Merriam-Webster Unabridged* online, s.v. "pioneer."

8   *Online Etymology Dictionary*, s.v. "leadership," accessed June 18, 2018, https://www.etymonline.com/word/leadership.

9   Peter G. Northouse, *Leadership: Theory and Practice*, 5th ed. (Los Angeles: Sage, 2010), 3.

10   John Maxwell, "Are You Really Leading or Are You Just Taking a Walk?," The John Maxwell Co., August 7, 2012, http://www.johnmaxwell.com/blog/are-you-really-leading-or-are-you-just-taking-a-walk.

11   James Cameron, as cited in the video *James Cameron to Dive to the Ocean's Deepest Point*, National Geographic, 2012, https://video.nationalgeographic.com/video/cameron-deepsea-mariana?source=searchvideo.

12   Angela Duckworth, *Grit: The Power of Passion and Perseverance* (New York: Scribner, 2016), 54.

13   Proverbs 4:23 NLT.

14   Ernest Shackleton, *South: The Story of Shackleton's Last Expedition (1914-1917)* (Digireads.com Publishing, 2009).

15   Adam Skolnick, "Colin O'Brady Completes Crossing of Antarctica with Final 32-Hour Push," *The New York Times*, December 26, 2018, https://www.nytimes.com/2018/12/26/sports/antarctica-race-colin-obrady.html; Roland Oliphant, "American Beats British Army Captain in Becoming First Person to Cross Antarctic Unaided," *The Telegraph*, December 27, 2018, https://www.telegraph.co.uk/news/2018/12/27/american-beats-british-army-captain-becoming-first-person-cross/.

16   Alexandra Shackleton (@shackletonlondon), Instagram.com, December 14, 2018, https://www.instagram.com/p/BrXfxpTnB7E/?utm_source=ig_embed.

Chapter 2

1   BLTC Research, "Horace Wells (1815–1848)," n.d., accessed February 20, 2018, https://www.general-anaesthesia.com/people/horace-wells.html.

2   Cincinnati Children's, "Craniosynostosis," accessed February 15, 2018, https://www.cincinnatichildrens.org/health/c/craniosynostosis; Mayo Clinic, "Craniosynostosis," accessed February 15, 2018, https://www.mayoclinic.org/diseases-conditions/craniosynostosis/symptoms-causes/syc-20354513.

3   Laurie Wilk, personal communication, February 11, 2018.

4   Wilk, personal communication, February 11, 2018.

5   Wilk, personal communication, February 9, 2018.

6   Wilk, personal communication, February 9, 2018.

7   *BLTC Research*, "Gardner Quincy Colton," accessed December 24, 2018, https://www.general-anaesthesia.com/people/gardner-colton.html, originally from Tercentenary Commission of the State of

Connecticut, *The Discoverer of Anaesthesia: Dr. Horace Wells of Hartford Tercentenary Commission* (Yale University Press, 1933).

[8] Wilk, personal communication, February 9, 2018.

[9] Leslie Wylie, "Olympic Girl Power: The Incredible Story of Lis Hartel," Horse Nation, November 17, 2014, http://www.horsenation.com/2014/11/17/olympic-girl-power-the-incredible-story-of-lis-hartel/; *History of Hippotherapy and AHA Inc.*, accessed February 18, 2018, http://www.americanhippotherapyassociation.org/hippotherapy/history-of-hippotherapy/.

[10] Wilk, personal communication, February 9, 2018.

[11] Northouse, *Leadership*, 182.

[12] Wilk, personal communication, February 9, 2018.

Chapter 3

[1] Marvis Olive Welch, *Prudence Crandall: A Biography* (Manchester, CT: Jason Publishers, 1983), 8.

[2] Welch, *Prudence Crandall*, 1.

[3] Welch, *Prudence Crandall*, 8.

[4] Welch, *Prudence Crandall*, 18.

[5] John Piper, "The Image of God: An Approach from Biblical and Systematic Theology," Desiring God, March 1, 1971, https://www.desiringgod.org/articles/the-image-of-god.

[6] Welch, *Prudence Crandall*, 22.

[7] Ecclesiastes 4:1 KJV.

Chapter 4

[1] Proverbs 3:27 KJV, emphasis added; James 4:17 KJV, emphasis added.

[2] Welch, *Prudence Crandall*, 25.

Chapter 5

[1] Charles Dickens, as quoted by R. Dalzell, "How Charles Dickens Saw London," *Smithsonian Magazine*, June 5, 2011, https://www.smithsonianmag.com/travel/how-charles-dickens-saw-london-13198155/.

[2] The YMCA, "The Story of Our Founding," 2019, https://www.ymca.net/history/founding.html.

[3] Rob Rains, *James Naismith: The Man Who Invented Basketball* (Philadelphia: Temple University Press, 2009), 32.

[4] Rains, *James Naismith*, 32.

5   James Naismith, as quoted by Rains, *James Naismith*, 32–33.

6   Carol Ferrans, personal interview, October 27, 2018.

7   Ferrans, personal interview, October 27, 2018.

8   The National Kidney Foundation, "History," 2019, https://www.kidney.org/about/history.

9   Ferrans, personal interview, October 27, 2018.

10   James Naismith, *Basketball: Its Origins and Development* (Lincoln, NE: University of Nebraska Press, 1996), 38.

11   Naismith, *Basketball*, 39.

12   Naismith, *Basketball*, 42.

13   Naismith, *Basketball*, 43.

14   Naismith, *Basketball*, 46.

15   Naismith, *Basketball*, 41.

16   Naismith, *Basketball*, 53.

17   Naismith, *Basketball*, 56–57.

18   NIH: National Cancer Institute, "Karnofsky Performance Status," n.d., accessed July 2, 2018, https://www.cancer.gov/publications/dictionaries/cancer-terms/def/karnofsky-performance-status.

19   Ferrans, personal communication, October 26, 2018.

20   Ferrans, personal interview, October 26, 2018.

21   UIC: College of Nursing, "Cancer Detection: Carol Estwing Ferrans," September 13, 2018, modified September 14, 2018, http://nursing.uic.edu/news-stories/carol-estwing-ferrans-phd-rn-faan/.

22   Rains, *James Naismith*, 51, 54.

23   National Wheelchair Basketball Association, "History of Wheelchair Basketball and NWBA," n.d., accessed July 2, 2018, https://www.nwba.org/history NWBA.

24   Ferrans, personal communication, October 26, 2018.

Chapter 6

1   T. Fright, "The Original Nimrod Expedition," 2007, accessed November 21, 2018, http://www.shackletoncentenary.org/about/the-original-nimrod-expedition.php.

2   National Library of Medicine, "1925: Emergency Vaccine Delivery Helps Stop Diphtheria in Alaska," *Native Voices*, n.d., accessed December 31, 2018, https://www.nlm.nih.gov/nativevoices/timeline/435.html.

3   Christopher Klein, "The Sled Dog Relay That Inspired the Iditarod," History.com, March 10, 2014, updated August 31, 2018, https://www.history.com/news/the-sled-dog-relay-that-inspired-the-iditarod.

4   Karl Clauson, personal communication, December 6, 2018.
5   Alfred Lansing, *Endurance: Shackleton's Incredible Voyage* (Wheaton, IL: Tyndale House, 1999), 14.
6   Lansing, *Endurance*, 15–16.
7   Margot Morrell and Stephanie Capparell, *Shackleton's Way: Leadership Lessons from the Great Antarctic Explorer* (New York: Penguin Books, 2001), 61.
8   Lansing, *Endurance*, 15.
9   Morrell and Capparell, *Shackleton's Way*, 60.
10   Morrell and Capparell, *Shackleton's Way*, 61.
11   Clauson, personal communication, December 8, 2018.
12   Clauson, personal communication, December 8, 2018.
13   Jim Collins, *Good to Great: Why Some Companies Make the Leap... and Others Don't* (New York: HarperCollins, 2001), 41.
14   Clauson, personal communication, December 8, 2018.
15   Clauson, personal communication, December 8, 2018.
16   Sir Earnest Shackleton, *South: The Story of Shackleton's Last Expedition: 1914–1917* (Digireades.com Publishing, n.d.), 66.
17   Clauson, personal communication, December 8, 2018.
18   Melissa Hogenboom, "Dogs Can Tell If You're Untrustworthy," BBC.com, February 20, 2015, http://www.bbc.com/earth/story/20150220-dogs-know-if-youre-untrustworthy.
19   Clauson, personal communication, December 8, 2018.
20   Morrell and Capparell, *Shackleton's Way*, 107–108.
21   Clauson, personal communication, February 14, 2019.
22   Morrell and Capparell, *Shackleton's Way*, 117.
23   Lansing, *Endurance*, 75.
24   Shackleton, *South*, 199.

Chapter 7

1   Richard Milner, *Charles R. Knight: The Artist Who Saw through Time* (New York: Abrams, 2012), 11.
2   Darren Naish, "Those Giant Killer Pigs from Hell Aren't Pigs," *Scientific American*, August 25, 2011, https://blogs.scientificamerican.com/tetrapod-zoology/entelodonts-giant-killer-pigs/.
3   Naish, "Those Giant Killer Pigs from Hell Aren't Pigs."
4   Charles Knight, *Charles R. Knight: Autobiography of an Artist* (Ann Arbor, MI: G.T. Labs, 2005), 39–40.

5   Centers for Disease Control and Prevention, "Travel to High Altitudes," CDC.gov, accessed October 21, 2018, https://wwwnc. cdc.gov/travel/page/travel-to-high-altitudes.

6   Joe Rankin, "Krummholz: The High Life of Crooked Wood," *Northern Woodlands*, April 7, 2014, https://northernwoodlands.org/ outside_story/article/krummholz-wood.

7   Milner, *Charles R. Knight*, 11.

8   Juni Felix, personal interview, October 10, 2018.

9   KZ-Gedenkstätte Dachau, Visitor Information, "Introduction," accessed October 2, 2018, https://www.kz-gedenkstaette-dachau.de/ index-e.html.

10   Felix, personal interview, October 10, 2018.

11   Knight, *Charles R. Knight*, 42.

12   Milner, *Charles R. Knight*, 174.

13   Felix, personal interview, October 10, 2018.

14   Felix, personal interview, October 10, 2018.

15   B. J. Fogg, BJFogg.com, accessed February 18, 2020, https://www. bjfogg.com.

16   Felix, personal interview, October 10, 2018.

17   Felix, personal interview, October 10, 2018.

18   Milner, *Charles R. Knight*, 16.

19   Milner, *Charles R. Knight*, 17.

20   Charles R. Knight, *Animal Drawing: Anatomy and Action for Artists* (Mineola, NY: Dover Publications, 1959; first published, 1947), 119.

21   Felix, personal interview, October 10, 2018.

Chapter 8

1   Welch, *Prudence Crandall*, 26.

2   Welch, *Prudence Crandall*, 45.

3   Welch, *Prudence Crandall*, 57, 56.

4   Welch, *Prudence Crandall*, 69.

5   Malcolm Gladwell, *David and Goliath* (New York: Little, Brown and Company, 2013), 10–11.

6   Welch, *Prudence Crandall*, 108.

7   Letter by Prudence Crandall Philleo, May 5, 1881, in "Students at Prudence Crandall's School for African-American Women, 1833–1834," n.d., compiled by the Prudence Crandall Museum (Canturbury, CT), accessed September 16, 2018, https://glc.yale.edu/students-prudence-crandalls-school-african-american-women-1833-1834.

8   "Simeon Jocelyn," in "Yale, Slavery & Abolition," n.d., accessed September 17, 2018, http://www.yaleslavery.org/Abolitionists/jocelyn. htm.

9   Lanson's obituary, *Norwich Courier*, June 6, 1836, as quoted in "Students at Prudence Crandall's School for African-American Women, 1833–1834."

10   Welch, *Prudence Crandall*, 215.

Chapter 9

1   Richard A. Swenson, M.D., *The Overload Syndrome: Learning to Live within Your Limits* (Colorado Springs: NavPress, 1998), 31, 32.

2   Swenson, *The Overload Syndrome*, 33.

3   Shackleton, *South*, 102, 108, 110.

4   Don Pettit, #WhyIMake, Infosys Foundation USA, February 6, 2018, https://www.youtube.com/watch?v=Xbxw4V69IzU.

5   Morina Koren, "Sunrise, Sunset, Sunrise, Sunset, Sunrise…," *The Atlantic*, September 15, 2015, https://www.theatlantic.com/ notes/2015/09/sun-international-space-station/405463/.

6   Don Pettit, "Zero G Coffee Cup," *Space Week Live*, Channel 4, March 16, 2014, https://www.youtube.com/watch?v=oG8JSNvuMuw.

7   Pettit, #WhyIMake.

8   The UK Society for Play and Creative Arts Therapy, "Definition of Play," PTUK, 2017, accessed February 18, 2020, https://playtherapy. org.uk/ChildrensEmotionalWellBeing/AboutPlayTherapy/Main Principles/PlayDefinition.

9   An LNB is a low-noise block downconverter, which is the receiving device mounted on satellite dishes. It collects the radio waves from the dish and converts them to a signal that is then sent through a cable to the receiver inside the building.

10   Cale D. Magnuson and Lynn A. Barnett, "The Playful Advantage: How Playfulness Enhances Coping with Stress," *Leisure Sciences: An Interdisciplinary Journal*, vol. 35, no. 2 (March 20, 2013), 139, http:// dx.doi.org/10.1080/01490400.2013.761905.

11   Shane Kimbrough, *Peanut Butter and Jelly in Space*, YouTube, April 21, 2017, https://www.youtube.com/watch?v=Z2szk-NuKWg.

12   Lori Meggs, "Growing Plants and Vegetables in a Space Garden," NASA.gov, June 15, 2010, https://www.nasa.gov/mission_pages/ station/research/10-074.html.

13   Sue Diamond, "The Sailor Zoo and Farm in Portsmouth: Re-enchantment and Necessity (Part 1 of 2)," *Port Towns & Urban*

Cultures, July 31, 2018, http://porttowns.port.ac.uk/sailorzoo-farm-part1/.

[14] Lansing, *Endurance*, 91.

[15] Montana.gov, "Animal discoveries," Montana Fish, Wildlife and Parks, n.d., accessed July 25, 2019, http://fwp.mt.gov/education/youth/lewisAndClark/animals/.

[16] Lansing, *Endurance*, 14.

Chapter 10

[1] Clauson, personal communication, December 8, 2018.

[2] Lansing, *Endurance*, 83.

[3] Ken Schuetz, Aligned Influence: Beyond Governance (New York: Morgan James, 2020), n.p., prepublished manuscript.

[4] Ken Schuetz, personal communication, September 20, 2019.

[5] Schuetz, personal communication, September 20, 2019.

[6] "The Policy Governance˚ Model," accessed October 5, 2019, http://carvergovernance.com/model.htm carvergovernance.com.

[7] Schuetz, personal communication, September 20, 2019.

[8] Ken Schuetz, "The Discipline of Governance: Defining Roles to Support the Goals," Alignedinfluence.com, accessed October 6, 2019, https://alignedinfluence.com/aligned-influence-and-policy-governance-compared-and-contrasted/.

[9] Ken Beere, "Obituary: David Beaty," *Independent*, December 22, 1999, https://www.independent.co.uk/arts-entertainment/obituary-david-beaty-1134036.html.

[10] John K. Lauber, "Resource Management on the Flight Deck: Background and Statement of the Problem," in George E. Cooper, Maurice D. White, G. E. Cooper, and John K. Lauber, eds., "Resource Management on the Flight Deck," Proceedings of a NASA/Industry Workshop held at San Francisco, California, June 26–28, 1979, https://ntrs.nasa.gov/archive/nasa/casi.ntrs.nasa.gov/19800013796.pdf.

[11] Lauber, "Resource Management on the Flight Deck," 14.

[12] Lauber, "Resource Management on the Flight Deck," 14, emphasis added.

[13] Bill Murphy Jr., "This United Airlines Pilot Saved 184 Passengers' Lives and Taught an Incredible Lesson in Leadership: Here's Why His Heroic Legacy Is So Extraordinary," *Inc.*, August 31, 2019, https://www.inc.com/bill-murphy-jr/this-united-airlines-pilot-saved-184-

passengers-lives-taught-an-incredible-lesson-in-leadership-heres-why-his-heroic-legacy-is-so-extraordinary.html.

14   Schuetz, personal communication, September 20, 2019.

15   Schuetz, personal communication, September 20, 2019.

16   Schuetz, personal communication, September 20, 2019.

17   Schuetz, personal communication, September 20, 2019.

Chapter 11

1   Kate Morin, "Too Much of a Good Thing? Foods That Can Be Toxic If You Eat Them in Excess," *Fix*, August 26, 2016, https://www.fix.com/blog/foods-that-can-be-toxic/.

2   Proverbs 27:6 BSB.

3   Karl Clauson, "Boys to Men," June 11, 2018, http://www.karlclauson.com/blog.

4   Clauson, personal communication, December 2018.

5   Clauson, personal communication, December 2018.

6   Emily E. Gifford, "Horace Wells Discovers Pain-Free Dentistry," ConnecticutHistory.org, December 11, 2015, https://connecticuthistory.org/horace-wells-discovers-pain-free-dentistry/.

7   Rajesh P. Haridas, "Horace Wells' Demonstration of Nitrous Oxide in Boston," *Anesthesiology*, vol. 119 (November 2013), http://anesthesiology.pubs.asahq.org/article.aspx?articleid=1918086.

8   Haridas, "Horace Wells' Demonstration of Nitrous Oxide in Boston," emphasis in the original.

9   Haridas, "Horace Wells' Demonstration of Nitrous Oxide in Boston."

10   Ron Grossman, "The World's Fair and the Fairer Sex," *Chicago Tribune*, April 18, 1993, https://www.chicagotribune.com/news/ct-xpm-1993-04-18-9304180141-story.html.

11   Grossman, "The World's Fair and the Fairer Sex."

12   Grossman, "The World's Fair and the Fairer Sex."

13   *American Architect and Building News* (1892), vol. 38, no. 883, p. 134, https://books.google.com/books?id=CohMAAAAYAAJ&pg=RA1-PA132&source=gbs_toc_r&cad=3#v=onepage&q&f=false.

14   *American Architect and Building News* (1892).

15   Haridas, "Horace Wells' Demonstration of Nitrous Oxide in Boston."

16   Haridas, "Horace Wells' Demonstration of Nitrous Oxide in Boston."

17   "Charles Thomas Jackson," *Encyclopedia Britannica*, https://www.britannica.com/biography/Charles-Thomas-Jackson.

18   Gifford, "Horace Wells Discovers Pain-Free Dentistry."

19 M. S. Desai and S. P. Desai, "Discovery of Modern Anesthesia: A Counterfactual Narrative about Crawford W. Long, Horace Wells, Charles T. Jackson, and William T. G. Morton," *American Association of Nurse Anesthetists* (December 2015), vol. 83, no. 6, abstract, emphasis added, https://www.ncbi.nlm.nih.gov/pubmed/26742335.

20 "Charles Thomas Jackson," *Encyclopedia Britannica.*

21 "William Thomas Green Morton (1819–68)," n.d., sciencemuseum. org, http://broughttolife.sciencemuseum.org.uk/broughttolife/people/ williammorton.

Chapter 12

1   Thomas Wessel and Marilyn Wessel, *4-H: An American Idea, 1900– 1980* (Chevy Chase, MD: National 4-H Council, 1982), 18.

2   Wessel and Wessel, *4-H*, 1, 2.

3   Suzanne Steel, "A. B. Graham's Legacy," College of Food, Agricultural, and Environmental Sciences, Ohio State University, March 9, 2018, https://cfaes.osu.edu/stories/ab-grahams-legacy.

4   Loren N. Horton, "Shambaugh, Jessie Field," *The Biographical Dictionary of Iowa* (University of Iowa Press, 2009), accessed November 30, 2019, http://uipress.lib.uiowa.edu/bdi/DetailsPage. aspx?id=336.

5   4-h.org, *4-H: An Idea Is Born*, video, accessed December 1, 2019, https://4-h.org/about/history/.

6   4-H History, "1914: Cooperative Extension System Is Created," accessed February 18, 2020, https://4-h.org/about/history/.

7   William Bratton and Zachary Tumin, *Collaborate or Perish!: Reaching Across Boundaries in a Networked World* (New York: Crown Business, 2012), 24.

8   Aristotle, *On the Heavens*, trans. J. L. Stocks (Ann Arbor, MI: University of Michigan, 1930), bk. 2, pt. 14, http://classics.mit.edu/ Aristotle/heavens.2.ii.html.

9   Aristotle, *On the Heavens.*

10 Tim Sharp, "How Big Is Earth?," Space.com, September 15, 2017, https://www.space.com/17638-how-big-is-earth.html.

11 Gladys Mae West, *Navy Hidden Hero: Gladys Mae West and GPS*, You. tube, video, U.S. Navy, December 19, 2018, https://www.youtube. com/watch?v=McIemoQWv64.

12 Air Force Space Command Public Affairs, "Mathematician Inducted into Space and Missiles Pioneers Hall of Fame," Air Force Space Command, December 7, 2018, https://www.afspc.af.mil/News/

Article-Display/Article/1707464/mathematician-inducted-into-space-and-missiles-pioneers-hall-of-fame/.

13   Amelia Butterly, "100 Women: Gladys West—the 'Hidden Figure' of GPS," BBC, May 20, 2018, https://www.bbc.com/news/world-43812053.

14   Schuetz, personal communication, September 20, 2019.

15   Ferrans, personal communication, October 26, 2018.

16   Schuetz, personal communication, September 20, 2019.

17   International Astronomical Union, "Constellations," n.d., accessed December 4, 2019, https://www.iau.org/public/themes/constellations/.

Chapter 13

1   Kathy Hartley, personal communication, November 1, 2019.

2   Hearthside House Museum, "Architecture," History, 2020, accessed January 25, 2020, https://www.hearthsidehouse.org/architecture.

3   Hearthside House Museum, "About."

4   Kaitlyn Murray, "The History of Love at the House That Love Built," *Engaged in Southern New England*, June 10, 2016, https://www.engagedsne.com/2016/06/the-history-of-love-at-the-house-that-love-built/.

5   Hartley, personal communication, November 1, 2019.

6   Hartley, personal communication, November 1, 2019.

7   Hartley, personal communication, November 1, 2019.

8   Don Larson, personal communication, November 14, 2019.

9   Larson, personal communication, November 14, 2019.

10   Larson, personal communication, November 14, 2019.

11   Larson, personal communication, November 14, 2019.

12   Hartley, personal communication, November 1, 2019.

13   Hartley, personal communication, November 1, 2019.

14   Hartley, personal communication, November 1, 2019.

15   Ed Peters, "Cocoa Exporter Ghana Now Makes Its Own Chocolates, with a Deeper Taste," *South China Morning Post*, September 3, 2018, https://www.scmp.com/country-reports/country-reports/topics/ghana-country-report-2018/article/2162187/cocoa-exporter.

16   Hartley, personal communication, November 1, 2019.

17   Hartley, personal communication, November 1, 2019.

18   Roger Trapp, "For Leadership, Like Everything Else, Practice Makes Perfect," *Forbes*, May 25, 2016, https://www.forbes.com/sites/rogertrapp/2016/05/25/for-leadership-like-everything-else-practice-makes-perfect/#12b692e22b3c.

[19] Hartley, personal communication, November 1, 2019.

[20] Larson, personal communication, November 14, 2019.

[21] Larson, personal communication, November 14, 2019.

[22] Larson, personal communication, November 14, 2019.

[23] Sunshine Nut Co., "Business Model," the Sunshine Approach, 2017, accessed February 15, 2020, https://sunshinenuts.com/sunshine-approach/our-business-model/.

[24] Larson, personal communication, November 14, 2019.

[25] Larson, personal communication, November 14, 2019.

[26] Don Larson, *Running a Business with a Social Mission*, YouTube, June 3, 2015, https://www.youtube.com/watch?v=XB7xAEuwhDo.

[27] Larson, personal communication, November 14, 2019.

[28] Larson, personal communication, November 14, 2019.

[29] 1 Corinthians 13:7 ESV.

[30] Hartley, personal communication, November 1, 2019.

[31] Hartley, personal communication, November 1, 2019.

[32] Larson, personal communication, November 14, 2019.

[33] Larson, personal communication, November 14, 2019.

[34] Larson, personal communication, November 14, 2019.

[35] Hartley, personal communication, November 1, 2019.

[36] Hartley, personal communication, November 1, 2019.

Chapter 14

[1] *Merriam-Webster Unabridged*, s.v. "canvas," accessed February 12, 2020, http://unabridged.merriam-webster.com/unabridged/canvas.

[2] Antoine de Saint-Exupéry, *Le Petit Prince* (Orlando, FL: Harcourt, 1943), 1–2.

[3] Ed Yong, "Meet the Squidworm: Half Worm, Half Squid…er, Actually All Worm," *National Geographic*, November 23, 2010, https://www.nationalgeographic.com/science/phenomena/2010/11/23/meet-the-squidworm-half-worm-half-squid-er-actually-all-worm/.

[4] Don Larson, "Our Approach," Sunshine Nut Co., 2017, accessed February 15, 2020, https://sunshinenuts.com/sunshine-approach/our-story/.

[5] Thesaurus.com, s.v. "principled," https://www.thesaurus.com/browse/principled?s=t.

[6] Colin Schultz, "Blame Sloppy Journalism for the Nobel Prizes," *Smithsonian Magazine*, October 9, 2013, https://www.smith

sonianmag.com/smart-news/blame-sloppy-journalism-for-the-nobel-prizes-1172688/.

7   Jeff Desjardins, "How Many U.S. Dollar Bills Are There in Circulation?," Visual Capitalist, April 17, 2018, https://www.visual-capitalist.com/many-u-s-dollar-bills-circulation/.

ACKNOWLEDGMENTS

A PIONEER NEVER ACCOMPLISHES ANYTHING ALONE. THIS IS ALSO true of anyone who writes a book. It is a journey that an author has the privilege of taking with the help of others. The hoped-for result is that new ground has been covered by exploring a subject in a deeper way and, in this case, offering a fresh perspective on a smaller segment of leaders, though the larger topic of leadership has been well researched and much discussed.

Heartfelt appreciation goes to Robert McFarland for encouraging me to take the initial steps in this journey. Thanks to your constant reminders that "I can do this," I can now say that I did!

To Bill Watkins, many thanks for your friendship, reassurance, and for liberally providing your expertise that guided me every step of the way.

Sincere appreciation goes to David Bernstein and the team at Bombardier for believing in the value of this project and for your professional support throughout the process.

To those who first gave me opportunities to break new ground: Mike Bingham, Bill Blount, Collin Lambert, and Dave Young: I am profoundly grateful for your belief in me.

My support network was invaluable to me throughout the book-birthing process: Cherrilynn Bisbano, Yvonne Carlson, Barbara Gauthier, Rima Jabbour, Elsa Mazon, Laurie Wilk, and so many others. Thank you for playing a significant role in this process by providing encouragement along the way.

My admiration and thanks go to the pioneers who personally shared their stories with me: Haley Wilk, Dr. Carol Ferrans, Karl Clauson, Juni Felix, Ken Schuetz, Kathy Hartley, and Don Larson. Keep doing what you do, making this world a better place for others.

Deep gratitude goes to my family: To my father, LeForrest Hayden Jr., for reading along as I wrote, offering feedback and praise; to my brother, LeForrest "Skip" Hayden III, who kept me laughing; and to my husband Jack, who took up life's slack, enabling me to complete this project. Your constant love and commitment made this work possible.

Finally, to all the pioneers who tirelessly apply their possibility-driven, probing, persistent, "peau-mantic," principled, and persuasive personalities to your individual quests. We all need you to keep solving new problems, exploring new places, plumbing new depths, and inspiring a new generation of pioneers.